Tales of Mountain Maryland

Tales of Mountain Maryland

✦

with a special section on the C&O Canal

Paula M. Strain

Potomac Appalachian Trail Club
Vienna, Virginia
2005

iUniverse, Inc.
New York Lincoln Shanghai

Tales of Mountain Maryland
with a special section on the C&O Canal

iUniverse books may be ordered through booksellers or by contacting:

iUniverse
2021 Pine Lake Road, Suite 100
Lincoln, NE 68512
www.iuniverse.com
1-800-Authors (1-800-288-4677)

First edition, 2005

ISBN-13: 978-0-595-38004-6 (pbk)
ISBN-13: 978-0-595-82375-8 (ebk)
ISBN-10: 0-595-38004-2 (pbk)
ISBN-10: 0-595-82375-0 (ebk)

Printed in the United States of America

Blue mountain walls divide Maryland into cultural regions: one in which the Choptank and the Nanticoke, the Patuxent and the Potomac, and the Chesapeake Bay encouraged a water-facing society, the other, a valley and highland region with a culture created by the steep slopes that hindered east-west travel for almost two and a half centuries.

Today, the mountains are no more than low garden walls, offering some protection from the expanding cosmopolitanism of the Baltimore-Annapolis-Washington corridor. This urban culture is absorbing the recognized culture of the Tidewater, and the less known one of Maryland's mountains. Before the protection of the blue hills fails, the mountain culture should be recorded.

Vignettes from three centuries of history in five Maryland counties attempt to illustrate what that culture was and is. While the tales may read like folk tales, only one chapter actually is such. The others tell the story of places and people worth remembering.

The C&O Canal Today

All internal photos courtesy of the National Park Service

Contents

I

A Walk in Spring

It happens every five years—a repetition of an eight-day hike that focuses public opinion on the Chesapeake and Ohio Canal as a recreational resource of value and that foreshadows wide participation in backpacking, hiking, and running as sports for the individual. When I chaired a program on the interaction of the Potomac Appalachian Trail Club with the canal, I discovered how little most of us today know about the original hike, the William 0. Douglas/Washington Post hike on the C&O Canal towpath in March 1954. These pages tell what happened on the hike, and a little about its place in canal history.

The Background

After carrying freight and passengers between Washington, D.C. and Cumberland for a hundred years, the old canal was no longer competitive with rail or highway. When the floods of 1924 ripped into the canal, no effort was made to bring it back to use. A dozen years later (1938) the federal government purchased it; the Civilian Conservation Corps was put to work restoring canal, towpath and some structures. The work halted with World War II (1939–1945). When the war ended, the automobile had become America's pride and joy.

It wasn't surprising that the National Park Service/Bureau of Public Roads study, "The C&O Canal" (1950) proposed that the canal become a 185-mile "Potomac Drive." The canal bed and towpath were quite wide enough for a scenic parkway, but the fourteen access interchanges required, and adjacent picnicking and camping areas planned would need the purchase of another 14,000 acres of land. The study also suggested that a few parts of the canal might be re-watered for fishing and boating.

1

Many residents of Allegheny and Garrett counties, including Maryland Senator J. Glenn Beall, thought the proposal an excellent one: western Maryland was accessible only by US 40 which twisted its way over three mountain ranges. The Congress, which had ordered the study, thought the proposal good enough to approve building the road—if Maryland would acquire and donate the needed 14,000 acres. The Maryland legislature had mixed feelings; it thought the idea good enough to authorize the purchase, but not sufficiently good to appropriate money for purchase.

There the matter rested until the fall of 1952, with apparent public support of the parkway rising. Then both the Audubon Society of the Central Atlantic (now, the Audubon Naturalist Society of the Mid-Atlantic) and the Potomac Appalachian Trail Club began to think about the proposed parkway.

PATC's Excursion Chair, John W. (Bill) Schorr, started a series of hikes December 5, 1952, to familiarize club members with the canal towpath. President G. Frederick (Fred) Blackburn appointed a committee to study the parkway proposal. The committee suggested the club do two things: adopt the Audubon Society's December suggestion to write Maryland legislators expressing opposition to appropriating funds to buy parkway lands, and call a meeting of representatives of all outdoors and conservation organizations in the region to discuss the parkway plans.

In March 1953, Fred Blackburn chaired a meeting at the District Government building in Washington, attended by 89 people. Harry Thompson, Assistant Superintendent, National Capital Parks, National Park Service, spoke on the parkway plans, emphasizing how the twenty-mile eastern end of the canal would be developed for recreation. He was followed by Dr. Irston Barnes, usual spokesman for the Audubon Society, who talked of the natural history and beauties of the canal, especially of its western end, which adjoined mountain wilderness areas.

A work trip of PATC members was scheduled that summer to help Park Service staff clear part of the towpath. And in May, an informal meeting of Audubon Society members was held at the home of Mrs. Gifford Pinchot to discuss the canal. Records of what they discussed are limited, as is a full list of the attendees. They do show that attendance included Dr. Barnes, Constant Southworth (an Audubon Society activist, and also a PATC member) and Anthony Wayne (Tony) Smith (active in both the Audubon Society and the National Parks Association). Smith was associate general counsel of the national Congress of Industrial Organizations, and chair of its Conservation Committee; he was also a friend of Associate Justice of the Supreme Court William O. Douglas, an enthusiastic outdoorsman who was a familiar figure on the trails of the Washington region. (His *My wilderness: east to Katahdin,* Doubleday, 1961, tells of his experiences hiking in the east.)

The PATC series of hikes on the C&O towpath continued at roughly two-month intervals all during 1953, drawing as many as fifty hikers on some walks. Irston Barnes used his nature column in the Washington Post to urge preservation of the canal for its beauty and its bird and animal life, but he failed to convince the Post editors.

Justice Douglas (right) hiking on the C&O Canal towpath in 1954

Endorsement and Challenge

On January 3, 1954, the Washington Post carried an editorial endorsing the proposal to build a parkway along the Chesapeake and Ohio Canal. "The old canal/has/no longer a commercial and economic aspect." Paving it over would cost a mere $100,000 a mile and doing so would make the Potomac Valley accessible to the many with "little detraction to its beauty." The wilderness areas along the river especially would be easily accessible to the public.

Justice Douglas read the Post. He sent a six-paragraph letter to the Post editors, which was published on January 19. In it, he recalled Justice Brandeis' canoe trip up the Potomac to Cumberland, and praised the beauty of the canal. He also said:

> I wish the man who wrote your editorial of Jan. 3, 1954, approving the parkway, would take time out and come with me. We would go with packs on our backs and walk the 185 miles to Cumberland. I feel that if your editor did, he would return a new man and use the power of your great editorial pages to help keep the sanctuary untouched.

Two days later, on January 21, "We Accept" headlined the editorial page of the Post. The editorial said in part:

> The Skyline Drive is doubtless more heavily traveled than the proposed Potomac parkway would be, but it has not destroyed the beauties of the Blue Ridge...He/Douglas/has only to name the time and the starting point of the journey and to prescribe the equipment to take along.
>
> We are sufficiently enthusiastic about it to wear some blisters on our feet, but we do not believe that this backyard wilderness so near to Washington should be kept closed to those who cannot hike 15 or 20 miles a day.

Preparation

Letters to the Post from other people supporting a natural canal began to arrive. Early in February, Anthony W. Smith arranged to have Jack Durham, a recent addition to the Wilderness Society staff, handle day-to-day planning of the hike for Douglas. Tony Smith also suggested that the six-day, 30-plus-mile-a-day hike Harry Thompson had outlined might be altered to a 20 to 25 mile a day hike. ("I doubt you will find other than me...willing to do 30 miles a day, and I am not sure whether performance will keep to ambition."). He also gave Douglas the names of two dozen men with conservation interests who should be invited to hike with him.

Some of the men Smith suggested were invited by letter; others may have received phone invitations since no record remains. Some asked to be invited—the author of the only history of the Chesapeake and Ohio Canal

Company, Walter A. Sanderlin, was one who did. Another was George F. Miller, aged 72, who, the year before, hiked the entire Appalachian Trail as the thirteenth person to do so. And at least one hiker, Jack Pearman, seems to have joined the hike at Cumberland on his own. No woman hiker was invited; at least one received a diplomatic letter of refusal. Conveniently, Douglas ignored all this when he told newsmen in Cumberland that the expedition was unique. No one had been asked to come; every one had asked to join.

The PATC six-ton truck and its regular driver were volunteered to carry hikers' duffel during the hike. William E. (Bill) Richardson, one of the Club's best camp cooks, would plan and cook meals for the hikers, and Charlie Thomas, aged 76, would act as general handyman. Richardson's menu and shopping list for one meal survives. The dinner included beef stew, salad, bread, fruit, coffee and tea. The shopping list for 12 pounds of meat, 30 potatoes, 36 carrots and a couple other illegible items totaled $43.50, to which bread ($1.61) and tea ($.45) were added for a total cost of $45.45, or a little over a dollar per person.

The Hike Gets Underway

The instructions sent the hikers by Jack Durham read:

> Hiking party assembles, with duffel, at Union Station in Washington at 12:45 on Friday, March 19. No diner on train, so lunch is to be eaten beforehand. Train leaves for Cumberland at 1:45, a special club car to be attached at end of train for party. Fare ($5.75) to be collected on train.

> Train arrives in Cumberland about 5 o'clock. Party will be met at train by cars (arrangements made by Senator Beall) and taken to Algonquin Hotel. Arrangements should be made by individuals, preferably by sending a card in advance, for lodging and breakfast at the hotel. (Single rooms with bath, $4.00 and $4.50, double rooms with twin beds, $7.50 and $8.00. Breakfast 45 cents and 80 cents.)

> After a brief stop at the hotel, the party will be taken to the Cumberland Country Club where they will be the guests of Mr. John McMullen, president and publisher, Cumberland Times and Cumberland News, at dinner. Hiking clothes will be worn. A few local residents will be present at the dinner, and a few speeches will be made, limited to 5 minutes each. The party will return to the hotel around 9 o'clock.

> Saturday morning hikers will be called at 6 o'clock for breakfast at the hotel and assembly for start of trip.

The National Park Service chief naturalist, Drew Chick, who accompanied the hikers, noted in a report that there were fewer hikers in the party than anticipated but that it contained "internationally and nationally-known names" and that "few knew each other before the hike and many never have participated in such an event before." As a matter of fact, neither had Justice Douglas; this was his first major conservation effort.

After the train ride actually began, the informal atmosphere in their special car encouraged getting acquainted. George Bookman sent this dispatch to TIME:

> Justice Douglas ambled to the platform just in time to catch the train. The youthful looking jurist was the jauntiest looking member of the party. He arrived dressed Western style with a Stetson hat, Levis, a striped dude shirt and short necktie, new high-cut hiking shoes, and light grey poplin jacket...Slouched in a parlor car chair in his blue jeans he looked very unlike a member of the High Court. In fact, a credit manager for U.S. Steel Co., traveling on the same train, heard his name was Douglas, mistook him for the Senator, and spent an hour upbraiding him for Paul Douglas' Senate speeches.

Later a Washington Post reporter augmented this tale.

The "five minutes only" speeches at the Cumberland Country Club began with Toastmaster J. Glenn Beall suggesting the hikers, when they arrived in Washington, would be singing hosannas for the inventor of the wheel and would unanimously support building the parkway. A later speech produced a quotation frequently repeated by the hikers. Walter A. Gunter, a former state senator, viewed the canal argument as a conflict between the twentieth century and the Stone Age. "The question is, whether the canal should be converted into a reserve for gold-plated Cadillacs of the Machine Age, or whether it should be preserved as a footpath for pedestrians of the Paleolithic Age?"

Douglas called the canal "one of the prettiest stretches in any part of the world I have ever visited" which, properly developed, would attract tens of thousands of tourists. "Think of being able to get on a horse at Washington, D.C., and riding all the way to Cumberland, Md., without climbing a hill or crossing a fence."

He asked Robert Estabrook, the Washington Post and Times-Herald editorial writer, and Associate Judge George Henderson, who, in the early 1920s, had canoed down to Harpers Ferry and then driven the mules of a canal barge into Washington, to join him in singing the canal song Henderson had just told him about, "Oh, the old Potomac's rising."

This became the theme song of the hikers, with Sigurd Olson and others making up new verses on incidents of the hike almost every day. There are thirty-two stanzas in the version preserved by the C&O Canal Association.

Saturday, March 20

Next morning, hikers were carried by auto to the Blue Spring and Lock 72 about seven miles downstream from Cumberland because of a number of fences crossing the towpath and a sewage discharge nearer town. Their actual start was delayed almost an hour because of photography by journalists, television and movie news cameraman, and the hundred or so local residents.

James "Little Scat" Eaton, son of George "Big Scat" Eaton, once a canal barge captain, presented Douglas with the last bell used on a mule on his father's barge. He also joined the hikers as far as Oldtown, where they left the towpath for a 45-minute visit to the home of Thomas Cresap, an early pioneer and Indian trader.

Signs of spring—spring peepers peeping, skeins of geese flying north—were observed as they hiked a towpath muddy from Friday night's rain. Irston Barnes identified birdcalls and excitedly recognized two Brewer's blackbirds, a western species rarely seen so far east. Louis Shollenberger recorded the spring sounds on his fifteen-pound CBS tape recorder for later playing over the air—after the tape was wiped of comments of hikers on walking in mud.

Aubrey Graves, a Washington Post reporter, said the hike used the "fifty minutes walking, ten minutes rest" system of the infantry but some hikers felt Douglas watched the second hand rather than the minute hand in counting the ten minutes. George Kennedy, Washington Star reporter, said the day's hike was twelve miles by map, but fourteen miles on the pedometers some hikers wore.

The day's hike ended at the Cardinal Club, but seventeen hikers accompanied Douglas an additional five miles to the western end of the Paw Paw Tunnel, so that it could be said Douglas went from Walla Walla (his birthplace) to Paw Paw. The Potomac Appalachian Trail Club truck carried them back to the Cardinal Club, where Secretary Sam Schwarz had arranged for dinner.

The Washington Star reporter, in the column he wrote that night, re-told Douglas' after dinner tale of roping mountain lions in Arizona for a rancher to use in training his dogs to hunt lions. Drew Chick recorded that Douglas asked him to comment on the plants and birds seen during the day. William A. Davies, from the U.S. Geological Survey, talked about the geology of the Potomac. ("Here the mountains were caught with their synclines down" was how he described the ridges and valleys of the region.) Bernard Frank (U.S. Forest Service Water Resources) explained why Town Creek was muddy and the Potomac clear. Olaus Murie commented on animal tracks he had seen during the day, and Walter Sanderlin talked about the history of the canal.

Chick also recorded that, despite the comfortable warmth of the club building, an overly-solicitous member of the Cardinal Club went around with a flashlight, even after lights were out, to wake sleepers with, "Are you warm enough?" And he draped Jack Pearman, who slept on a billiard table in the basement, for want of a cot, with an American flag to be sure he was comfortable. This stanza was added to the hiker's song:

> Oh, the bunks were soft at Cardinal
> And we snuggled in to rest;
> But our guardian angel spoiled it all,
> For he thought he knew best.

Sunday, March 21

"A wonderful breakfast of bacon and hot cakes dished out...by three members of the Potomac Appalachian Trail Club," wrote George Kennedy. And:

> The way he/Bill Richardson/takes care of men constantly coming back for more pancakes is amazing. There is only room on the griddle for two at a time. But he keeps popping them on to the plates as fast as they are brought to him. The bacon is cut by hand and cut thick. Bill's recipe for his cakes, which were delicious, is a simple one: One-third water-ground corn meal, two-thirds white flour pancake mix.
>
> He adds two tablespoons full of dried milk powder, one teaspoon of baking powder and an egg for every cupfull of the dry mix.

A minor blizzard, according to the newspapers, and "wind-driven snow in our faces" according to Grant Conway, accompanied the hikers as they walked from Maryland 51, where the truck dropped them, to Paw Paw Tunnel. Here "Little Scat" Eaton and some of his family met them. The day before, two men from Paw Paw, West Virginia, had cleared the worst of the debris off the walkway through the tunnel and hauled in planks to cover the largest holes.

Also, George Claggett and his two boys, who were hiking up river, joined the party to walk through the tunnel, which they had by-passed the night before by climbing up over it on a path new to Drew Chick. With the flashlights and lantern provided by the Eatons and the Claggetts, the hikers managed the tunnel well.

In the deep cut at the tunnel's eastern end, the walkway had rotted away, leaving only the narrow ledge where the supports had rested. Grant Conway reported that George Miller slipped there and, with another hiker, gone into the canal bed.

When the hikers passed the riverbank property of the Cumberland Outdoors Club at 9:30 a.m., a sign welcomed them across their bridge for lunch. Early as it was, they stopped for ham sandwiches, coffee and beer, and spent about an hour there.

"Cut across a loop a mile or so beyond Paw Paw Tunnel by going through the Western Maryland railroad tunnel," Durham's instructions for the day's hike suggested. Some hikers, including Robert Estabrook, did just that, gaining two hours on the others. Douglas and Pusey among others stayed on the towpath for the extra miles. The truck met the hikers at Little Orleans to pick up many; according to Chick, the hikers were strung out for over a mile.

George Kennedy, who had ridden half of Saturday's hike, elected to walk all the way to the Woodmont Gun and Rod Club. His story reads:

> I strolled the last six miles from sheer exhaustion. I began seeing a mirage. The parkway had been finished through this beautiful scenic stretch, and kindly people in gold-plated Cadillacs were asking me to ride with them.
>
> Anthony Wayne Smith, associate general counsel of the CIO, lagged back to see to it that I wasn't alone. And a Methodist minister from nearby joined us. He said he had witnessed the beginning of the hike near Cumberland and was so disappointed that it had not been started with prayer that he decided to walk a stretch with the group.

Grant Conway's account is somewhat different:

> On the second day, George, brimming with confidence, decided to hike a long stretch without access roads. Near a lockhouse, Kennedy collapsed on a log with exhaustion. When after half an hour he couldn't seem to regain his feet, preparations were made to send a rescue party. George said he could walk any time he wanted but he was having trouble getting the top off his bottle of whiskey.
>
> At this point, a local Methodist minister arrived and took over. He had wished to start the party off with a prayer at Cumberland but arrived too

late and it had taken him a couple of days to catch up. He had always wanted to rescue a fallen newspaperman, and here was the chance. He got George on his feet and even agreed to carry his pack. When George asked for a drink along the route, the parson obliged by passing the bottle. George finished so strong that he insisted on walking the last two miles where he could have ridden. The minister credited George's strong finish to his faith and Kennedy's own whiskey.

> Oh, the Old Potomac's falling,
> The river's running dry,
> But Kennedy'll float on down to town
> On good old Rock and Rye.

Dinner was at the Woodmont Gun and Rod Club, and was "a sumptuous meal, served in courses with champagne, cocktails, and a choice of after-dinner liqueurs." Other guests included Senator Beall and Judge Henderson. The hikers:

> slept in beds with sheets and inner-spring mattresses. We admired the 'Presidential Chair,' a cane-bottomed rocker with a wild-cat skin, where six U.S. Presidents had sat. Arrangements were made for Justice Douglas to sit in the chair and a silver plate with his name engraved on it was placed on an arm. Justice Douglas responded with the gift of a skin of a mountain lion which he had roped the previous year. The air was saturated with benevolence and we were not prepared for the Club official's postscript.

> 'And right under the plate for Justice Douglas, we expect soon to have another plate dedicated to the Prince of Wales...' Quiet prevailed in the room, and we looked inquiringly at each other. It developed that a member of the Club has dreamed for many decades that the Prince of Wales, now the Duke of Windsor, would accept an invitation to Woodmont and grace the confines of the 'Presidential Chair.' The dreamer was Henry F. Bridges, secretary-treasurer of the Club, who was responsible for inviting the hikers there.

A number of hikers left that evening or next morning to return to work in Washington. It is a little difficult to determine, from existing records, who went, because almost all returned toward the end of the hike.

Monday, March 22

Twenty-three hikers "got off the champagne circuit in perfect weather" at 9 a.m., rather later than the usual 7:30 to 8 a.m. departure. They walked out of the mountains about twenty miles to Ernstville, where most boarded the truck to carry them the last few miles to Fort Frederick State Park, so that camp could be set up before dark. Sigurd Olson, and four others, declined the ride and walked into camp, where they arrived at 7 p.m., two hours after the main party.

Several incidents made the day memorable. Near one of the locks (probably Lock 54 or 53), a farmer (whose name Chick recalled as Weaver) had brought an autograph book and a basket of apples. Each hiker was asked for his autograph and in return received a polished apple.

At Hancock, part of the towpath and canal bed was used as city dump, and hikers could choose to ride around it on the truck. The Post editors were among those who did, thereby missing the "derisive comments" from some townspeople that Chick reported. The Cumberland News story said, "Hikers said that, along the route, various residents have been shouting at them, 'We want the parkway,' 'Develop the canal,' 'Git rid of the mosquitoes.'"

A civics class with their teacher met the hike, and were asked by Douglas, "How many Justices have there been in the Supreme Court since it began?" They didn't know; nor did he, he admitted.

A few miles below, at Millstone Point, Louis Shollenberger reported,

> an official greeting in penciled handwriting was nailed to a tree along the bank of the canal. It read:

> Welcome to Millstone Point
> Population 40
> Speed limit 105
> Mayor A.E. Eichelberger
> Special rates to hitchhikers
> Sloan's Liniment and Blue Jay Cornplasters
> Good Luck and Watch your step!

It was there that someone noted the order in which the hikers were walking. In the lead was Grant Conway, followed by George F. Miller, Constant Southworth, Fred Blackburn, Harvey Broome, Justice Douglas, Drew Chick, Jack Pearmain, Dr. Irston Barnes, Smith Brookhart, Cohn Ritter, Sigurd Olson, Dr. Olaus Murie, Albert Farwell and William Davies. The other nine were presumably still in the truck circumventing the city dump. By then, only fifteen of the hikers had walked every step of the way.

Later that afternoon, Conway remembered:

A lady on horseback bore down on us from the rear. She was riding from the wilderness in the west and we expected at any moment to see Indians emerge from the thickets and overtake her. She skidded her horse to a stop and slid from her English saddle and held out her hand to the Justice. 'I'm Mrs. Snodgrass. Glad to know you, Justice Douglas. The mosquitoes are frightful here. Sometimes they almost eat my horse and myself alive.' After a few more comments on mosquitoes, she mounted her horse and started to ride away. Turning in the saddle, she shouted to Justice Douglas, 'See what you can do about those mosquitoes, my boy!'

At Tonoloway Creek, four Eagle Scouts and the editor of their high school paper joined the hike to go with it as far as Williamsport in order to get an interview with Douglas for the school paper. Chick commented that the young editor earned his interview because he was an inexperienced hiker and his equipment was poorly chosen.

Bill Richardson had arrived at Fort Frederick by truck an hour and a half before the hikers to prepare dinner (the beef stew of the menu and shopping list preserved). Tents were set up in a "Civil War encampment." Despite the 20° F. temperature, some, including the Justice, preferred to sleep under the starry sky. This stanza resulted:

> Last night we took to sleeping out
> Beneath the open skies
> The ground was hard, the dew was wet
> But stars were in our eyes.

Tuesday, March 23

"The night in the open proved no hardship. The air mattress on the leaves was as comfortable as any innerspring mattress. It was cold, but warm inside the eiderdown sleeping bag," George Kennedy wrote. The Star carried a picture of Douglas in his sleeping bag. (According to Paul Hauck, Kennedy had borrowed his equipment, most of it from Grant Conway.)

Breakfast was eggs and bacon and coffee.

Durham's advance instructions said that this day's hike was "very bad along slack water just below Four Locks in 1951" when Corporal Howar made his last inspection trip. It wasn't any better in 1954. Conway wrote:

> Above Dam No. 4, there wasn't a canal for several miles and there never had been one. The barges floated in the Potomac and the narrow towpath near the water's edge was covered with oozy mud. We mucked our way, with gobs of mud clinging to our tired feet.

A reporter wrote:

> On the move, the hikers listened to a bird talk by Dr. Irston Barnes.../who/pointed a finger skyward with surprise at a flight of American merganser ducks and a Brewer's blackbird.
>
> Around noontime, they encountered 87-year-old Ezra Bargoff who described his labor on the canal 66 years ago. He told Douglas that he first worked as a mule driver and then as a barge steerer at 50 cents a day.
>
> 'That', said Bargoff, 'was a good wage in those days.' He then offered welcome cups of coffee to all hands.

At Williamsport, an elementary school band and chorus offered music, and young Judy Smith handed out several copies of the pamphlet "Williamsport and Vicinity Reminiscences." A sign advised the hikers, "Cumberland 84 miles; Washington 100 miles." There were also framed pictures showing the Potomac in flood. Later, at the Potomac Rod and Gun Club at Falling Waters, four school children came out from Williamsport to sing their canal song, "I've got a mule and her name is Sal." Sigurd Olson led the hikers in singing in response, all the existing verses of their canal song.

By this time, foot trouble was appearing. Kennedy's dispatch for the day included:

> This is a tough hike and even the experienced young hikers are beginning to feel it. The Justice is 55. There are no serious casualties yet, but there are some swollen ankles and sore knees, not to mention feet.

In Conway's article on the hike, he says that Dr. Barnes had written a column in an earlier Washington Post on the art of walking in which he recommended walking flatfooted for ease and comfort.

> Irston has fallen arches and walks flatfooted naturally...At a lecture when Justice Douglas was prevailed upon to discuss his technique of walking on

the Canal, his answer was 'putting one foot in front of another'...Merlo/Pusey/was a good sport but the pace was too fast.

Paul Hauck sent me his reminiscences of the Douglas hike, which he joined at Williamsport, arriving by Greyhound bus, which Jack Durham met to carry him to camp.

But first we stopped at Hooper Wolfe's general store in the Square where Jack bought out Hooper's entire stock of moleskin. I had never heard of the stuff before, but over the next few days I was to learn to appreciate its soothing qualities as I drew on Jack's precious supply. In 1954 most of us were still hiking in surplus GI boots or common sneakers. Except for a few trail-wise veterans like the Justice and Harvey Broome, special boots or hiking shoes were not much in evidence. I remember that Merlo Pusey walked in his old high top black Keds. My own shoes were Marine boots I had worn in Guam. I recall that Colin Ritter also hiked in his old military footwear—Army boots with the over-the-ankle strap. By the end of the hike his feet were so swollen that he did not take his boots off at night for fear he'd not get them on again in the morning.

Hauck also described "the regular pattern of activity after the day's walk."

First, after picking out a spot on the grounds each man would tend to that day's aches and sores. Those personal chores done, the group would then enjoy a hearty meal, and finally would relax with good conversation, restorative liquids and session of song before turning in for the night. A couple of verses of the 'canal song' were already being sung with great enthusiasm to the tune of the old Erie Canal song. If a piano was available, Connie Southworth accompanied the singing in his inimitable style, bouncing up and down on the piano stool for emphasis.

Hagerstown attorney Charles F. Wagman had offered the hospitality of the Potomac Rod and Gun Club to the hikers. Cots under the roof were available, but some of the hikers preferred the porch, and a couple chose to sleep completely outdoors.

"Perhaps one secret of Douglas' stamina was his ability to sleep soundly," Robert Estabrook wrote recently:

We discovered a contributing factor at one of the fish and game clubs that offered us use of its dormitory after a day's trek. One of the hikers produced a bottle of bourbon and asked me to pour the justice a drink. Douglas held out a tumbler and said: 'I'll tell you when!'

'When' turned out to be an entire tumblerful, which the justice proceeded to down in short order. Soon after, he retired to a sleeping bag, snores emanating as if he had sawed several cords of wood.

Wednesday, March 24

One of the sore ankles belonged to Drew Chick so he traveled by road that day, reducing the number who had walked every step of the way to ten. The 24-mile hike took nine and a half hours, including some rest stops, and an hour spent for lunch. Hiking continued difficult because parts of the towpath had been recently flooded, and the damp river silt clung to hikers' feet.

At Taylor's Landing, just beyond the halfway mark of the hike, Mr. and Mrs. L.H. Miner, Mr. and Mrs. R.E. Stover, Mr. and Mrs. S.J. Gower and Mr. and Mrs. William A. Startzman set up a long table in the Miner garage and served luncheon—hamburger, boiled ham, Swiss cheese, potato chips, pickles, cake, and coffee. Was this the occasion for which this stanza was created?

> The people swarm around us
> With cookies, fruit and cheer.
> This is the consarned dangdest thing
> That ever they did hear.

After lunch, Grant Conway wrote:

A farmer intercepted us on the towpath and presented his problem to the Justice. It seemed that carp entered the Canal from the river and the dying carp attracted buzzards. When the buzzards had eaten the carp, they stayed and ate his young pigs as fast as his sows could bring forth the litters. Some seventy little piglets had been devoured by the buzzards. He had called the sheriff, game warden, and county agent and they hadn't given him any satisfaction. The Judge, who wasn't one to tarry along the trail, finally commented, 'Yes, we've got to do something about those buzzards,' and led his stalwart band down the trail to Washington. The story soon spread, and this was the evening's creation:

> "Buzzards are a-killin' pigs,"
> The irate farmer swore;
> "If, Justice, you don't stop them birds
> There's goin 'to be a war!"

Later near Shepherdstown, the first welcome on the towpath was "Our thanks to the Washington Post and Times-Herald" nailed to a tree. The second greeting was tacked to a stake planted just to the right of a mud puddle. It read, "Justice Douglas, keep to right. Booby traps to left are for Post editors." A few feet farther on, also nailed to a tree, was this "poem:"

> Henry Kyd Douglas
> Stonewall Jackson's aide
> Got a hill named after him-
> You keep our sanctuary,
> We'll have another hill named Douglas.

About a hundred residents of Shepherdstown were on the towpath to greet the hikers. Douglas maintained his pace of 112 steps a minute, pausing only long enough to greet each well-wisher by name and introduce those hikers that happened to be walking with him. Then he was off down the towpath, allowing well-wishers and hikers to catch up if they wished.

The hikers reached the Conococheague Club about 5:30 p.m. PATC staff again provided dinner and breakfast.

Thursday, March 25

Because this was expected to be the toughest and possibly longest day of the hike (covering 26 miles), five hikers started out at 6:20 a.m., with others getting off a quarter of an hour later. Walter Sanderlin and Bernard Frank rejoined the hike, as did Post writer Aubrey Graves. He brought with him his two sons, three horses and a burro. The horses were immediately put to use. Merlo Pusey was one of the riders. Another was Don Stough (a PATC member, whom Graves identified in a photo caption as a man "who once outran a band of revolutionists in the wilds of Brazil"). One of the leading hikers posted a sign on a tree by the towpath, "Jackasses have traveled this way before."

Paul Hauck told me this story, though he remembers it happening at Point of Rocks a day late:

Olaus Murie was a world famous biologist from Moose, Wyoming. The Justice invited Olaus along to provide expert observations on the wild life along the trail. And Olaus didn't disappoint. We all marveled, for example, at his ability to read animal tracks. Each morning he would identify the tracks of nocturnal visitors to our camp. No matter how faint the tracks, Olaus was able to identify the critter for us. On the next to last night out, Aubrey Graves, the Post's outdoors editor, had his son transport Aubrey's pet Mexican burro from his suburban Virginia farm to our camp at Point of Rocks. Arriving at the camp after dark, Aubrey's son led the little burro, Jose, to a distant tree to be tethered for the night. Early the next morning, Aubrey made a point of showing the burro tracks to Olaus. Olaus looked puzzled and hesitated for some time before speaking. 'This has got me stumped,' he said finally. 'If I didn't know any better I'd say a Mexican burro came through here last night, but of course that's impossible.'

Aside from the usual obstacles of brush and rocks, the difficult point of the day's hike occurred above Harpers Ferry between locks 33 and 32, where the rising river had inundated the canal and the towpath was either crumbled away entirely or an island in the racing river. Conway wrote "following the steep banks/on the berm, side/we found ourselves in a box canyon. We had the choice of retracing our steps or climbing the cliffs to the parapets of Fort Duncan above." Grapevines provided holds up the 150 foot cliff for Douglas and a dozen others. The newspaper correspondents took the truck by back roads to by-pass the obstacle. The Keepe Tryst-Sharpsburg road brought the hikers back to the towpath at Lock 32.

Bird life was more colorful than usual on this stretch. Albert Farwell sighted a cerulean warbler. A large flock of white swans was on the river.

"Harpers Ferry was covered with a blanket of mist and we could not even see across the river." No one detoured to visit the town—perhaps because Harry Bowers was serving lunch to the hikers in his summer home, Potomac Shores, at Weverton. Bowers and nine associates served 42 steaks to 37 hikers. Graves commented, "They're still trying to figure out what kind of arithmetic that is, but nobody's confessing." ABC sent camera crews to film a live interview with Douglas, Estabrook and Pusey.

At Brunswick, a banner the width of the towpath informed the hikers local citizens preferred a parkway; however, those that met the hike were welcoming.

That day, thanks to Constant Southworth, the hikers had two new marching songs. One was to the tune of "Where do we go from here, boys?"

Where do we go from here, boys?
Where do we go from here?
We hope to go to Washington
Although that is not yet clear.
This we know before we go
We'll give a lusty cheer.
So that is the way it stands today;
Where do we go from here?

The other parodied the Marine song:

From the genial hosts of Cumberland,
To the girls of Washington.
We have set our sights on foot to go
Be it walk, or be it run.
The sedentary man will humbly gaze
With envy and with awe
And stride beneath the banners of
The press and of the law.

It is perhaps fortunate neither song lived beyond the hike.

The Kanawha Club at Calico Rocks, near Point of Rocks, has a unique setting of high-thrusting limestone conglomerate rocks, and is perhaps the most attractively located of all the clubs the hikers visited. It belongs to the Frederick County Fish and Game Protective Association. Alton C. Whitmore, club secretary, served the hikers and many Association members a steak dinner. Among the prominent Frederick County businessmen present were Will Delaplane, publisher of the Frederick News Post; Russell McClain, chairman of the State Roads Commission; Dr. Eddie Thomas; and Col. Elmer Munshown, Superintendent of State Police.

Friday, March 26

The history of the twenty-seven miles from Point of Rocks to Seger's store at Seneca, Maryland, is not as well reported as earlier days. The headline over Aubrey Graves' evening dispatch to the Post evidently reflects the hikers' mood: "Canal hikers just 18 miles from (Sigh!) Washington."

At 6:05 a.m., Douglas and six others started hiking, forgetting their lunches. Corporal Sam Howar chased them six miles by road to deliver them.

It was a pleasant spring day with temperatures in the 70s. Innumerable turtles sunned themselves. A groundhog ambled by. A flock of Canadian geese went over. Drew Chick identified spring wild flowers for the hikers—bloodroot, toothwort, deadnettle, speedwell, chickweed, spring beauty.

Justice Douglas is welcomed at Fletcher's Boathouse

At White's Ferry, a beagle attached himself to the hikers, and, at a rest stop, was photographed panting between Bernard Frank's bare feet. A collie also followed the group. Both dogs were left stranded when the hikers were picked up at Seneca. Ray Riley, a boat concessionaire, penned the dogs and took them home to Germantown. The owner of the collie recognized the dog on that day's television news and asked the National Park Service to return it. Both dogs were returned to their owners April 2, when a Park Service policeman made his inspection trip that way.

At Broad Branch, above Edwards Ferry, "the rain-swollen river had washed out the towpath. A few hikers took off their shoes, rolled up their jeans, and waded across. Then, a hundred feet below the gulch, somebody discovered a walk of rocks, thoughtfully laid by Hugo Habbutzel, United States Parks maintenance foreman."

Robert Estabrook rode one of Graves' horses during the day. "After riding six miles, he dismounted, claiming he had been lured into the saddle for the foul purpose of aggravating his only two 'unsore' muscles."

At Seneca, private automobiles took the hikers to the Izaak Walton League club house and conservation farm at Poolesville. A Boy Scout troop prepared "a fabulous feast. The choice was buffalo or salmon steaks. The former had been given a liberal treatment of 'tenderizer' and were just what the doctor ordered. At feast's end, all hands agreed that 'hospitality means McKee.' A.B. McKee is president of the League's local chapter." He also brought three political figures from Montgomery County to meet the hikers.

Following dinner, Chick reported, "The group met spontaneously to organize into an association for the purpose of expressing its views and to keep the close friendships created by this experience." Bernard Frank was the temporary chairman but Douglas was elected the permanent chair and was instructed to name a committee to solicit the views of all the hikers—both nine-day and two-day—on the canal's future. A report summarizing their views would be prepared for delivery to the Secretary of the Interior.

Saturday, March 27

By seven a.m., the hikers were again at Seneca walking south. They reached Great Falls by nine, still maintaining the three plus miles an hour pace they had developed. Here a large contingent of people supporting the preservation of the canal joined them for the "triumphal last miles," as Chick put it. Two kayaks paced the hikers in the canal. At Cropley, the last meal of the hike was prepared by PATC cooks, but Chick does not mention whether they attempted to feed the day hikers who had joined them.

At Lock 6, Secretary of the Interior Douglas McKay, National Capital Parks' Superintendent Edward Kelly, NCP'S Assistant Superintendent Harry Thompson, and Sutton Jet, National Park Service historian, met the hike. "Justice Douglas, I presume" and a handshake was McKay's greeting, according to a Washington Star photographer. The Justice's reply, as quoted by George Kennedy, was, "You've got some wonderful country up there. I'm going to write you a little letter."

The hikers gather at a lockhouse

All walked the half-mile to Lock 5, where the National Park Service's mule-drawn barge waited. All thirty-seven Douglas hikers got aboard, more or less just as Sigurd Olson's last composition describes:

> Glory to the Immortal Nine
> The waiting thousands roared.
> The conquering heroes hit Lock Five
> And hurled themselves aboard.

"Wrapped in blankets, the triumphant hoofers ate doughnuts, drank steaming coffee, and waved to friends and greeters who crowded the towpath by the thousands as their magic carpet floated them home" is the Post description.

Half a dozen canoes followed the barge. One carried two signs: "Scratch the Parkway at the Post" and "May Justice (Douglas) prevail."

Chick concluded his report with the opinion that the hike "was probably the most significant event in the history of the canal since the government acquired and reconstructed the first twenty miles in 1938–48." George Kennedy, in his final dispatch to the Star, called it a stunt, and suggested the future of the canal would be as a Mecca for Sunday drivers in their Cadillacs. A Park Service historian, writing in 1991, has probably the best assessment of the hike. "The real purpose of the hike was publicity, of course, and in this its leaders were not disappointed."

Afterwards

The C&O Canal Committee appointed after the Poolesville meeting by Douglas consisted of Dr. Irston Barnes, Fred Blackburn, Harvey Broome, William Davies, Robert Estabrook, Bernard Frank, Olaus Murie, Sigurd Olson, Louis Shollenberger, Anthony Smith and Howard Zahniser. Their report was delivered to Secretary McKay in mid-April, but it wasn't until January 1961 that the canal received protection from parkway construction by the creation of the C&O Canal Historic Monument. It took another ten years for protection from dams on the Potomac and probable flooding of the canal and towpath to be assured when the Monument became a National Park. All this is a story better told elsewhere.

In early winter 1954–55, Constant Southworth, Grant Conway, Paul Hauck and Jack Durham organized a reunion for the original hikers in spring 1955. A private get-together for the hikers was held Friday night at a small cabin on the berm side of the canal just below Paw Paw Tunnel, with PATC truck and cooks on call. A hike and a banquet on Saturday were open to the public. The banquet, arranged with the help of Frank Wachter of the Hagerstown Chamber of Commerce, was held at the Alexander Hotel in Hagerstown. Friday and Saturday nights were stag affairs. The second reunion, at Fort Frederick State Park, drew much larger attendance from the public. When time for the third came, the C&O Committee had taken steps to turn the Canal Committee into the Chesapeake and Ohio Canal Association. The Association has its own history.

The Hikers

It's not exactly clear how many Douglas hikers there were—meaning how many started out with the intention of hiking one or more days with Douglas. A list in Douglas' 25 papers has 43 names on it, with penciled notes on some attempting to show how many days were actually hiked. The first Washington Post story on the hike itself headlined 39 hikers as beginning the hike, but the next day's headline made the number 37. Aubrey Graves, in his final story on the hike, said 37 hikers began the hike and 37 ended it, but not the same 37.

What is certain is who the "Immortal Nine" of Olson's verse are. They are the "simon-pures" who walked every step of the way. They are Harvey Broome, Grant Conway, Justice Douglas, Albert Farwell, George F. Miller, Olaus Murie, John Pearman, Colin Ritter and Constant Southworth.

The hikers classified themselves into several other categories, too. There were the dragons, hikers who walked most of the way, sometimes barely dragging themselves in. (Estabrook and Pusey fell into this category.) There were the snapdragons, who were dragons who occasionally lagged behind to take pictures. Taillights were those who were habitually in the rear out of sight, sometimes by miles. Finally, there were the duffers, who hitched frequent rides in the truck.

George Bookman's early dispatch to TIME described the group well:

> Experienced outdoorsmen, officials and members of such groups as the Wilderness Society, Potomac Appalachian Trail Club, Audubon Society, National Parks Association…The party included a military geologist, economists from five government agencies, a history professor, and an economics professor. All have love and knowledge of the outdoors.

Memorial bust of Justice Douglas

II

A Modest Marathon

Almost as rare as a $20 gold piece in a church collection plate are organizers of an athletic event who, having achieved sponsors and enlarged attendance, back off from the glory and publicity. But that was what the Cumberland Valley Athletic Club did in the mid-1970s and has held to since. Even the JFK Hike/Run remains a modest ultra-marathon for amateurs.

Bruce Burnside wrote an excellent account of the early history of the event for the Cumberland Valley Athletic Club which is reprinted here with the permission of author and club:

> Teddy Roosevelt had the idea in 1908.
> John Kennedy revived it in 1963.
> The Cumberland Valley Athletic Club couldn't forget it.
>
> For six years a small group of runners kept the JFK 50-mile hike/run alive. From Boonsboro to St. James, Md., until unexpectedly in 1968 it began phenomenal growth. In ten years, it went from 11 participants to more than 1700.
>
> In 1963, William J. (Buzz) Sawyer placed a notice in the Hagerstown Morning Herald that the Cumberland Valley A.C. would do a 50 mile hike on Saturday March 30th. It was very informally arranged. Buzz thought this would be a change for his CVAC boys and he had picked out a route two weeks before. All of them were runners who had never before tried such a long hike. At 6 A.M., eleven of them started slowly up South Mountain, traveling as light as possible. They carried only canteens, and bought food and soft drinks at several stores along the way. After 13 hours and 10 minutes, Sawyer and three others reached the finish line in darkness, hiking most of the distance and running only a short part.
>
> Not yet thinking of himself as a 50-mile race director, Sawyer assumed it would be only a one-shot event. But the next year the CVAC boys wanted to do it again, and seven of the nineteen finished, the three co-leaders

boasting a time of 12 hours 33 minutes. For the next several years near the end of March, the group would set out over the horseshoe-shaped course…Each year the winning time crept downward and the Morning Herald carried an account of the event…

By 1966 the word had spread over the mountain to the next county, and the Frederick News began to write about the enthusiastic few who liked to hike, run, limp and ache their way for so many miles. With the field in 1968 totaling only 36, the race was recognized for the first time in the Baltimore Sun…The first woman completed the course.

In 1969, without any warning, four times as many starters showed up…151 starters eager to battle with the long path over the mountain and beside the river…Sawyer believed "The jogging craze had been building up for about a year. Many people now had better conditioning and increased confidence, and they wondered if they could meet the challenge of our mountain trail."…

More race officials were needed as the race grew in size, and formal checkpoints were established at trail intersections…Volunteers have also come recently from the Mack Truck Company, where Buzz has worked since 1961 as a gear design engineer. He is pleased with the community spirit which has developed, although he admits he could still use more help.

That was written for the program of the 1974 race, which was also supported by the Washington County Tourism Council and the Hagerstown television station. The 1974 race began with 1366 participants. Soon after the race began, a cold rain carried by a nasty wind began and continued all day; by afternoon, bare twigs and greening bushes were coated with ice. Only 225 of the 1355 participants finished the course in what some called the "Campaign of second degree hypothermia."

The date for the 1975 race was changed to November, in the hopes of better weather: the change has been permanent. Buzz Sawyer and the CVAC stepped back from the big time also…The Cumberland Valley Athletic Club set the registration date for participants very early, so that the number was held to a more manageable size—usually between 300 and 350. Although local sponsors continue to support the hike/run, organizations outside the region are neither solicited nor accepted. A further change was made in 1980, when the last few miles of the course were changed to bring the race to conclusion at the Springfield Middle School in Williamsport. This did not change the distance of the race, which remains at 50.2 miles.

One rule remains inflexible: to earn a plaque as one of the top ten finishers, or a certificate as a participant, the participant must finish the course within 14 hours. Over the years the completion time of winners has gone down from the original 13 hours plus to under six hours. The first such win was in 1973 with 5 hours, 55 minutes, 30 seconds. In 1994, the winning time was 5:46:22, with the second man coming in just 12 minutes later. The number of participants finishing has increased as well. In the last half dozen years, the number of finishers has been over, sometimes well over, two-thirds of the number who began the race.

Buzz Sawyer continued to organize the event after his retirement in 1980, giving the job up only in 1992. He registered as no.1 participant for the 1993 race but was prevented from running by a hairline fracture a month earlier. He is still keeping the statistics of the race: times of winners; the oldest participant; the first ten year old to enter the race; who ran the race most often. In 1994, Mike Adams and Kim Byron (brother to politician Goodloe Byron who also ran in the JFK during his lifetime) completed running 1300 miles in the JFK. Carl Mahoney completed his twenty-fifth consecutive run. Paul French, of Williamsport, the first Washington County man to be in the top ten finishers for three consecutive years, commented to a reporter that running the JFK "is like a tradition. This is like a holiday: when it comes to this time of year, you stop everything because it is the time to run the JFK."

More than 3500 people from 13 states and Canada have participated in the JFK over the years, and it is the oldest continuously run ultra-marathon in the country. It is also over a challenging course.

It begins with a three-mile warm-up on the streets of Boonsboro and a 1190 ft. climb up South Mountain on Alternate US 40, the old National Road. Then there is 12.7 miles of the Appalachian Trail, which was not designed with runners in mind. As a reporter-runner of the JFK wrote:

> terrain like a roller-coaster—a narrow path with boulders, hard stone and razor-sharp rocks, in gullies of different depths we climbed up one way and down another.

In fall the trail is often slippery with leaves or mud. Nor is it always obvious: one man raced out to the brink of the 550-foot Weverton Cliffs because he failed to note the double blaze marking a turn in the trail. The Appalachian Trail has absorbed the wear of so many racers surprisingly well; I (Paula) have maintained three and a half miles of part of the course for twenty years and, despite my watchfulness, have seen no significant damage to the treadway.

After the mountains comes 26.5 miles of approximately flat C&O Canal towpath. "The towpath determines the race," the 1994 winner told a Hagerstown Mail reporter. The final 6.3 miles are the mostly asphalted roads that roll through southwestern Washington County.

Buzz Sawyer's description of the course is the best:

> Mainly it's the appeal of a unique course with a tremendous variety of scenery. You have paved roads at the beginning and end, the Appalachian Trail and the canal towpath. The main thing is you're completely away from crowds and automobiles for most of 39 miles. It's not like most marathons—running through streets or along highways. It's just you on the mountain or you beside the river, or as Teddy Roosevelt put it, "The only others are the people in the arena with you." for miles and miles. I think there are few events where this is duplicated, where you're isolated from the modern world for so long a time...

The JFK remains a modest neighborhood event. The participants and the Cumberland Valley Athletic Club like it that way just fine.

III

Spirits, Legal or Otherwise

Making and drinking whiskey has been an important part of life in western Maryland from the earliest days, although, perhaps, it has had less importance in the most recent half-century than it did in earlier periods.

Even before the region was settled, rum almost caused a war between Indians and Europeans. Settlements were accompanied by small whiskey stills. Williams, in his histories of Washington and Frederick counties, pointed out that, while wheat could be made into flour and shipped economically, corn and rye had to be made into the less bulky whiskey to send profitably to a distant market.

Frederick County had, in 1790, 400 stills, one for every seventeen families. A few years earlier, the British officer, Thomas Ansbury, writing about the prisoners of war held in Frederick after Burgoyne's surrender, said:

> Spirits are easily procured in Frederick County and at a cheap rate as there are an abundance of stills around the county and the soldiers were in a constant state of intoxication…Within the fortnight we have lost two in a most melancholy way, who during the absence of the man who attended the still on the Colonel's plantation, drank the liquor hot out of the pipe and the next morning were found dead in their beds.

It was much the same in Washington County:

> The manufacture of whiskey, being almost the chief industry of the County, there was a considerable number of brass-workers and coppersmiths to make and repair distilleries. (Williams)

The Frenchman, Bayard, traveling through Maryland and to the valley of Virginia in 1791, observed:

> It would be difficult to tell which offers the greater attraction, the hunt or the drinking bout. When they would propose that I go fox-hunting, they would not forget a good dinner, the good porter, and the excellent rum that would be found after the hunt. Americans like to lose their dignified reserve in a tavern. It seems the national timidity and reserve can be overcome only by drink.
>
> A circle of drinkers in the United States is not as noisy as in France: each speaks in his turn. When one of them sings, he is not accompanied nor interrupted, and if these quiet tipplers did not move from the table it would be difficult to discover their intemperance...
>
> In the cities, every one has his glass for beer and wine, though the *tody* and punch are drunk out of the same bowl.

In a footnote, Bayard explained that *tody* was a drink made of brandy, sugar, and lukewarm water, in which one or two roasted apples and a little nutmeg are placed. Elsewhere he expressed disgust at the common drinking bowl, primarily because of the stains and bits of tobacco left on its rim by the tobacco-soaked mustaches and beards of the drinkers.

With whiskey-making so commonplace, it is not surprising that, when Congress imposed a seven to eighteen cents a gallon tax on whiskey (the amount depending on the strength or proof), or an alternative tax upon the stills, the farmers of western Pennsylvania and Maryland were outraged and regarded the tax as unjust oppression. The Whisky Rebellion began.

President Washington regarded it as serious enough to call out 15,000 troops and to take command of them himself at Cumberland. However, in the South Mountain area, the Whisky Rebellion sputtered like a defective rocket.

> Along the base of South Mountain it is probable there were at that time a great number of small stills. An organized body of men armed themselves and proceeded toward Frederick town with the aroused determination to attack the town and take possession of the magazines there deposited. Frederick had already been notified by messenger from Hagerstown of the meditated attack but as there were five hundred enlisted men in the town and a large number of Baltimore militia within easy reach no fear was felt nor was there any occasion for apprehension for the attack was not made. The Governor of the State hastened to the scene of the disturbance. He arrived in Frederick on Saturday, and remained over Sunday, returning to

Annapolis on Monday…The arrival of Washington at Cumberland where troops were assembled speedily put an end to the troubles. (Williams)

When Jefferson became President in 1802, the excise on whiskey was reduced to a minimum. "There followed, roughly between 1810 and 1840, the heaviest drinking in American experience," according to Bready, in the *Maryland Historical Magazine*. Williams said this about the use of whiskey in Washington County in this period:

The amount of whiskey consumed…at that time and down to recent years, is fearful to contemplate. It was cheap and fortunately it was pure. There was no adulteration and no excuse for any. The prices for drinks for many years was regulated by law. If a man wished to "treat" he would not order so many drinks but a pint of whiskey more or less, according to the number called up to drink. For many years there was a fashion of whiskey bottles, blown into a likeness of Washington and nearly every man in the county has his "George Washington" which he took to the nearest grocery to be filled. Every grocery sold whiskey and many other stores kept a bottle in a back room to "treat" customers. On Saturday a grocery clerk in Hagerstown was kept busy from morning to night filling "George Washingtons" from a barrel until frequently a boy engaged in this work would topple over drunk from the fumes. Sometimes the storekeeper would make the boy drink a small quantity of the whiskey and that would at once render him proof against the overpowering effects of the vapor. For many years and down to the time when the Franklin Railroad, the Canal, and the National Turnpike were constructed, it was a matter of contract with laborers the amount of whiskey to be dealt out. A regularly employed functionary on these and other works employing a large number of men was the "Jigger Boss" who made constant rounds among the men, with his "jigger," a small tin can, doling out whiskey. The men working on the Canal agreed with the contractors to receive eighteen of these jiggers and a "chance at the jug"—that is, at the close of the day's work each one should have the privilege of drinking from a jug all that he could take in a single draught. Possibly this will account for a number of riots that occurred during the prosecution of work on the Canal.

Nathaniel Row, an Emmitsburg gunsmith interviewed at age 87, about the turn of the twentieth century remembered prices when he was a young man:

Ah, yes. We knew what whiskey was in those days. It was good whiskey, too. There were lots of distilleries around here. Whiskey only cost twenty cents a gallon and sold in the taverns a gill for a fip. A fip was a Spanish coin worth six and a quarter cents, about the size of the old three-cent piece. Most all of our silver coins were Spanish. But about the whiskey. It was usually bought by the barrel for household use and everybody could help himself when he wanted a drink. Ah, those were the good old days. There was much less drunkenness than there is now in spite of the fact that whiskey then was as cheap as Emmitsburg water is now.

While drinking liquor might be commonplace, it was not universally approved. In 1829 and 1830, temperance societies formed, especially in Washington County, some under the aegis of the Lutheran Church. Society members pledged not to drink ardent spirits, nor to furnish them to families, workers or laborers they might employ "except when necessary as a medicine." They also pledged to give preference in hiring to those who abstain from use of ardent spirits.

The first step they proposed was to abandon whiskey in the harvest and hay fields and to increase wages to the amount the whiskey would cost. A genuine temperance excitement was started, which lasted nearly two years. Many storekeepers joined the society and abandoned the sale of whiskey in the stores, and it was gravely announced as the crowning triumph of the movement that…at two taverns the practice of tippling on Sunday had been abandoned. (Williams)

The temperance societies did not long survive. Perhaps they had some effect on the amount of liquor consumed. Seabright's 1883 account of tavern life along the National Road in its busiest years suggests this:

Many old waggoners were fond of fun and frolic, but very few of them were intemperate, although they had the readiest opportunities for unrestrained drinking. Every old tavern had its odd shaped little bar, ornamented in many instances with fancy lattice work, and well stocked with whiskey of the purest distillation, almost as cheap as water. In fact, all kinds of liquor was kept at the old taverns of the National Road, except the impure stuff of the present day. The bottles were of plain glass, each marked in large letters with the name of the liquor it contained, and the old landlord would place these bottles on the narrow counter of the little bar, in the presence of a room filled with waggoners, so that all could have access to them. None of the old tavern keepers made profit from the sale of liquor, they kept it more for the accommodation of guests than for money-making purposes. There was probably a tavern on every mile of road…and all combined did not realize as much profit from the sale of liquor in a year in that time as is realized by one licensed hotel keeper of Uniontown at the present day.

Seabright was writing in 1883. By the middle of the nineteenth century, distilleries were fewer but larger. Frederick County had nine distilleries, when Outerbridge Horsey built his distillery south of Burkittsville. General Franklin's Union troops destroyed his buildings (1862) carrying away the machinery as well as whiskey barrels. Horsey rebuilt on a larger scale three years later. By 1875, the Horsey distillery was the most prosperous in Maryland, producing 3000 barrels of Very Fine Outerbridge Horsey Rye Whiskey a year. Horsey imported a special strain of rye from Ireland to be grown locally and used in making the whiskey. The liquor was aged six months in the warehouse before being taken to Knoxville, Maryland, for shipment to Baltimore docks where, he advertised, it was carried by steamer to California for storage for another two years before it was shipped back to Maryland. The two sea voyages supposedly added special smoothness to the liquor. Grant Conway, who collected oral history from local residents between the 1950s and the early 1960s, recorded a Burkittsville resident told him such shipment was done but once, and was not repeated thereafter. Whether that was true or not, sales records seem to show that about a third of the Horsey production was sold on the west coast. In 1901, after Horsey's death, when his children were in control, the production of bourbon was added.

The Ahalt distillery was built after the Civil War, between Burkittsville and Knoxville, also its shipping point. The Ahalts did not claim any special virtues for their product due to particular methods of shipping. They advertised it was triple-distilled (two distillings are usual). It was widely regarded as excellent whiskey.

To the west of South Mountain, there were other distilleries. Russell Hicks, in his history of Washington County for the schools, said there were seven distilleries on Antietam Creek alone. The best known of these was that run by the Weast brothers in Boonsboro. Horine Weast, who named his product Horine Whiskey, after himself, liked his own product too well. He was also a rabid supporter of states' rights and the Southern position. In 1861 or 1862, he got into an argument with Dallas Smith, an equally ardent supporter of the North. Meeting Smith in the Boonsboro town square one evening, Horine shot him. Although very seriously injured, Smith recovered and did not prosecute Weast. Speculation at the time was that Horine had made a monetary settlement on Smith. In later post-war years, the two became quite friendly.

In the late nineteenth century and early twentieth, 51 commercial distilleries operated in Washington County, according to research by the Washington County Historical Society. The largest of these was the Roxbury distillery at

Benvola outside Boonshoro, which had a 50,000-gallon capacity, and operated between 1888 and 1910. Roxbury closed when its owner went into bankruptcy.

By the early 1900s, whiskey was no longer considered a medicine by doctors. A renewed temperance movement made notable successes, one being in Burkittsville, which closed its saloons in 1905 to assure that black farm workers did not miss work because of drunkenness. A number of Maryland counties, including Frederick and Washington, voted themselves dry in 1916; by 1918, most counties of the state had joined them.

Then came the passage of the Eighteenth Amendment and the Volstead Act that prohibited the sale of whiskey throughout the country. Neither the Act nor the Amendment was popular with many Marylanders, including Governor Albert C. Ritchie. At a luncheon meeting with President Harding and fifteen other governors Ritchie delivered a lecture on the foolishness of federal prohibition itself. He noted that before the Eighteenth Amendment, Maryland had met the temperance issue quite well on a local basis. Naturally they resented the Volstead law. "In the main," declared Ritchie, "they regard it as an unnecessary and drastic federal infringement on their State and personal rights"…Besides a focus of local pride, the Maryland governor became a national rallying point in the struggle against dry tyranny.

So Robert Bruger, a modern Maryland historian, writes. This attitude in top state officers was reflected to some degree in the events around South Mountain that followed.

When the Eighteenth Amendment came into force, those distilleries still active shut down and their warehouses were sealed and guarded. The filled barrels inside remained a magnet to the thirsty.

The Burkittsville distilleries were in a relatively isolated area. Former U.S. Senator Charles McC. Mathias wrote this about the Outerbridge Horsey distillery located on the Maryland Tract. His father was the trustee responsible for the security of the whiskey until it could be lawfully liquidated.

> The barrels of "Old Horsey" were locked up in a strong warehouse built of field stone, the walls of which are still visible. It was formidable, but was also remote from surveillance and from assistance if any should be necessary. My father, who lived twenty miles away in Frederick, put the keys to the warehouse in the hands of a local lieutenant, a Mr. Myers.
>
> The large stock of famous whiskey of high quality and reputation was a lure that attracted the attention of the "Mob" or whatever passed for organized crime in those days. The isolated warehouse with its valuable contents seemed to be a target for a raid that would richly reward the bold and the law-

less. A gang, reported to be "from New Jersey," decided to risk a raid and invaded the Maryland Tract...There must have been some sort of warning because Mr. Myers recruited a defensive force and occupied the warehouse. The Mob attacked with live gunfire, but were finally defeated and beaten off...I have no record of casualties, but "Old Horsey" survived intact.

In the fulness of time, the "Old Horsey" stock was sold, still under bond, for export to the British Isles. It was hauled to Baltimore and loaded on board a merchant ship bound for Scotland. My father had grave doubts that it ever reached its destination and suspected that the ship might have off-loaded the rye as it passed the New Jersey coast and that the raiders may have been successful in the long run.

The Ahalt warehouses were broken into several times, the guards having been bribed to look elsewhere during the break-in. The fourth of such raids in two years occurred at 3:30 a.m. on the bitterly cold morning of March 31, 1923. Six barrels of whiskey were taken. The state police set up a road block near Frederick, toward which the raiders were said to be fleeing, and also sent out a police car whose radiator burst before it got very far. The raiders were not caught. The April 1 Frederick Post published the story of the raid; it did not publish again until Monday, April 3. That issue carried the obituary of the respected Burkittsville physician, Dr. George Wilmer Yourtee, who had been previously in good health and been ill "only 24 hours, dying at 8 p.m., March 31"—sixteen hours after the raid on the warehouse.

A legend of the event has been repeated over the years, its first written record being in Conway's notes. It was published in 1978 by a Frederick Post reporter, and was told to me in 1990 by a member of the Ahalt family. The legend is: the raid was by Burkittsville men. They had bribed the guards, as usual, but one guard, new to the job, was unaware of the protocol. He fired at the thieves and hit one. "If I'd ha' knowed it was Dr. Yourtee, I wouldn't have shot," he said. The Frederick journalist gave his judgment that this was only a legend. It was improbable because, although he could find no death certificate on file for Dr. Yourtee, he thought it unlikely both the attending physician and the Frederick police would cover up a death from gunshot wound. My informant's comment was simply, "Dr. Yourtee, like all the Yourtee and Ahalt men, liked his whiskey."

During the years Prohibition was in force, the southern parts of both Washington and Frederick counties saw the operation of many hidden stills. A Knoxville resident told a reporter in 1979 that in those years, "There was more whiskey and more moonshine in a ten-mile radius of here than anywhere else in the United States." The hollows of the mountains were thick enough with briers and trees to provide hiding places. Springs still provided the cold pure water that made Horsey, Ahalt, and Horine whiskeys so good. Nor were all the stills in the mountains. Officers of the Maryland State Penal Farm, south of Hagerstown, were on continual alert for "jump study" as the inmates called the liquor they made from fruits and other fermentables obtained from the prison cannery. Jump study rarely passed off the penal farm but there was a steady market for the product of mountain stills.

The Knoxville man recalled he was part of an operation "which supplied the doctors of Washington, D.C., and the equestrians of Middleburg, with the purest, smoothest liquor in the country." He mentioned delivering the product as if he was delivering milk, to planned hiding places behind bushes, etc.

Making moonshine became organized. Individual distillers sold to a man who handled further distribution of the whiskey. In turn, the distributor provided certain benefits to the distillers.

One such entrepreneur was the owner of the Salty Dog tavern at the base of Maryland Heights. Spence Weaver had his first still in a cave or rock shelter, on the Heights, which revenuers raided at least once. Later, he occasionally operated a still at the spring below the Naval Gun Battery site on the Heights. Conway's informant said that the still's output was piped downhill to a cistern in the basement of the Weaver tavern. Another told Conway he had seen copper pipes in the arched vault of the ruined tavern after the 1956 flood. Conway was of the opinion that it was more likely Weaver had piped spring water, rather than whiskey, to the house. Another of Conway's informants said that he regularly delivered a ton of sugar a month to Spence Weaver, and also to another man distilling on Elk Ridge. A ton of sugar makes a lot of whiskey!

Besides making whiskey, Weaver hired mountaineers to supply him from small stills in the mountains of Maryland, West Virginia, and Virginia. He kept these men on a monthly payroll. If the man went to jail, his salary was paid to his wife and family. At the death of such supplier ("Sudden death was not a requirement," Conway noted.) there was a $300 death benefit to the local mortuary and a pension for the widow. One Conway informant thought there were about 30 such suppliers and that Weaver paid off state enforcement officers. Another put the number of suppliers as only eight or ten.

Weaver drove his car into the C&O Canal near his tavern and drowned. It was never decided whether he had a heart attack or was drunk. When the accident was reported, the reporter wrote he had been driving a Model T. Mrs. Weaver was indignant. "He never owned anything less than a Buick!" Enough cash was recovered in his house that burlap bags had to be used to carry it to the bank.

Elk Ridge and its hollows were favored by moonshiners. Over a three-day period in July 1926, three federal agents seized eight stills and hundreds of gallons of mash and whiskey, and arrested eight persons. Of the eight, three men were arrested in the Frog Hollow area; the others were caught at Mt. Brier, Red Hill, and Trego, all adjacent to Elk Ridge.

One federal agent, named Cushwa, is especially remembered for his activity against moonshiners. He may have been involved in the raid on a Knoxville still that was described by the moonshiner in 1979:

> The first time we got broke up was on Sunday, March 6, 1936. It was a terrible blizzard. I'd worked all night with the brew downstairs. A car drove up. All four doors opened. There was revenue men out both sides. I climbed through the window. My friends and I ran out the towpath. They did some shooting. I knew I couldn't make it. I watched my friend disappear into the falls. He still had his hat on.

He himself managed to swim ashore downstream, and he and his buddies were back in operation next day, but in a different location, back of a Knoxville church. His wife also observed the raid and remembered, "They were busting the kegs open. I watched them pour it into the stream."

The story of the July 1928 raid on the Blue Blazes still in the Catoctin Mountains, in which the deputy sheriff was shot in the back, possibly by one of his posse, is still recounted by Catoctin Mountain Park rangers as part of their demonstration of how a still operated. Their product, I regret to say, is undrinkable, being laced with something that produces nausea.

The places where moonshine could be obtained were well known. A former resident of Pleasant Valley told me that, when she was a girl in the 1930s, young men got their whiskey "below Buggy Rock on Elk Ridge." A Hagerstown resident told me that, as a young man, he bought oogleberry wine at Poundsville for $1 a gallon. "I don't know what went into it, but it was wine, not whiskey."

Half a century ago both the Eighteenth Amendment and Volstead Act were repealed, but the urge to evade taxes is still active, as these stories collected by Conway confirm.

In 1969, Squirly (sometimes Curley) Lambert was arrested for drunkenness. The judge in Frederick asked him if he had anything to say to the court. "Yes, sir. I'm going to have to raise my price on liquor to make up for the fine."

In 1972, the historian of Harpers Ferry National Historical Park, Archie Frazen, told Conway of a local man who had brought a gallon jug of colored glass to a still to be filled from the spigot. After the jug was filled, the customer said he couldn't pay. The moonshiner grabbed the jug and emptied it in the barrel, returning the jug with a "Get out!" The customer went down the trail. Out of sight, he retrieved a wide-mouthed jug from the bushes, broke the colored jug, and squeezed the sponge inside. He got almost a pint of whiskey.

Making moonshine is still quite dead. An undated news story commented that, in 1985, an average of five stills a year were broken up by Maryland revenue agents.

Legal commercial distilling in the mountain counties of Maryland did not resume when it again became legal to make whiskey. Vineyards and wine-making have replaced them, but that's another story.

IV

The Hagerstown Almanack

Every Maryland home had one, in the days before weather reports came over the radio or the television. Most present-day Maryland homes still have a current Hagerstown Almanack, because its weather prognostications, especially for winter storms, are considered more reliable. There are other reasons: the monthly calendar also tells what astronomical events to expect along with the weather for the day. There are pages of additional information, much of it useful (tables on when to plant, the Presidents in order, etc.) and some interesting but not directly useful (how much tea is drunk in China, whether a cat sees colors, etc.). The information pages change from year to year, along with the jokes, riddles, and puzzles.

Aside from that, not much else has changed in the Almanack from when it began publication. The size, two to three dozen pages, has not changed. Some time in the late nineteenth century, the publisher put a loop of string in a hole at the top of the spine so the almanac could hang on a nail for easy access.

The biggest change in the Almanack occurred in its first quarter century of life: the language in which it was published changed from German to English.

John Gruber published a German-language newspaper, the Western Correspondent, in Hagerstown for the Jeffersonian Democrats. To its publication and that of a number of other German hymnals and books, he added the Volkfreund unter Hagenstaunen Kalendar in 1797. In 1822 he added an English language edition, with the name The Hagers-Town and Country Almanack, and in 1833, he stopped publishing the German Almanack and all other publishing in German.

Gruber's son-in-law continued publishing the Almanack until mid-century. A series of publishers (T.G. Roberts, the Hagerstown Herald Mail, the Hagerstown Book-Binding and Printing Company) continued it until 1935. That year, the Gruber Almanack Co. was formed to produce the Almanack. The company has been doing so ever since.

Putting the calendar, astronomical data, information and puzzle pages together is straight forward. How the weather forecasts are made was secret for over a century until F.J. Watz gave this explanation in the Popular Science Monthly of October 1905:

> In America, probably the almanac which has been more widely read and its weather forecasts more generally credited than any other, is the Hagerstown Almanac...Predictions...were based entirely upon the time of day the moon entered into any one of her four quarters. For instance, if this happened between midnight and 2 a.m., it indicated fair weather in summer, and fair with hard frost in winter, unless the wind is south or southwest. While, on the other hand, if this change occurred between noon and 2 p.m., it indicated very rainy weather in summer, and rain or snow in winter. And so a table...was prepared for all the hours, and thus was weather forecasting simplified and made easy.

After this disclosure, the Almanack publishers allowed the names of its weather forecasters to be known. One was Charles Flack, a blacksmith; another was W.A. Shoemaker, business manager for a school district in Pennsylvania. The present forecaster for the Almanack is William A. O'Toole, professor of mathematics and computer science at St. Mary's College in Emmmitsburg.

While he reviews in this year's Almanack the success or failure of his weather conjectures for last year, O'Toole does not reveal much about his methods. In one newspaper interview of 1995, he admitted to giving more emphasis to phases of the moon in current forecasts, than to sunspots, which were of more importance, and greater number, five years previously.

The Hagerstown Almanack's reputation for accuracy in weather prediction has been long-lived, though the story most often heard of its greatest success is just a tale. The often-repeated story is that the 1874 Almanack weather conjecture for July 4 was for snow—*and it snowed*! Alas! The actual conjecture for that date reads, "July 4...fair." And the Weather Bureau records for July 4, 1874, in Maryland report a mean temperature of 64 degrees and no precipitation. It was, indeed, fair. (The conjecture was accurate; the legend not.)

Another story seen in print but whose citation is lost was that the Governor of Maryland, William T. Hamilton (1880—1884), depended on the Almanack for selecting dates for executions, then still done in public. He did not want to inconvenience spectators by exposing them to snow or rain!

The Almanack predicted snow for the day William Howard Taft was inaugurated; the Weather Bureau predicted fair weather. It snowed.

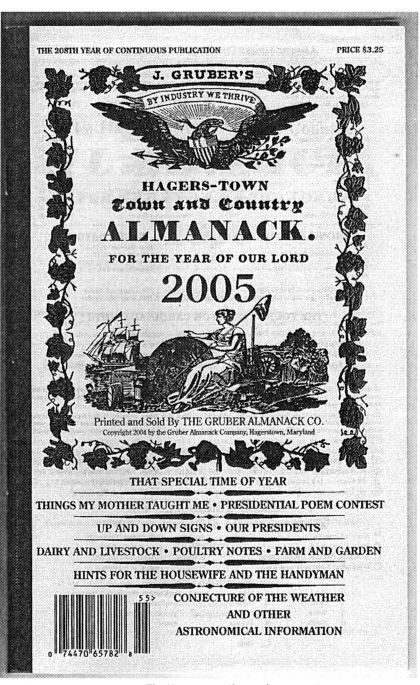

THE 208TH YEAR OF CONTINUOUS PUBLICATION   PRICE $3.25

J. GRUBER'S

BY INDUSTRY WE THRIVE

HAGERS-TOWN
Town and Country
ALMANACK.

FOR THE YEAR OF OUR LORD
2005

Printed and Sold By THE GRUBER ALMANACK CO.
Copyright 2004 by the Gruber Almanack Company, Hagerstown, Maryland

THAT SPECIAL TIME OF YEAR

THINGS MY MOTHER TAUGHT ME • PRESIDENTIAL POEM CONTEST

UP AND DOWN SIGNS • OUR PRESIDENTS

DAIRY AND LIVESTOCK • POULTRY NOTES • FARM AND GARDEN

HINTS FOR THE HOUSEWIFE AND THE HANDYMAN

CONJECTURE OF THE WEATHER
AND OTHER
ASTRONOMICAL INFORMATION

The Hagerstown Almanack

O'Toole reviews the accuracy of his predictions for the preceding winter in the current almanac. In each of the last dozen years but one, accuracy was 51% or higher (his worst year was 1985 when he was 49% correct). Most of his conjectures are 75%-80% correct. 1994 was the best ever. His weather conjecture for January hit every one of the ice and sleet storms that hit Maryland one after another, on the nose. One of the television weather forecasters noticed and remarked on this accuracy, and Professor O'Toole was the target of several dozen interviewers.

Need we say sales of the 1995 Almanack rose 77% over the previous year's sales of 150,000?

Two features added in the past quarter century are unique to the Almanack. In 1962, "Aunt Lydia" Chase's formula for successfully predicting the sex of unborn children other than the first born was printed, and was so appreciated that it continues to appear even after her death. The formula, like the weather conjectures, is based on astronomical signs

A 1983 contest initiated by the Almanack's publisher on the accuracy of weather forecasting by woolly bear caterpillars attracted enough interest that each Almanack now reports who brought in the cutest woolly bear (named "Alma") and who the biggest (named "Hairy Hager") last year.

The Hagerstown Almanac is the second-oldest almanac published in the United States, a mere two years younger than the oldest. It will continue into a third century as a regular feature in Maryland households.

V

Game in Western Maryland

The regrowth of forests in western Maryland in the twentieth century has been accompanied by a steady increase in the number of the larger game species, giving hunters opportunities missing for a century or more.

Although elk and bison wiped out in the eighteenth century have not returned, deer and turkey populations are now large enough to justify annual open seasons for hunting, which was not considered possible fifty years ago. The sightings of black bear in parts of the region are frequent enough that hunters speak hopefully of a short open season on bears.

The reported sightings of other native game animals—wolf, panther, snarly yow, snallygaster, and dwayho—are not sufficiently frequent to encourage hopes of an open season on any of the five species. But, perhaps in another quarter of a century?

Mammals of Maryland, which repeats and expands on the wisdom of the U.S. Bureau of Sports Fisheries and Wildlife, assures us that the panther (*Felix concolor*) is extinct in Maryland, while also admitting there have been unsupported sightings of the animal. Such a sighting, in the McKee-Breshears Wildlife Management Area in Montgomery County, was reported in some detail in a spring 1997 issue of Audubon Naturalist.

The grey wolf (*Canis lupus*), which the historians Williams and Scharf reported as being especially numerous in the thick woods of Pleasant Valley south of Boonsboro in the early eighteenth century, were exterminated very early. Any nineteenth and twentieth century reports of wolf-like creatures around South and Catoctin mountains undoubtedly were of the wolf's cousin, the snarly yow (seen but never captured).

The snarly yow (*Canis zittlei*) is also called the Black Dog, because of its usual coloration and its generally dog-like configuration. Its habit of baring sharp white teeth and fiery red mouth and tongue occasion the descriptive name, snarly yow.

43

The nocturnal, usually solitary animal, has been known in the South and Catoctin mountains for over two hundred years, with its largest populations always centered near Zittlestown, where the type specimen was identified, and Emmitsburg.

Considerable variation in the behavior of individual animals has been observed, within the pattern of the species…For instance, a path to a certain spring has been used by snarly yow for almost a hundred years, although each animal disappears from the observer's view at one or another point on the path before the spring is reached.

The Snarly Yow

The snarly yow can be playful. One mountaineer, known as "Big Joe," pursued on horseback a snarly yow along a woods road. The animal easily kept ahead of the horse, flicking up stones and gravel to sting horse and rider. Occasionally it looked back, tongue lolling in a canine grin. At last, tired of the game, it vanished. Another mountain resident, large in size but equally large in his capacity to drink whiskey, was riding home one night when a snarly yow appeared on the road ahead. The horse stopped dead and refused to move, even when the whip was applied vigorously. It panicked and threw the rider, who broke his collar bone in the fall. The Black Dog vanished forthwith.

Its ability to vanish at will appears to be related to its limited vulnerability to available weapons. Witnesses have fired rifles at the snarly yow without harming the animal. As excellent marksmen, they claimed that the bullet passed right through the animal. Perhaps, they were not the good shots they claimed to be? Another Zittlestown resident, coming up from an evening at a Boonsboro tavern, saw a black dog "big as a calf" prancing in his path. On seeing him, the yow's red mouth opened menacingly. He swung the ax he carried and cut the animal in half. Disconcertingly, the two halves continued to prance, without attempting to rejoin. They swelled to an even larger size, "big as a cow," and the halves jumped over the church before they disappeared.

The snarly yow has solid weight, as a couple discovered, returning just after sunset from the Washington Monument to the old National Road. A big black dog appeared suddenly in their headlights. A thump, and the feel of a heavy impact. The driver got out to assess damage to car and animal. The snarly yow, unharmed, was snarling viciously: then it vanished. Damage to car, unreported.

It does not always menace. One animal, whose home range was in the Catoctins, would walk parallel to the foot traveler for several hundred yards, nonchalantly and harmlessly walking right through fences and bushes in its path. If the traveler indicated friendship in any way, the snarly yow walked to heel. However, the animal only did this once. No matter how often the traveler was again in the neighborhood, the snarly yow ignored him thereafter.

Sightings of the snarly yow have been infrequent of late; so have walkers after dark on local roads. It is, therefore, unclear whether the lack of sightings indicate a decline in the snarly yow population. Certainly, with less frequent sightings, no hope for an open season soon is possible.

The snallygaster (*Schnellgeister middletownii*) was first reported about the beginning of the twentieth century. The sightings are grouped in time, suggesting a population that varies in numbers for specific reasons, such as extended incubation periods. (Also seen but never captured.)

The first observations of the snallygaster were made by "colored farmers" south of Burkittsville early in the twentieth century. Mothers warned children the snallygaster would carry them off if they continued to misbehave. Undoubtedly, the snallygaster flock was largest in that area. By the end of the first decade, sightings of the snallygaster were reported elsewhere—in Cumberland, where the ungainly creature cooled its wings over the chimney of a pottery kiln; in the Middletown valley where the Valley Register reported frequent sightings; in Sharpsburg where an informant thought that an egg had been laid, though he could not locate the nest. Children, especially those in the Middletown valley, and some adults, refused to go outdoors at night, lest they be carried off. One unreliable report claimed an unusually large snallygaster was seen flying off with an adult rapscallion: the report did not mention his fate.

The Snallygaster

An expert from the Smithsonian Institution in 1909–10, after studying a report from a Shepherdstown, West Virginia, witness declared: "The beast is either a winged Bovolopus or a Snallygaster; it has some characteristics of both. These animals are rare, and a hide is worth $100,000, as it is the only substance known to man that will polish punkle shells." (The Valley Register noted that punkle shells are prized as ornaments by the Umbepelao tribe of deepest Africa.)

The expert's added comments bewilder. "It is a native of Senegambia where only colored people live, and so it has never acquired a taste for white persons." (The expert, and the Valley Register, failed to explain why an African animal should suddenly appear in mountain Maryland. As the newspaper failed to cite the expert's name and credentials, we cannot know on what data his assumptions were based.)

A hiatus in sightings occurred. Not until the 1930s was the snallygaster again observed in the air above the Catoctin and Middletown valleys. Witnesses now described it as "large as a dirigible," with "arms like an octopus," or "an aerial dragon." They also said it changed size, shape, and color at will. Such variation in detail confirms the unreliability of visual observation alone.

At some point in this series of sightings, an artist interviewed witnesses and produced a sketch of the snallygaster. Unfortunately, the accuracy of some of the details is questioned. The forelimbs are shown as vestigial, a survival from the "bird's" saurian ancestry; obviously, they are non-functional. The tail is probably out of proportion to the body. Reported behavior strongly supports binocular vision, though the artist depicts only one eye, as do witnesses' descriptions. None of the observers, it is to be regretted, are helpful about the color and extent of the feathers of the snallygaster. The head, unquestionably, is naked and horny, but the rest of the body must have feathers to aid in its flight. No witness has been a careful enough observer to report their color, or how much of wings and body they cover.

Timothy J. Cannon and Nancy F. Whitmore, in 1979, brought together most earlier observations of the snallygaster. Studying them, they concluded that it was some species of bird; that a favored nesting site was on the mountain above Burkittsville; and that an egg might be in incubation for as long as twenty years.

All the facts collected to date suggest that there is not a large population of snallygasters at any one time. Fortunately, there is little chance today that any will suffer the fate of the only snallygaster observed to die. That snallygaster followed the scent of an active moonshine operation in Frog Hollow on the west slope of Elk Ridge. Here a 2500-gallon vat of moonshine was steaming. The bird, drunk on the steam, plunged into the vat and was drowned. Within a very few minutes, far too short a time for the still operators to get the bird out of the mash, two federal revenue agents, George Danforth and Charles

Cushwa, arrived in a raid. They used 500 pounds of dynamite to blow up the vat, moonshine, other parts of the still, and the snallygaster, thus costing science the opportunity to examine Maryland's unique descendant of the dinosaur.

Another twenty-year cycle may be coming to an end. In the very late 1980s, a maintainer of a section of the Appalachian Trail south of Brownsville Gap reported extensive damage to the bark of trees there that suggested a snallygaster nestling was learning to find its own food. The report does not seem to have been acted on by the Department of Natural Resources. If the reported evidence does indicate snallygaster hatchings, the population may increase enough for the bird to be seen more frequently—with luck, often enough to justify a one-day open season. In any case, hunters and outdoorsmen, keep a camera handy. Get its picture!

Mountain Maryland's fifth big game animal, the dwayho (pronounced dwy yo) has been so shy that only within the last quarter century have there been reliable sightings, and identification as a separate species. The identification and naming was made November 27, 1965, and reported in the Frederick Post.

"John Becker" (the observer used a pseudonym to avoid publicity) heard a strange noise outside his house, which is near Gambrill State Park. Upon investigation, he saw an animal "big as a bear, with long black hair, a bristly tail, and which growled like a dog or wolf in anger." It reared up on its hind legs, standing at least seven feet high, to attack him. After a brief struggle, it fled into the woods, leaving "Becker" and his family astonished." His report to the state police was filed under the pseudonym; in it, he called the animal a dwayho—on what authority we do not know.

Shortly thereafter, a Washington Post reporter, George May, wrote that zoology students at the University of Maryland said the dwayho came from the upper Amazon highlands and also the Yangtze Plateau of China. The specimen on the College Park campus was, they said, quite friendly.

A few days later, the Frederick Post noted that the county's License Bureau had received an application and a $2 fee for licensing a dwayho as a pet. The Post failed to say whether the license was granted or to whom.

Over the next few months, a rash of other sightings was reported in Carroll and Frederick counties, some of a "strange dog-like" animal which suggests a snarly yow. Most sightings ceased after Christmas, 1966, possibly because of an excess of Christmas spirits. However, rangers in Cunningham Falls State Park reported seeing a large hairy creature, walking on two legs, at several times in 1978.

Until there are further eyewitness reports, preferably accompanied by photographs or other physical evidence, science cannot assign the dwayho to any order. There is tentative agreement among Maryland zoologists that it may belong to the *Ursus* (bear) family. Zoologists from other states disagree and say the *Canidae* order is more likely. One or two even hint that the dwayho may be an early branch of the genus Homo and be related to the sasquatch of the west coast. Hunters who photograph this elusive animal will improve possibilities of establishing an open season on it as well.

VI

Celebrations and Superstitions

Customs are interesting because they differ from place to place, even within a region. They also change with time, and half-forgotten customs are even more interesting. This is particularly true in western Maryland.

How great some of the changes have been is most clearly shown in how holidays are celebrated. Until two or three generations ago, western Maryland celebrated Christmas quite differently than did Tidewater Maryland.

The Christmas season itself differed. Ours begins with the shopping frenzy of Thanksgiving weekend; theirs began only a few days before Christmas itself but ended at Epiphany, twelve days past. There were Christmas trees, because that custom came from Germany with the German immigrants. Santa with his reindeer and sleigh of gifts was missing. In German-speaking Maryland, Belsnickel (or Pels Nichol, Furred Nicholas) walked in the evenings just before Christmas. He walked the streets and visited houses where children waited. He wore an outlandish costume, often a warmuss, or Indian hunting shirt, perhaps fur-trimmed. His face was painted or he was masked; he carried a switch to punish bad children and a bag of candy to distribute to good ones. Naturally, all children were good the evenings Belsnickel was expected. The limited gifts of the day—clothing, simple toys—might appear under the tree after a late night visit from Belsnickel. Soon after Christmas, the tree disappeared, also overnight; where it had stood, there might also be an additional gift or two for the child.

A week later, on New Year's Day, Belsnickels sometimes reappeared. In Emmitsburg tradition, Belsnickles appeared on New Year's Day, on horseback, wearing black hats and strange costumes, waiting at the door silently for a handout, usually a warm stirrup cup. In response, they sang Christmas carols, usually German ones. In the Pleasant Valley area, costumed young men also belsnickeled. They visited neighboring farms, where their identities were guessed and refreshments served—usually so much that three or four farms were all that could be visited in one evening.

In the early days of the twentieth century, in the far western counties of Maryland, the upper Shenandoah valley and West Virginia, shanghaiing was a practice. It could occur any time from Christmas through to Twelfth Night, always in the day, with both adult men and women taking part—though usually more young men than women. Participants dressed in some sort of costume, blacked their faces or used masks, and rode horseback or in buggies, wagons or sleighs, all gaily decorated. All they did was ride through the neighborhood calling attention to themselves. The object was to be seen, admired, but not to stop anywhere. The tours often took much of the day to accomplish. As autos replaced horses, shanghaiing died.

The pioneers of Scotch-Irish background brought the custom of "first footing" on New Year's Day, which is still dimly remembered by older people. The Scotch-Irish believed that the first person to enter a house after the New Year brought luck to the household for the year. If a tall, dark-haired man came, very good luck was assured. Any man, but a bald man, a red-haired man, or a deformed man, brought good luck—but should a woman be the first to enter it was very bad luck indeed. The person who stepped the "first foot" brought a small gift—a sprig of mistletoe, a piece of firewood, a lump of coal—because there was a related belief that something should come into the house before anything went out. Of course the "first footer" was rewarded with a gift, usually something to eat. In later years, "first footing" was such a general practice in some western Maryland communities that whole neighborhoods set up buffets in every home, and neighbors went from door to door visiting and sampling from midnight to dawn.

The Christmas season ended, for German descendants, with the burning of juniper berries on the hearth on Twelfth Night.

For perhaps the first third of the nineteenth century, another holiday was celebrated in the region. Western Maryland communities sometimes created a grotesquely dressed "St. Patrick" effigy and displayed it on March 17. The "Paddy" quickly was considered an insult by the Catholic Irish workers who were building the C&O Canal. Confrontations between the canal workers and townspeople resulted, usually without injury to either side. The three-way Funkstown "insurrection" of 1824 between the citizens of Funkstown, the "turnpikers," and the "sons of Hibernia" was the most notable of these. The Hagerstown Torch Light ended its story of the fracas this way:

> The result of the campaign may be summed up as follows:—None killed, one wounded by the kick of a horse, some a little and some a good deal · frightened; a few made prisoners—and the *insurrection* quashed!

The Fourth of July has always been an important celebration, though it has changed significantly over the centuries. A Liberty Pole once was commonly erected in honor of the day; there would be speeches, and toasts were drunk. At first there were thirteen, one for each of the states. As states increased in number, so did the toasts—until it became necessary to change. The firing of cannon became a substitute, though sometimes the results of too enthusiastic loading of powder produced explosions and injuries.

Celebrating weddings differed more from what we do now. Williams tells that, in the early days, weddings might be held in Hagerstown, with the wedding party celebrating all night eating and drinking in a tavern. Return home began at dawn. At the edge of town, the groomsman went back to the tavern, returning with a bottle of wine and two glasses on a tray. The bride and groom each drank a glass of wine and then, bottle, glasses and tray were dropped in the road as the party went on. Not infrequently, near home, the party would meet a strongly barricaded fence erected by neighbors who hadn't been invited to the wedding; passing this might require inviting the neighbors to the celebration at home. A related custom (probably later in time) had the bride's father prepare a gaily-wrapped bottle of the best liquor and stand in the door of his house after the wedding. Male wedding guests would leave the reception, mount their horses, and take off across country in a race to get the bottle. The winner brought the bottle back to the wedding party, with the bride and groom drinking first but then sharing the bottle with all the party.

Another custom involved stealing the bride's shoe after the wedding. She was protected by the best man and her bridesmaids. The wedding guest who was quick and dexterous enough to steal a shoe exhibited it to the party. The best man had to redeem it with a bottle of wine or $1 (a considerable sum then). The bride could not dance until the shoe was returned.

A custom that is better remembered today was serenading the newly married couple the first night they were in their new home. (It was also called belling, or shivaree.) Neighbors and friends arrived outside, preferably well after the couple was expected to be abed; they carried and used noisemakers—bells, whistles, drums, and fired guns. After dynamite became available, a stick or two might be shot off. The newly married couple was expected to invite the serenaders in for food and drink.

The birth of a baby called for two customs now forgotten. Black mothers living near the Mason-Dixon Line gave the newborn its first drink of water from a silver thimble. Was this to insure its future wealth? In Westminster the young children of the town were dressed in their best and brought to call on the baby.

A century ago the closer connection with the land and its products made for customs now forgotten. One of these was nutting parties. Chestnuts grew so sturdily and produced so many nuts that city and farm folk alike went out in groups to gather chestnuts. Only after the chestnut blight came in the early part of the twentieth century did "No Trespassing" signs go up and such parties cease.

Harvesting another native plant ceased much earlier. Ginseng is and was a remedy for many ailments though its principal market is China, where it is sought as an aphrodisiac. George Washington's journals mention his meeting packhorses laden with ginseng root going to the ports. By the mid-nineteenth century, ginseng was no longer worth seeking in Maryland woods. Today, only a few of the most enterprising Marylanders have learned to cultivate the plant in gardens.

Two hundred years ago, almost everyone treated illness or accidents with plants, because doctors were few and medical knowledge limited. Some of the remedies have survived. A Quaker cookbook, published in Montgomery County, advised treating dysentery or diarrhea with a pint of new milk in which a tablespoon of bruised berries of the spicebush was infused, and treating colds and coughs with elderberry jelly; sore throat with black current jelly. (Efficacious or not, spicebush berries and fruit jellies taste good.) Another writer suggested using may apple root mixed with whiskey as a purgative, but failed to give proportions, a serious fault since root and foliage of may apple are poisonous. He also recommended using jewelweed as a remedy for itches and rashes, a safer suggestion.

Grant Conway, who collected local history around Harpers Ferry, recorded meeting, in 1948, a man going to Herr's Island to collect "vanbert buds" for his grandmother, who fried them to render a grease which she mixed with lard and used in curing burns and open sores. Conway did not see what was being collected and was unable to identify, in reference books, any plant with a name sounding like "vanbert." The grandmother was using old medicine that may well have worked.

This unidentified person, who was quoted in a 1984 paper, evidently felt confident in this suggestion:

> An Indian in Frederick gave my father a receipt for burdock tea which he drank for twelve years for his diabetes, and never had any trouble. You go out in the fall, after frost, gather the burrs, and boil them, just like tea. My father never took any insulin when he had this tea.

That remedy and some that follow sound more like superstition than medicine. A remedy for hemorrhoids, said an old man living below Crampton's Gap to an anonymous recorder in 1912, was: "Dig a new potato in the full of the moon, and carry it in the right hip pocket. It is a sure cure for piles." He produced a dried-up potato from a pocket as proof.

He also told how carbuncles or boils could be cured. Circle the boil three times with the right thumb; with each circuit, say this verse and call on the Holy Trinity by name:

> The Dragon and the Bile
> Went over the creek.
> And the Dragon drunk
> And the Bile thunk.

Mrs. Dahlgren's "South Mountain Magic" also has this same charm and states the viable word is "thunk," not "sunk".

A number of spells for curing afflictions are included in her book. This one, for curing a scald or burn, may be worth knowing:

Say,—"The holy woman went over the land. What carries she in her hand? A *firebrand*. Eat not in you, fire!—eat not around you, fire! In the three highest Names, Amen." Then say these words, and rub three times with the right hand upwards and downwards over the part three times, and blow three times—each time three times.

This charm may be a spell used in fire blowing, an art practiced by a few people not considered witches, who kept their methods secret. The young evangelist who preached the revival at Frog's Eye Church in the 1920s observed the practice, and seemed to feel it relieved, to some degree, a man seriously burned in a gasoline fire.

Luck and superstitions interact in odd ways. Williams told how fall hunting parties of the days of first settlement "rested from…labors on Sunday, but more from superstitious fear than from religious motives. Hunters believed, he said, that unless they rested, their operations would be attended by ill-luck "the remainder of the week." Today, the law, not belief in ill luck, says No Hunting days.

A shiny brown bean from the Kentucky coffee tree is often found in Maryland pockets or handbags "for luck." It began, the story goes, when a

Delaware Indian told Jonathan Hager of the bean's luck-bringing properties and gave him a necklace of the seeds of the Kentucky coffee tree (*Gymnocladus dioica*). Hager, in turn, gave a bean to Andrew Calvert Bridges, who recorded the story and Hager's decision to build by a spring fed pond where a lucky Kentucky coffee tree grew. Hager's house is still there. During the eighteenth century, the bean was often seen as jewelry or used to make a coffee-like drink, which is, according to some who have drunk it, unwholesome though not poisonous. The shinier the bean, the better luck it brings. It may be given away without harm within the first seven days of possession; to do so after that brings bad luck. The nut of the buckeye tree is somewhat more readily found and many use it instead of the Kentucky coffee tree nut.

Good luck follows finding a red ear of corn; finding an egg with a double yolk; entering church right foot first; carrying a coffee tree bean or a buckeye; finding a penny or a homemade nail.

Working on Ascension Day was unlucky because everything would go wrong. However, it was a good day to go fishing. (That was usually the day fish began to ascend the rivers!)

Pillows were removed from beneath a dying patient, lest a witch have placed a wreath of feathers inside a pillow. Such a wreath would keep the soul from leaving the body. At all funerals, male mourners kept their hats on during the ceremony in church.

Death of an inmate of the house could be presaged in several ways—a spade or hoe brought indoors; a bee heard inside a kitchen cupboard; or the unexplained fall of a piece of furniture by itself.

Bad luck could be brought on by singing at table; hanging clothing on a bed post; destroying a spider web; burning locust wood; stepping over a person lying on the floor; walking on a grave.

Never ask the name of the horse being purchased; name it anew to avoid bad luck.

Observe animals as a journey is begun. If a rabbit or squirrel crosses before you to the right, the journey will be successful. If the animal crosses to the left, misfortune follows unless the traveler immediately makes a cross in the dust with his foot. If a black cat crosses before the traveler, he must immediately turn back. A crow flying over him also presages bad fortune.

Neither custom nor superstition, some of the words and expressions heard in western Maryland are also relics of an earlier time. Many folk call the wild azalea with its clove and cinnamon scent "wild honeysuckle"; some long settled families in the Catoctins call the rhododendron "deer laurel" or "deer tongue laurel." Both terms go back to long ago lack of botanical knowledge.

Other expressions may be remembrances of how it was said in German. Farm wives talk about a "cluck" when a hen has chicks, and a farm boy told Grant Conway, "I was charged by a skunk" in explaining the lingering odor that accompanied him. Another invited a passer-by to "Light and rest your hat" when offering hospitality. Even these small differences are fading as radio, television, and movies influence everyone.

Those that remain reflect western Maryland's past.

VII

Balls, Bats and Picnics

Kids today play Little League Baseball, football, and soccer. Adults play golf or watch football and basketball on the television. Did grandpa or great-grandfather play games or did he prefer to watch? The record-makers of the past left limited information about how our ancestors enjoyed themselves. We do have some records of what western Marylanders, male Marylanders mostly, enjoyed in granddad's time.

Balls to be tossed, kicked, run with, or hit have attracted men and boys for centuries. Maryland soldiers were playing "base," an early form of baseball, at Valley Forge. It was a simple game. "Any number from two and on up could play; rules were for the players to agree on." By the 1840s, the game, which was being called baseball, was played widely enough that rules began to be standardized. James Bready, who has made the only study of baseball in Maryland, though he confined himself to baseball in Baltimore, commented that the rules for number of players, innings, bases, etc., required an urban population from which to draw players. Some evidence says the growing towns of western Maryland had their own teams from about the same time as Baltimore formed its first team in 1855.

In 1872, the organized baseball team in Williamsport was challenged by a team made up of the employees of a local contractor. The game was played with a "Dead Red ball," and the account says it was "merely dropped." The score? Home team, 120 runs; challengers, 63.

By the first decade of the twentieth century, amateur baseball teams existed in Allegany, Frederick, Garrett, and Washington counties. While the Baseball Edition of the *Maryland Cracker Barrel* wrote this about Washington County interest in the game, it was probably true of the other counties as well:

Small towns through the county had great pride in their team, whether it be Mt. Brier, Gapland, Sharpsburg, Boonsboro, Keedysville, Yarrowsburg, or

Weverton to the south, or Clear Spring and Hancock to the west, or the river town of Williamsport, or the various teams in and around Hagerstown, such as Funkstown, Maungansville, Harristown, Security, Antietam, Mt. Lena, Chewsville, Cavetown, Middleburg, Hoffman Chevies, and Victoria. The list goes on and on.

There was also a professional league, the Tri-City League, which was first made up of teams from Frederick, Hagerstown, and Martinsburg, West Virginia, and later expanded as the Blue Ridge League by including teams from Chambersburg, Gettysburg, and Waynesboro, Pennsylvania. This league survived into the 1920s. Its days of glory were in 1921. The Hustlers team of Frederick was league champion, and it played Princess Anne, champion of the Eastern Shore League, for the state championship, in a six-game playoff, of which they won four. The first two games were at Frederick and drew 1100 fans. The next two at Salisbury drew 1184 fans. Even larger crowds attended the last two games held at the Orioles' stadium. (The Orioles were, at that time, a minor league club, though it was managed by Jack Dunn and Babe Ruth was a team member.)

Grandfather enjoyed baseball; great-grandfather had other ball games as well. There are two that are mentioned frequently enough in the old records, that we have a few clues about their rules. One of these is alleyball. Alleyball was played in any western Maryland village that offered a flat wall and a quiet street or alley. A soft ball was bounced by the hand repeatedly against the wall. The goal was to keep it in the air longest without its touching the ground. A reasonable guess is that this was a game played more by boys.

Another ball game popular on both sides of South Mountain was played by men and is now, fortunately, forgotten. It was called long ball in the Emmitsburg area. A heavy ball about the size of a croquet ball was thrown at a target. The player whose ball was the farthest from the target had to buy drinks for the other players. Or so it was played in 1837 as an elderly gunsmith recalled seventy years later. "It wasn't much of a game, and was dying out when I came to town to live."

Long bullets was the name west of South Mountain. The ball used, Scharf said, was a four-pound iron ball. Getting it nearest to or touching a given point in the fewest possible throws seems to have been the goal. Wagers were laid on the throws. This, too, was a street game whose popularity offers a possible reason for the iron bars on the ground floor windows of some of the older buildings in Hagerstown. Long bullets were banned by ordinance as early as 1819 because of the danger posed to pedestrians and horses. The ordinance remained on the city books until the end of the nineteenth century.

Marylanders even found a way to use a ball in politics. In the political campaigns of 1840 and 1845, enthusiasm ran high among the Whigs of Maryland, and the male electorate turned campaigning into entertainment. The Emmitsburg gunsmith recalled the campaign:

> A national election is a pink tea affair by comparison with the "Tippecanoe and Tyler, too" campaign. You know Tippecanoe was the nickname given to General Harrison.../who fought Indians/on the Tippecanoe River...He and John Tyler were nominated by the National Whig Convention in December 1839, and...the fight was red hot...One end of his/Harrison's/house consisted of a log cabin covered with clapboards and it was said that he placed hard cider instead of wine on his table. The Democrats, I believe, were really responsible for the log cabin and hard cider becoming issues in the campaign. They ridiculed Harrison for his primitive standard of living, and the Whigs accepted the challenge and made the log cabin and hard cider emblems of democratic simplicity which, of course, was very effective.
>
> In our parties in that campaign we had a log cabin built on a wagon. It was six feet wide, about sixteen feet long and one story high. Coon skins were nailed beside the door and inside on the walls. The door of the cabin had the latch string hanging out and everybody was welcome to go inside and tap the barrel of hard cider that was kept on hand. The inside walls of the cabin were hung with traps, powder boxes and buckskin ball pouches. The wagon was driven by a man dressed in hunting shirt made of linen or tow which came to the knees and was hung with a three inch fringe around the bottom and held with a broad belt of buckskin. His hunting breeches of buckskin and a cap of coon skin completed his costume. The horses wore bonnets of coon skin with the heads and tails on. The whole outfit made an impressive appearance.
>
> ...The Whigs added the coon as a political emblem to hard cider and the log cabin...
>
> We made a big campaign ball of muslin stretched on a wood frame. It was twelve feet in diameter. Through the centre of the ball a long pole ran horizontally so that the ends stuck out about five feet on each side. It rolled on the ground on a wooden flange, running around the outside at right angles to the pole. Men would trundle the ball through the streets, by taking hold of the end of the poles on each side and pushing it ahead of them. It was painted with cartoons and political mottoes. I remember one of the cartoons was a picture of a fox getting his paw caught in a trap. The fox's head was the head of Van Buren. James Hickey, professor of drawing and music at Mount St. Mary's, did some of the painting and so did my brother-in-law, Joshua Rowe. Once we rolled the ball to Frederick for a meeting

there. We left here in the evening and rolled all night, getting to Frederick after daylight next morning. We took a wagon along with straw on the floor and plenty of provisions. When a crew got tired, they would climb in the wagon and go to sleep and another crew would keep the ball rolling through the night. That showed our enthusiasm. Would any of the young men now do as much for Taft or Bryan?

"Harrison & Tyler" campaign emblem of 1840.
(from Library of Congress Website)

Other balls appeared in that Maryland campaign. A ball ten feet in diameter was rolled from Cumberland to Hagerstown, Williams reported, noting one of the young men rolling it later became one of the leading lawyers of the state. As the ball reached villages along the way, it stopped to allow political speeches to be made. A similar ball was rolled from Waynesboro, Pennsylvania, to Hagerstown in February 1841 to welcome President-Elect Harrison as he passed through on his way to inauguration.

The gunsmith remembered political songs during this campaign but not the words or music. Williams did record the refrain of a song sung during the Cumberland-Hagerstown ball-rolling:

> With heart and soul
> This ball we roll.

A more common political activity of the period was the erection of a liberty pole. The partisans of any party might erect it. First, a sufficiently tall and symmetrical tree had to be found, felled, trimmed, and then brought to the chosen site in the village. Skill and labor also were needed for the erection, which was accompanied by political speeches. Unfortunately, once the speeches were over, there was no assurance the pole would remain erect. All too frequently the opposition party cut it down quickly.

The liberty pole was raised in protest as well as in support. During the Whiskey Rebellion, a mob calling themselves the Whiskey Boys set up a liberty pole in Westminster. Old Colonel Joshua Gist, who had been a member of the Carroll County Committee of Safety during the Revolution, rode into town with drawn sword and ordered the boys to cut the pole down. They did. Gist stayed there, foot planted on the pole, until it was cut in short pieces. By the time of the Civil War, erecting a liberty pole had stopped being a form of political expression. Was it because suitable trees were no longer easily found in the woodlands?

Men also found fun in making or meeting challenges to skill or strength. Marksmanship was a common challenge in newly settled Maryland because skill in using the gun procured food from wild animals. The troop of western Maryland men under Colonel Cresap, who arrived in Boston in 1775, astonished other American troops from longer settled areas with their marksmanship. Shooting matches, with prizes of a bear or a wild turkey, continued to be popular in the early nineteenth century. The prize might well be the target. Later, as wild animals became less common, a hog or a domestic turkey was substituted as the prize. Today's turkey shoots often lack even the turkey, the prize being money.

The elk chase vanished with Maryland's elk, the last recorded chase being held in 1822. Williams said participants in the chase paid to chase and either catch or shoot the elk, which had been let loose in the streets of Hagerstown.

Ownership of fine horses made it inevitable that there would be races to determine whose horse was the fastest. Almost every town had its racetrack, certainly not the formal structures of the automobile age, but a course of agreed on length. Williamsport laid its course out between town and river. On December 29, 1791, a race in three-mile heats was held there which was open to any horse, mare or gelding. The purse was a sizable 15 pounds. Aged horses carried nine stone; half a stone was allowed for every year of a younger horse's age. A second race was held the following day, open to any horse except the winner of the previous day. Its purse was 7 pound 10 shillings.

Bets were often laid on the outcome of cockfights

A quarter century later, races at western Maryland's towns usually lasted three or four days. Booths were set up to serve liquors and edibles. Sometimes there were stands for the guests, because both men and women attended. Both men and women laid bets on the outcome of the race. Usually the owners of the horses, who might also double as their trainers, were local men. "Colored lads" were the usual riders. Such race meetings usually ended up with festivities. In Williamsport, the festivity always included an oxen race, in which the beasts were trimmed with gaily-colored ribbons and "little picaninnies were the riders." This race always provided amusement, hilarity and applause."

Wagers were also laid on feats of strength—how far a man could carry a barrel of flour or something similar. A Samuel Shaw carried three bushels of wheat over a mile to a Washington County mill to win a wager. It is regrettable he died soon after from the exertion.

Bets were laid on the outcome of cockfights. Hagerstown men bred game birds that were famous in the early nineteenth century. The fights that were held on Easter were the biggest and best attended of the year.

Besides such records of what grandfather and his father enjoyed, there are accounts of when whole families and neighborhoods gathered for recreation in communal work parties or picnics.

Our Emmitsburg gunsmith described two work parties: corn-husking and apple-butter making:

Corn-huskings/were/generally held in October when the moon was full. It was the custom to allow the corn to ripen thoroughly on the stalks...When the corn was full ripe the ears were pulled off and hauled to the barn...

The day before the husking, the neighbor women would come and help get ready the harvest supper. What did we have for supper? Good things, let me tell you. Chicken pot-pie, roast pork and apple sauce, cakes and every kind of pie you could think of—plenty of everything. Well, the ears of corn would be laid out near the barn in long rows about three feet high and three feet wide. As many men as could get to a row would fall to with their husking palms. We began about dark and worked until about ten o'clock. If there was no moon great bonfires were made to give us light. Most every farmer had at least one or two slaves and the darkies would bring their banjos and sing the good old songs while we worked. It was a thirsty business and a bucket of water was kept going up and down the rows. The water bearer would carry the bucket in one hand and the whiskey bottle in the other for some needed a little stimulation to sustain them at their labors.

Sometimes as many as seventy-five men with their women folk would come to a husking and they could shuck the corn crop of a big farm in one evening. No, the women didn't do any husking. They helped put the finishing touches on the supper and served it when the men were ready. Between the hard work and the whiskey we had hearty appetites by quitting time and what we could do to a pile of grub would astonish you.

The gunsmith's description of apple-butter making is quite different from the exhibit now staged at county fairs and possibly it was more fun:

I believe the young people got more fun out of the apple butter boilings than out of the huskings. The night before the boiling the neighborhood boys and girls would come to core and "snits" the apples, as they called it, and that was always a great frolic...The next night was more interesting for the young people who were inclined that way. In the morning a big copper kettle in the yard would be filled with cider, as much as a barrel sometimes, and the fire would be lighted. The cider was boiled down one half; that generally took until noon. Then the apple snits were added a little at a time. Then the stirring began and never stopped until the apple butter was done. A paddle fastened at right angles to a pole about six feet long was used for stirring and it was kept going slowly round in the kettle until way into the night. The young people in pairs would take turns in stirring, one on each side of the pole facing each other. When a boy and girl had held the paddle you can guess what might happen in the evening when it was dark except for the light of the fire under the kettle.

When work wasn't being made into fun, picnics and barbecues provided pleasure for friends, relatives and neighbors. "An abundance of fat edibles and a little 'suthin' of John Barleycorn" is how a Williamsport writer explained their nineteenth century popularity. Picnics in the eighteenth century weren't much different, according to the French visitor, Bayard:

Among the pleasure parties which bring together a large number of farmers in the seasons of fine weather, I shall not forget the one at which members of both sexes and of all ages are gathered. The families of a district agree to meet in a woods in the neighborhood: the site is good if there is a spring whose clear and cold water can contain the punch, beer, rum, and wine. The old people, women, young people, and children set out on horseback, in carriages and in wagons and proceed merrily to the meeting place.

The man who is giving the feast has borrowed horses to convey the food, the drink, the table service, the cooking utensils and the boards which must be fashioned for the tables and benches.

That deserted place is filled with people in an instant. The horses graze freely around the banqueting hall whose ceiling is formed by the bushy tops of beautiful trees.

Not far from there, Negroes can be seen digging a pit: others are felling trees to fill it, and soon sheets of flame will rise from that furnace: when it no longer contains anything but live coals, there will be placed thereon a half of a beef, a veal, and some suckling pigs, attached firmly together on the trunk of a young oak which serves as a spit.

The women go by turns to the pit of live coals to baste the meats, then return to the spring to put the bottles in order. The young ladies squeeze the lemons in large porcelain bowls. The young men help the Negro boys place the plates on the long tables made of boards placed on upright stakes.

The old people sit in a group on the grass and their grandchildren play around them. The married women assign themselves to all the places where the young ladies are occupied, and encourage them to work.

When everything is prepared for the dinner, the women take the right side and the men the left. The old people of both sexes face each other.

The children under the care of their nurses have the grass as a substitute for a table and benches. Everyone eats with a good appetite and with gaiety. The men, under the eyes of their wives, and watched by their children, leave the table without drinking to intoxication.

The Negroes show signs of the feast: meat grease gives a gloss to their ebony cheeks, and a few glasses of rum makes their eyes sparkle.

Bayard then describes an afternoon of leisure and talk, with the young people strolling in the woods. No games are mentioned. He also describes how the party breaks up in the evening, with children wrapped, old people helped into saddles or wagons, and all riding off together. He does not mention who cleaned up the picnic mess, however.

He also describes another party—one which may still be held on Chesapeake Bay or ocean beaches, but which Maryland or Virginia inland rivers cannot support today, and certainly did not support for many years after Bayard's visit. The last record of such a feast was one held at the Little Falls of the Potomac in 1810:

> In the country they are acquainted with another kind of pleasure party which is rarer, because it requires more preparation. The feast is given on the banks of a river and is called a *fish-feast.*
>
> Workers are sent the day before to cut boughs of trees and to make of them a large bower. This green bower is usually near the house of the person who lends his cooking utensils for frying the fish, but it is always built on the banks of a river...The only children present at this feast are those at the breast...
>
> The giver of the feast has cold meats and pastries brought in, and the chinaware and silverware are spread out on tables covered with beautiful linen. As soon as a guest arrives he is offered cold punch in a large porcelain bowl. This large drinking vessel, which often holds three or four bottles, is passed around in the circle of guests and is pressed to all the lips. Few Frenchmen can adapt themselves to this ancient manner of drinking, and in America, where nearly all the men chew tobacco, it is extremely nasty...In the cities, every one has his glass for beer and wines: but the *tody* and punch are drunk out of the same bowl.
>
> When all the party has arrived, boats, manned by servants, push off, and the nets are thrown into the water. The riverside resounds with great cheering if the fishermen catch some fine specimens. The fish is given to the spectators who send them to the frying pan or throw them back into the water. The ladies intercede for the pretty ones: but the epicures in America, much less gallant than those of Europe, would not let go a choice bit for the most beautiful eyes in the world.
>
> The husbands remain at the table a long time after the ladies have left; and this custom is established in the country as in the city.

Our grandparents had their own ways of having fun, like and yet unlike ours. Do you suppose the recreations of our great-grandchildren will be as unlike ours?

VIII

Frederick Occupied

This account was written, probably about 1879 or 1880, by Ann R. Lute Schaeffer; its final page, in a slightly altered hand, seems to have been written some years later to replace a lost page. The manuscript was deposited in the Maryland Historical Society in 1935 by a Mrs. E.R. Schaeffer; accompanying it is another manuscript on her experiences in an academy for girls in Frederick.

Here, the first paragraph of Mrs. Schaeffer's reminiscences, which apparently include portions of a journal written at the time, is omitted. The three dots that frequently appear in the text are hers.

...Some time since leaving Frederick City, which had been my residence for many years, I sought to dispel the sadness...My thoughts reverted to scenes occurring around this peaceful vale in 1862...

I have found melacholly/sic/pleasure in overlooking my journal, and copying some interesting facts relating to the occupation of Frederick in 1862 by the Rebel army.

About the 4th of September came rumors of the Rebel army crossing the Potomac into Maryland. But we had heard such reports before and gave little heed. At evening, while sitting quietly in my parlor conversing with several friends, we were startled by the cry of "Fire! Fire!" Then we heard the fire bells ringing the given signal of the approach of the enemy. No tongue or pen can describe our emotions. Seeing the street illuminated by a bright light, we learned Union troops were burning the Hospital stores, producing a grand bonfire in the street, of all the bedding that could not be carried away to prevent them falling into the hands of the Confederates and the soldiers themselves were "skedaddling" as fast as their horses and their own legs would carry them leaving the town defenceless. All sorts of reports were abroad and nobody knew what to expect. Fearing perhaps we would be obliged to fly during the night, or forced from our home by fire,

I packed up a few necessary articles of clothing, shawls, etc., in satchels, awaiting my Husband's coming home from his store. He confirmed the reports of the Rebels. Union men were fleeing fearing arrest. Among them our neighbors on either side. Finally we learned the Confederates had encamped six miles south of town and would not enter until the next day. Confident his drug store would be ransacked, my husband had the most valuable articles brought home, where we hid them away covered from view by ashes under an old-fashioned bake oven...

6th Sept. Woke up, found all quiet. The fires in the street dying out, leaving a horrible smell of burnt hair from the mattresses...I went up the street before breakfast to secure shoes for the children. Streets crowded with anxious faces. Returning home I got back together all the small valuable articles—silver spoons, etc., and put them in large pockets, which I fastened to a belt around my waist under my skirts. I learned afterwards many ladies carried around a similar burden for a whole week. After breakfast, my cook took leave—as the colored people are running away in all directions, and I am left alone with the children and the white nurse. About 11 A.M., the Rebels came in by the Southern Pike, led by a former citizen of Frederick and were received with open arms by those who favored their cause while the Union men hung their heads in sorrow and shame to see the Stars and Stripes pulled down and trampled on. Our own small flags were all hidden out of sight. Soon the streets were swarming with ragged, filthy men, yet every one (to our astonishment) respectful and polite. Soon they were thronging the stores, offering their Confederate notes which, not being regarded of much value in Maryland, about 4 P.M., most of the stores closed up.

7th Sept. Slept peacefully. The Sabbath Day, wanted to go to church but feared to leave home. Hear rumors of the Federal army but know not how to credit them as we are cut off from all communications with the outside world, guards and pickets on every side.

8 Monday I returned to the more public streets today to see the crowds and could not help admiring the conduct of these poor men. Although in need of every thing and our merchants refused to open the stores, they humbly acquiesced. I learned afterward, they were simply keeping orders, for it is the policy of their officers, to do nothing to offend in Maryland, still hoping she may be induced to secede. Generals Lee, Stonewall Jackson, Stuart, and Longstreet are all in Frederick. The men appear devoted to their officers, who seem to care kindly for them and cheerfully share their privation. The Southern sympathizers keep open house and our kind hearted Union citizens turn none away hungry who apply to them for food, so that they all declare Frederick is the best place they have quartered for a long time. Their hatred of the "Yankees" as they call all Unionmen is intense though they admit they are heartily tired of the war. We can learn

nothing of our troops approaching, although the slaves and contraband who wait at the table where the Rebel officers are dined and wined, listen attentively to all that is said and assure us "They are coming." Nobody pretends to work; everybody on the streets standing in groups, talking and eyeing the quiet passing soldiers...

9 Sept. The stores remain closed. Men still gloomy though getting a little accustomed to the state of affairs. Our supplies are all cut off—the bridge destroyed and R.R. tracks torn up—the mills taken possession of. Housekeepers are examining their stock of provisions. We succeeded today in getting a bag of cornmeal, with a prospect of some flour...I learned today with deep regret the brave scout who brought the news of their approach was arrested and yesterday shot at Camp Worman. Encouraging reports this evening of the Rebels leaving but our streets are still crowded with the filthy desperate looking, but polite strangers.

10 Sept. Very warm. At 12 M last night the Rebel army (the darkies were right) began moving and are passing through our streets out the Hagerstown pike as fast as they can travel. Their destination (they say) Pennsylvania, but many think to endeavor to cross into Virginia at Williamsport. I have had some interesting conversations with several soldiers. One especially is homesick—he begged me for citizen's clothing to facilitate his escape, which I supplied him, he promising to inform me when safe and far away. (I never heard from him and suspect he was, like many other stragglers, shot in crossing the mountains.)

This evening, my husband got hold of a newspaper, which had been smuggled into town, the "Philadelphia Inquirer." It was almost worn out, having passed through many hands. We read hurriedly, for others were wanting their turn and were much disheartened on reading the accounts therein given of a few panic stricken Rebels crossing into Maryland. They—the North—will not believe, with what a formidable force they may have to contend, until they see them at their door...

11. Still in suspense—Confederate army leaving—streets thronged— stores closed. I tried to calm my nerves this afternoon by sewing—but the excitement is too great. Every noise startles as we are listening intently for the booming of cannon announcing the arrival of the Federal army. Knowing friends North are all anxiety concerning us, I tried to send a letter but failed to get it through the lines. There is a great noise tonight and rumors of Stuart's cavalry preparing to leave. Wagons rumbling through the streets mingled with the lowing of the cattle they take with them. Almost afraid to go to bed...

12th. Our condition still the same. Our army said to be near the Confederates, evidently in great confusion. I added another page to my letter and put it in my pockets to send by the first opportunity. Compelled myself to remain quiet at home. About 4 P.M., my husband rushed into the house to tell me the Union troops were in sight and that from Canon Hill they might be seen fighting and driving the Rebels before them. I quickly donned my bonnet and going to a friend's house ran up to the observatory where with a glass we could plainly see our troops approaching.../She describes troops entering, fighting on Patrick Street, and at the square./As the shots whistled through the streets, citizens ran in every direction, seeking shelter. I started for home, but seeing the street deserted and hearing more shots, I returned to the observatory—We heard cheering and listening and watching we beheld the Stars and Strips born aloft at Patrick St. Good Lord! Could I believe the sight of the dear flag would ever so effect me thus! Unconsciously I screamed and shrieked, jumped for joy. Again we flew down to welcome the small body of troops coming up Church St. Oh, the frantic joy of that hour I shall never forget! and so will everybody. Some shouted, some laughed, some cried. Cheers and hurrahs rent the air. People ran out of the houses, clasped each other's hands. I went home to the children, and found my little five year old daughter had somewhere found a hidden flag and was waving it—the first I saw on our street. Then we went to Patrick Street. The Union troops were pouring in. Everybody at doors and windows, cheering and waving flags and handkerchiefs, many on the sidewalk, engaged with buckets, dippers, and cups giving the tired, heated soldiers water as they passed. After a while came Burnside himself. And how they cheered...Surely was army never given a more uproarious welcome. At last we came home to supper and this exciting day—another 12th of Sept. ended in a quiet night, or at least we felt we could lie down and sleep in safety.

One little episode I must here record and give the true history of Barbara Fritchie and her flag. A Confederate has recently said she was bedridden and probably never saw a Rebel soldier. This was untrue—I will relate here what one of her nieces told me, when Whittier's poem first appeared. Mrs. Fritchie was very old, upwards of eighty years, and looked much older. Before the door of her residence was a long, shaded porch, and during the warm September days of that memorable week, the poor, worn-out soldiers would often seek rest there. She, leaning on her staff, would sometimes come out among them and say, "Get out, you lazy, dirty Rebels!" Without replying, they invariably made way for her.

On the evening of the 12th she sat in her open window waving a small flag for the advancing Federal troops, who were led by Gen. Reno. They halted in front of her door just before crossing the town bridge. The soldiers seeing the *very* old lady cheered her and one and another begged for the little flag. At length she gave it to one, who fastened it to the headgear of Gen. Reno's horse. Stonewall Jackson had led his men, just a few hours previous, up an alley coming out on Patrick Street, a little distance from Mrs. Fritchie's house, and I doubt whether she ever saw him. This is, I believe, the true story. The gallant Reno passed on to South Mountain, where the next day he was killed in battle.

Sept. 13. Awoke to find our streets crowded with Union Soldiers. After breakfast I went to my sister's on one of the main streets. All bustle and excitement—McClellan expected. We heard a great noise, and looking out saw the Hero at the head of his staff approaching. Leaping down the steps we ran the square and were among the first ladies to grasp his hand. Shouts and deafening cheers! People seemed beside themselves and forced him to stop to receive their greetings. He sat as one confounded—the enthusiasm so unexpected, while ladies hung upon his horse's neck—patting his head, stuck a flag in the gearing. At last he galloped away and when the streets cleared, I hurried to the P—Office which had just opened to mail my letter. All the morning we have heard the booming of cannon for a battle going on at the foot of the mountain. Again McClellan and Burnside passed through town and now indeed came an army. Began passing at noon, and continued marching as rapidly as possible until eight. Oh, what a different day from last Saturday! Still, most of the stores were closed and it is difficult to purchase anything. All articles of food are very high, but we hope for a change next week.

14. The holy Sabbath and still the murderous work goes on. We have heard firing all day.

15. Still sounds of the battle in progress. Said to be between Boonesborough and Burkittsville, The wounded and prisoners constantly arriving.

16. McClellan gains victories, but Harpers Ferry has surrendered to the wizard Jackson who is always appearing where least expected. Wounded now constantly arriving in ambulances—churches all taken for their accommodation. The Ger. Reformed alone reserved for public worship. I sent provisions to the old Epis. church today. We heard most heartrending accounts of wounded, exhausted and dying men lining the roadside, and on the battlefield. If possible, I would go out but know not how, besides we have our hands full here in town.

17. I thought I would remain at home to accomplish some necessary sewing, but could not resist going to the street to see the prisoners passing through town on their way to Washington to be exchanged. First, the Rebel prisoners. After these about 8,000 Union soldiers just surrendered to Jackson on Monday last. A more humiliating sight to a loyal heart could not be conceived. Returning home I saw a number of wounded soldiers just arriving at the Seminary and hurried home to prepare bread, butter, and coffee for them.

18. Battle raging at Antietam.

19. Wounded arriving from battlefield. Strings of ambulances in our streets on their way to Baltimore from our churches, halls, and school house and some private homes are filled. I with our neighbors determined to confine our attention for the present to these poor fellows in the ambulances and found them sadly in need of refreshment.

20. All day in the kitchen preparing broth, porridge, and jelly for the wounded.

21. A lovely Sabbath day—but it does not appear like the Sabbath. Church filled with the wounded and dying, streets thronged with ladies and servants carrying baskets and buckets, endeavouring to minister to their comfort and alleviate their suffering, and the saddest sight of all, strangers going the rounds to find friends, only hoping they might be found among the wounded.

22. Busy preparing food for the sick.

23. Accompanied some ladies to the hospital at the Barracks. Time can never efface from memory the scenes of suffering witnessed then. Oh! this hellish war! I could not help thinking how ridiculous our world must appear to superior intelligences. Our incurring so much trouble, experience and suffering to maim and murder each other and, after accomplishing this object, laying the poor creatures side by side endeavouring to relieve their pain and save their lives...How terrible was the torture of some we saw. One especially who just had one jaw removed—another was dying far from home and friends. On our way home we stopped at the Methodist church. Saw two who will die tonight. One delirious; the other shot through the lungs was calm; said he had a Father and Sister in Pennsylvania. He trusted in God's mercy for his salvation. Really I can scarcely believe I am living in Frederick. Good old Frederick, once so quiet, orderly and clean, now all bustle and confusion. Sidewalks crowded with soldiers, ladies and /Here ink and writing change, though the handwriting is clearly that of the other pages—though less flowing./

Still we hope for a brighter future. A great battle has been fought at Antietam. The union troops, victorious. The Confederates are recrossing into Virginia. History will record this glorious victory. I have only record- ed some of the side scenes—the shadows cast by the cruel war...The des- olation of hearts and home spread abroad throughout the land, our happy land and then the rapture with members of my family for we were divided.

IX

Three Flags in September

Whittier's lines tend to stick in one's memory.

> "Who touches a hair of yon gray head
> Dies like a dog. March on!" he said.

The poem from which those lines come created a legend that still brings tourists, although most Frederick citizens know that Confederate General "Stonewall" Jackson and Barbara Fritchie, 96-year-old daughter-in-law of a man executed for treason eighty-two years earlier, never confronted each other over an American flag.

Barbara Fritchie certainly had a flag in her upstairs bedroom window. Some Confederates did march out of town past her house, though Jackson left Frederick by another street. But the departing troops left in the dark hours before dawn when a flag in an unlighted bedroom window couldn't have been seen by any one. Probably Barbara Fritchie shooed lounging Confederate soldiers off her porch some days earlier, as a neighbor recalled a few years later. She certainly gave a flag to Union General Jesse L. Reno when he visited her a day or so later. (That flag draped his casket three days later. Barbara herself was dead before 1862 ended.)

Whittier got his facts wrong but read Jackson's character accurately. A Marylander who was Jackson's aide, Henry Kyd Douglas, recorded an incident that occurred in Middletown a few hours after the Frederick departure:

> as for Barbara Fritchie, we did not pass her house. There was such an old woman in Frederick in her ninety-sixth year and bedridden. She never saw Jackson and he never saw her. In Middletown, two very pretty girls, with ribbons of red, white, and blue in their hair and small Union flags in their

hands, came out of their house as we passed, and laughingly waved their colors defiantly in the face of the General. He bowed and lifted his hat and with a quiet smile said to his staff: "We evidently have no friends in this town." The young girls, abashed, turned away and lowered their battle-flags. That is about the way he would have treated Barbara Fritchie.

Similar politeness was not shown other young women who flaunted the Stars and Stripes before the Confederates in western Maryland that September.

In Middletown, George Crouse displayed a Union flag in the upstairs window of his house on West Main Street. In mid-September, though the brief Valley News Echo story does not give a precise date, a squad of Confederate cavalry led by Captain Edward C. Motter, a resident of the Catoctin Creek valley, rode into town. They visited a known Confederate sympathizer, S.D. Riddlemoser, who offered hospitality—probably not cold well water, the paper hinted. After the visit, the squad passed the Crouse house where the flag hung. Here we pick up the expanded story that George F. Rhoderick, Sr., the 1862 editor of the local paper, told his son, George, Jr., who edited the paper in the early years of the twentieth century.

As the squad of fourteen reached the Crouse home, they reined in and a burly cavalryman dismounted. He demanded of the two young women standing by the door, "Take that damn Yankee rag down!"

As he climbed the porch to push past the two girls, 17-year-old Nancy Crouse and her bosom friend, Effie Titlow, Nancy dodged him with a taunt, and fled upstairs, where she wrapped the flag around her body. "You may shoot me, but never will I give up my country's flag to the hands of traitors!" she declaimed. (Did young women really talk like that then?)

He held a revolver to her head. They exchanged taunts. The soldier did get the flag from Nancy, and the troop rode off. According to the brief item in the paper, the cavalryman "tore the flag to bits." Rhoderick, Sr., told his son the flag was used to make a sunshade for the rider's horse.

The Confederate squad rode to the tavern of John Hogan, which was about three miles from the Confederate lines, where, the paper said, they stopped to refresh themselves again. There a pursuing squad of Union cavalry captured all but Captain Motter.

Rhoderick, Jr., recorded both Nancy and Effie married and continued to live in the region. After Nancy's death in 1908, Effie Titlow Herron confirmed to him the story of the flag and the Confederates.

Across the mountain, in Sharpsburg, another family displayed the Stars and Stripes. Their seventeen-year-old daughter was quicker of wit than Nancy

Crouse. The John Kreutze family lived on Main Street and, during the early days of the war, displayed a large flag on a rope over the street between their house and a neighbor's. This is the story that Marie Teresa Kreutze told to Fred William Gross, a Civil War buff, in 1929:

There were some Southern sympathizers in town…

When it became evident that the Confederates were going to occupy the town, I began to fear for the safety of the flag. Finally we took a box, wrapped the flag up, and placed it therein. Then father took the box and buried it in the ash heap which was banked up against the back side of the smoke house in our backyard.

I felt sure that some of the Southern sympathizers in town would tell the Confederates that we had a flag and that the soldiers would be after it. Sure enough, as soon as the Confederates occupied the town, a party of soldiers called at the door and demanded the "Yankee flag."

I said, "Gentlemen, there is no Yankee flag in this house."

"O yes, there is," was their reply. "We have heard all about the big flag that you have kept hanging across the street, and you must give it up."

I then said, "I knew somebody would tell you about that flag, and rather than have it fall into your hands, I laid it in ashes." They thought I had burned it.

Several times during the Confederate occupation of town, a demand was made for the flag. I always gave them the reply, "It is in ashes."

After the battle was over and the Confederates had left town, we took the box out of the ash heap, unwrapped the flag, and hung it between two of the upper windows on the street side of the house. Some of the Confederate prisoners who were still in the town saw it and cursed me right roundly, and said I had lied to them. I told them, "No, I told you what was absolutely true. The flag was in ashes."

That flag was used at funerals of Union soldiers in Sharpsburg until it finally wore out sometime about the turn of the century.

X

Clara on the Battlefield

A handwritten draft recounting her experiences on the Maryland battlefield exists in the Clara Barton manuscripts in the Library of Congress. Some pages are written on the letterhead of the Office of Correspondence of the Friends of the Missing Men of the United States Army, which has a printed date of 1866. This suggests the manuscript was intended as a lecture. The abridged draft that follows is her account of her experience going to and on the battlefield of Antietam/Sharpsburg.

She had been promised an army wagon with some supplies, driver, and four soldiers to take her to Harpers Ferry, then under siege by the Confederates. The officer giving permission also said significantly, "I wouldn't wait for Sunday to pass, if I were you." We begin with Clara Barton, early on the morning of Sept. 13, 1862, watching:

the approach of the long, high, white-covered, tortoise-motioned vehicle with its double string of little, frisky, long-eared animals, with the broad shouldered dutch driver astride, navigating his craft up to my door with the eternal jerk of his single rein...I found the "few things" which Maj. Gen. Ruckler had thought of to consist of pails, camp kettles, & lanterns by the score, tin plates & knives, forks, spoons, cups by the hundred & gross, hung & packed among the bows and canvassing of my wagon as to occupy the least possible space. Then & there, 7th St. just off Pa. Av, my vehicle was loaded with boxes, bags & parcels & last of all, I found a place to sit down with fair success...I remembered at the last minute to tie up a few articles/for myself/in a handkerchief.

Thus equipped and rested my chain of little uneasy animals commenced to straighten itself, and soon brought us into the center of Pa. Avenue in full gaze of the inhabitants of the whole city in their best attire and on their way to church. Thus all day we rattled on over the stones and dykes and up and down the hills of Maryland. At nightfall we turned into an open field, and dismounting, built a campfire, prepared supper, and *retired,* I to my room in my wagon, the men wrapped in their blankets camped around me. All night an indistinct roar of artillery sounded upon our ears, waking or sleeping we were conscious of trouble ahead and before day break, we had breakfasted and were on our way.

...We were directly in the midst of a train of army wagons at least ten miles in length moving in solid column, the government supplies of ammunition, food, and medicine for an army in battle.../Soldiers were failing and falling by the roadside./I busied myself as I rode on hour by hour cutting loaves of bread in slices and passing them to the pale haggard wrecks as they lay by roadside, or staggered on to avoid capture. At each little village we entered I purchased all the bread its inhabitants would sell...The residents began to tell us of a great battle fought last night, they said, a few miles up the mountains, and that a general had been killed. Hastened by anxiety and excitement we were urging on, when suddenly we found our wheels literally crushing the bodies of unburied slain...We had found a battlefield, for this ragged mountain rising heavily on our right was South mountain, and that fallen general—Reno.

/She walked over the battlefield on foot./Shocked and sick of heart we returned to our waiting conveyance. A mammoth drove of cattle designed as rations for our troops was passing at the moment.

...Scarcely was I seated in my wagon when the officer/in charge of the drove/rode up and said confidentially, "Miss Barton, the house on the lower side of the road under the hill has been taken as a Confederate hospital and is full of wounded rebels. Their surgeons have come out and asked me for meat, saying that their men will die for lack of animal food. I am a bonded officer and responsible for the property under my charge. What can I do?"

"You can do nothing," I said, "but ride on ahead. I am neither bonded nor responsible." He was wise and a word was sufficient—he had a sudden call to the front of his train and dashed forward.

Speaking to two of my men, I pointed out a large white ox slightly strayed from the drove and attempting to graze. He had been with Genl. Pope's army long enough to learn to "live off the country," and I directed them to drive him to the house inside the fence which surrounded it, put up the bars, and leave him there, asking no questions. I need not say that it was all performed with wonderful alacrity, and the last I saw of the white ox he had gone completely over to the enemy and was reveling in the tall grass about the house...

/Because of/the great length of the Army train...we could no more change our position than one of the planets unless we should wait and fall behind...The order of the train: first ammunition, next food and clothing for well troops; and lastly hospital supplies.../Delivery of medical supplies would/be two to three days coming up. I resorted to strategy.

We found an early resting place, supped by our camp fire, and slept again among the dews and damps. At one o'clock when every thing was still, we rose, breakfasted, fed, harnessed, and moved past the whole train, which like ourselves had camped for the night. At daylight, we had gained ten miles, and were up with the artillery, in advance even of the ammunition. All that weary dusty day we followed. And during all the afternoon the sullen roar of distant guns growing ever louder and nearer assured us that our haste had not been in vain. At nightfall brought us up with the great Army of the Potomac...Following close our pace-making leaders (the cannon) we drew up where they did among the smoke of a thousand camp fires...

In all this vast assemblage, I saw no other trace of womankind. I was faint but could not eat, weary but could not sleep, depressed but could not weep, so I climbed into my wagon, tied down the cover and dropped down in the little nook I had occupied so long. I prayed God...

/Next morning, after viewing the battlefield from a hill/We followed the artillery around eight miles and turning into a cornfield near a house and barn, and stopping in the rear of the last gun, which completed the terrible line of artillery...A garden wall only separated us...We had met wounded men walking or borne to the rear for the last ten miles, but around the old barn and in the field lay there, too badly torn to admit of removal some 300 thus early in the day, for it was scarce ten o'clock.

/She followed a path through head-high corn to the house/my arms full of stimulants and bandages and rags, and followed the opening, arriving at a little wicket gate, I found the door yard of a small house and, face to face, with one of the kindest and noblest surgeons I have ever met, Dr. Dunn of Connaughtsville, Pa. Speechless both for an instant, he at length, threw up his hands with "God has indeed remembered us. How did you get from Virginia here? and so soon? And again to supply our necessities—and they are terrible—we have nothing but our instruments, and the little chloroform we brought in our pockets. Have torn up the last sheets we could find in this house; have not a bandage, rag, lint or string, and those shell wounded men bleeding to death." Upon the porch stood four tables with a stupefied patient upon each, a surgeon standing over him with his knife and a bunch of *green corn leaves* for dressing.

/She devotes several pages to a description of how the battle-lines changed around them, and her effort to aid a wounded soldier on the field, during which a bullet passed between her supporting arm and her body to hit him in the chest killing him instantly./

At 2 o'clock, my men came to tell me that the last loaf of bread had been cut and the last cracker pounded and soaked. We had three boxes of wine still unopened. What should they do?

"Open the wine and give that," I said, "God help US!"

The next instant an ejaculation from Sergeant Field, who had opened the first box of wine, drew my attention, and to my astonished gaze, it was revealed that the wine had been packed in nicely sifted Indian meal. If it had been gold dust it would have seemed poor in comparison. I had no words. No one spoke. In speechless silence the men wiped their eyes & resumed their work.

A woman would not hesitate long under these circumstances. This was an old farm house. Big kettles were picked up, washed & filled with water and set over fires, almost as quick as I can tell it, and I was mixing meal and water for gruel. The thought occurred to us to explore the cellar.

The chimney rested upon an arch and forcing the door, we discovered three barrels and a bag. "They are full!" said the sergeant as he sounded them with his foot. Rolling them to the light, we found that it bore the mark of Jackson's army. These three barrels of flour and bag of salt had been stored there by the rebel army the week previous. I shall never experience such a sensation of wealth & complacency again. From utter poverty to such riches. All the night my men carried buckets of hot gruel for miles down the line to the poor wounded soldiers lying where they fell.

This time we had lanterns to hang in and around the barn & having directed it to be done, I repaired to the house & found the surgeon sitting alone beside a table upon which he rested his elbow, apparently meditating upon a tallow candle that flickered in its centre. Approaching carefully, I said, "You are tired, Dr.?"

He started up with a look almost savage, "*Tired*! Yes, I am tired. Tired of such heartlessness, such suffering" & turning full upon me he continued, "Think of the condition of things. Here we are at least 1000 wounded men—terribly wounded. 900 of them cannot live till daylight without attention. That two inches of candle is all I have or can get & we have only to sit helpless in the darkness & listen to their dying groans. What can I do? How can I endure it!"

I took him by the arm & leading him to the door pointed in the direction of the barn, where the lanterns glistened like stars among the moving corn.

"What is that?" he exclaimed.

"The barn is lighted," I said. "The house will be in a few minutes."

"Who did it?" he asked.

"I—I brought them."

"Where did you get the candles? How many have you?"

"All you want. Four boxes."

He looked at me a moment & turned away without a word & never afterward alluded to the circumstances, but the deference with which he ever after treated me was almost painful.

I could tell you how the following day, we roamed over the whole ground and gathered up the wounded & worked until the arrival of supplies on the third day—got the men in hospitals & reached home almost as weak & worn as they...

XI

The Half-Life of Ha'nts

Ghosts haunt the valleys, slopes, and houses of the blue hills, at Halloween and other times.

Some come from an almost forgotten past; others were prosaic neighbors. The stories of some are known; others appear but we know not why. Others appear only once or twice, and never again. Those that are seen by many have a half-life, like radioactive material. They are seen most frequently in the years close to their death, and less often as the years increase. Even after they are rarely seen, they are remembered. Here are accounts of some western Maryland ghosts whose half-lives continue today.

Ghosts walked even in the early days of settlement, and were fearsome to many, although not to the French traveler of post-Revolution days:

> Ghosts are often seen in the United States. The woods, the rivers attract them, and the simple minds of the inhabitants adapt themselves better to the companionship of a spirit than to knowledge of physical sciences which would reveal to them that it is an atmospheric phenomenon which frightens them. The fume of spirituous liquors, the shadows of the night and the woods are the elements which are very suitable to the formation of goblins.

Ghosts of Indians who had lived and hunted in Maryland woods were seen by those who supplanted them. Indians with fiery hands barred the fords to benighted travelers. Ghostly campfires sparked on distant meadows. By the latter half of the nineteenth century, however, when Madeleine Dahlgren collected material on regional ghosts, only the Negroes living up the rocky slopes saw Indian ghosts and heard their cries of "Ok-en-ja!"

The tale of the vengeance of one such ghost lingers. Chief Twenty Bones was buried, with his musket, copper beads, pots of food and other grave goods, on a hill near Linesboro. Settlers believed the mound and its treasure were

80

under a curse. A drifter, whom the original account describes as a philosopher, scoffed at the curse when he heard of it in the local tavern; late at night, he was observed going quietly out with pick and shovel in hand. He did not return by morning. When they went to look for him, the Chief's grave was open. The skeleton was exposed, but had not apparently been disturbed: his musket was still by his side, copper beads around the bony throat. The food pots were broken open, however. Spots of red trailed from the pots (dry like red ochre) into the woods, growing damp and sticky as it went. The trail led to an opening where a tree had fallen in some storm. Here, grass and fallen leaves were spotted with bright red, as if a rain of blood had fallen from above. The trail ended. Nothing was ever seen of the drifter. The good people of Linesboro closed the grave again—but more than a little of the grave goods went home with them. Chief Twenty Bones, however, took no more vengeance.

Another pre-Revolutionary ghost has had a long half-life. East of New Windsor, the neo-classical house Avalon stands. It was built as the mansion of Furnace Hill Plantation and its iron works. Like others of the period, the house was built with two separate fireplaces on the first floor whose flues joined higher up into a single chimney. In this house, the ground floor fireplaces were connected with brick walls leaving space behind. The English immigrant, Leigh Masters, who built house and iron works, used slaves to fire and operate the iron furnaces. He died shortly after Maryland ratified the Constitution of the United States. Soon after his death, the slaves of the neighborhood said they saw a ghost patrolling the boundaries of Furnace Hill Plantation. It cried aloud for mercy as it rode a gray horse, which was usually followed by three imps carrying lanterns as if they were searching. Some said the horse's nostrils emitted smoke and flame; others heard the clanking of chains. What had Masters done to become such an unhappy ghost?

Much or nothing. Nothing, if we believe a woman historian writing a generation or so after his death. She described Masters as an "honest, public spirited gentleman, though rough in his manners as people of the time often were."

Much, if we believe evidence found in the hidden space between fireplaces and an even later historian. In his lifetime, Masters was known as a brutal master to his slaves, especially to one called Sam. After Sam disappeared one night, Masters never mentioned his name again. Did Masters kill Sam, or did Sam walk a couple of hours north into Pennsylvania and freedom? Sometime toward the end of the nineteenth century, the chimney of Avalon had to be repaired, breeching the walls that connected the fireplaces. Bones were found in the vault, but whether they were animal or human was not recorded. A recent historian of black history in the county writes that Masters killed Sam, who objected to Masters' rape of a female slave, and buried him in the vault between the fireplaces.

In 1877, the brick vault in which Masters had been buried disintegrated and his bones were reburied in the Episcopal Church of the Ascension, Westminster. Since that time, the ghost and following imps has not been reported. Masters is usually remembered today as a colonial Maryland legislator.

In Auburn, an iron-master's house of the early nineteenth century, the younger brother, Edward, of the McPhersons who occupied the house during the Mexican War, took his brother's place to serve in the army. While in Mexico, Edward fought a duel, in which he was wounded so severely he died that same day. At his request, his body was sent home for burial, preserved in a barrel of whiskey for the long journey. ("What a waste of whiskey!" a relative is said to have commented.) Edward's ghost wanders the halls of Auburn, greeting guests with a nod and bow, and sometimes opening a door for them.

The nineteenth century produced many ghosts. One of these is the only ghost recorded from Boonsboro: a woman in white who looks wistfully toward Little Antietam Creek from an upper window of a shop building on Main Street. Another is the spirit who appears in Turner's Gap above Boonsboro, described by Mrs. Dahlgren:

> A spirit of very awful mien and huge proportions has been seen, in the guise of a Waggoner, to suddenly rise from the ground in the dell below South Mountain House and lifts his vast arms aloft. But no one has ever staid to see what else he did, or if he ever sank back to the same place from which he came.

A third is the tall, beautiful woman who has been in a number of places on or near South Mountain. Some called her a banshee because, when she was seen, the death of some relative near to the viewer followed in a short time. Certainly, each time she was seen bending over a child, the child died. To others who saw her, she brought only a feeling of intense cold.

"Middletown in song and legend" by T.C. Harbaugh has several ghost stories, only one of which seems to be based on history. Jim was the little black jockey of the racehorse, Selim. When Selim lost a race on which his owner had placed heavy bets, the owner was so enraged he shot Selim on the spot and then beat Jim so severely he later died. Harbaugh wrote that, later, Selim and his jockey were frequently seen by other jockeys practicing on the race course.

A ghost in Harbaugh Valley has been seen by many. Here on the last night of 1830, five members of the Newey family and an apprentice boy were murdered in their beds and the house set afire over them. For years after, in the cold dusks of December, passers-by told of seeing a man in old-fashioned clothes lurking in the bushes around the site of the burned house. Some thought it was the murderer returned to the scene of his crime. Others felt it was the ghost of the supposed accomplice, never identified, but known to have been with the murderer a few hours before the crime. Gossip said that, in Ohio, a man on his deathbed had confessed to have been an accomplice in the murders.

The old jail in Westminster has a ghost who wanders its hall and its yard with hands outstretched, pathetically seeking its missing head. It is the ghost of Big Tom Parkes, who came from Tennessee in 1840, and was arrested several times for blasphemy and for striking a woman. While the complaint on which arrest was attempted Christmas season of 1846 is not remembered, not forgotten is that the arrest was accomplished only by the sheriff, two deputies, and a pistol held to Tom's head. The enraged sheriff threatened Tom with a term in the penitentiary; Tom committed suicide, with his own knife, on Christmas night. The coroner was Dr. William Zollickhoffer, author of "Materia Medica of the United States," and a member of the Union Mills Scientific, Literary, and Philosophical Society. He asked for, and got, permission to study Parkes' head for phrenologic clues. Phrenology (the identification of criminal character traits by the shape of the cranium) was a subject of interest to science at that time. Tom Parkes' ha'nt has been searching fruitlessly for his head ever since.

A researcher at Beltsville's U.S. Department of Agriculture's offices heard this story of a mill near Westminster that was haunted one night a year. One summer night in the 1840s, a young farmer and his handsome mare were found dead in the millpond. No explanation for their death was discovered. On the night of the full moon next August, the miller, alone in the mill with his dog, felt great loneliness, isolation and unease. The dog crept whining under the bed and refused to stir. His feelings persisted until dawn, but did not return until the night of the next August full moon. That night, or the one the third year, the miller chanced to look up stream. A distant figure, white as milk, approached at speed. As it neared, it became a horse and rider galloping hard…Zigzagging ahead of the two was a ghostly fox, which raced toward the dam of the millpond. As the horse and rider passed, the miller recognized the rider as the young farmer whose death had never been solved. He heard a muttered, "I'll get that damn fox if I have to go to hell for him!" The fox leaped into the pond; horse and rider plunged after. The miller fainted, regaining consciousness only with the arrival of the first load of grain to be ground next morning. Thereafter, the mill never operated nor was occupied the night of the full moon in August.

The half-life of these ghosts is almost ended; they are rarely seen today. Ghosts who died later in the century have strong enough half-lives they are seen occasionally even today.

A pastor (now retired) of a Burkittsville church sometimes heard the sound of tramping feet on the warm nights of late summer, when ghostly campfires (which some said was marsh gas and others fireflies) flickered on the fields beyond the village. Were the sounds that of soldiers who died on South Mountain returning to the scene of their last battle?

On the western edge of the village, the tannery had served as temporary hospital after the battle of Crampton's Gap, but stood empty and abandoned in the early twentieth century. It offered a quiet parking place for young couples, who said they never heard or saw anything, but next morning, there would be human footprints on the hood and roof of the car that would not wash off. It was thought the unknown soldiers who had died in the tannery wanted recognition. A suitable monument was obtained. The American Legion post dedicated it with a prayer from a local pastor. The footprints stopped appearing. The tannery is now a residence.

The one soldier ghost of Fox's Gap was easily appeased. Burial of the dead after that battle was hastily done, so hastily a number of Confederate dead were thrown into the well of the Wise farm, and dirt shoveled over. When the Wise family returned home, old Mr. Wise frequently dreamed of a soldier beckoning to him. One evening, before retiring, he stood in the doorway looking out toward the well. He saw a dark figure beckoning as in his dreams. "What do you want?" "I'm Jim Tubbs, and I'm buried in a damn' uncomfortable position. Turn me over, will you?," the ghost demanded. Next day, Wise opened the well, and turned the topmost body over. Sergeant Tubbs was seen no more.

Turner's Gap has its military ghosts as well. Mrs. Dahlgren told of smoke that oozed out of the stone barn behind her South Mountain house when there was no fire in or near it. She told of hearing the clash of sabers, smelling burnt gunpowder, and seeing, at night, smoke coalesce into soldiers in battle line. Another anonymous writer said two hikers on the Appalachian Trail who were sleeping in the field below the South Mountain Inn (Mrs. Dahlgren's former home) were awakened by the same sounds and smells Mrs. Dahlgren had reported years earlier. They too, saw pale figures march past in battle line.

A little north, at Washington Monument, military ghosts left physical evidence of their presence. Between the battle of Turners' Gap and that of Sharpsburg/Antietam three days later, a Union soldier deserted and was hidden by his Zittlestown sweetheart. After the battle and the departure of the two armies, he came out of hiding and lived with his sweetheart. Suddenly, in mid-

September of 1863, both of them disappeared. "The fallen comrades he deserted came back for both of them," Zittlestown folk decided. "The ha'nts buried them near the Blue Rocks" close by the monument. They also said that, each September since, the soldiers fight, the girl cries and moans, and the proof of the ghostly battle is seen next morning in grasses flattened as if trampled by many feet—or by wind. The state caretaker who lived at the Monument for fifteen years after World War II never admitted he saw that ghostly sign.

The battle of Antietam/Sharpsburg created many ghosts, but the ones with longest half-lives are those known to the children of Sharpsburg. Ask any child in Sharpsburg to tell you a local ghost story. Like the Gale children, many others are not afraid of living in a "haunted house." They know ghost stories of their homes or lands. Jeffrey Rohrer's house used to be a part of John Brown's farm, and ghosts of soldiers supposedly walk around his lot. Jennifer Abel's mother and uncle saw a ghost on the battlefield when they were younger. Other children relate stories of doors closing, tin cups clanging, the eerie feeling of being touched, homes built over graves, drumming and the sound of gunshots on the battlefield on foggy mornings.

The C&O Canal saw armies come and go but only one Civil War ghost seems to be remembered. It made a desirable anchorage unusable after the Battle of Ball's Bluff. George Wolfe told what happened when a new canal boat captain anchored between Milepost 33 and 34 on the Nine Mile Level. Almost as soon as the lanterns were put out for the night, the mules at the feed trough on the towpath became very restless. The captain got up, lit a lantern and went to calm them. He found, to his surprise, the mooring line was untied and the boat was drifting away. He awakened the other crew members, and, after an hour's work, the boat was poled back and tied up. They retired again. Now there were sounds as if the hatches were being opened. Shotgun in hand, the captain emerged to find all secure, but the mules were still restless and had eaten nothing of the grain before them, which they would ordinarily have cleaned up. A third time the crew tried to sleep, but were awakened by the mules braying in fright—or hunger. The mate told the captain, "This is the Ghostly Bend. Maybe the mules don't like the ghosts. Maybe it's better to move the boat somewhere—fast." They moved in the dark a mile upstream. All was serene at the new mooring. The mules were already devouring their grain even before the lanterns were turned out.

A very few other ghosts along the canal are remembered. A headless man and woman haunted the towpath between Brunswick and Sandy Hook. A lady ghost walked the waste weir below the Catoctin tunnel toward the riverbank.

An Indian chief wandered a towpath he had never seen in life near Big Pool. They faded with the freight traffic on the canal.

Ha'nts that began their after-death careers near enough our time to have much of their half-life remaining are fewer now, or they have not been adequately recorded. Most of us, all born in the twentieth century, are unwilling to admit to a belief in ghosts or to seeing one. Should an unexplained specter be seen, we keep quiet. However, the few ghosts which have been acknowledged are much like their predecessors, only mildly interesting.

Aunt Mary White, who lived in Burkittsville, used to see a neighbor leading his cows out to pasture in the early dawn light—even though he had been dead half a year or more.

In Eldersburg, an eighteenth century kitchen was connected to a nineteenth century house by a hall, which had a stairway to the house's upper floors. Food had to be carried from the kitchen through the hall to the dining room in the newer building. The family and the farm workers eating in the dining room regularly saw a young woman in gray come down the stairs to look anxiously at the food passing by. As she never left the stairs, they all grew so accustomed that a son of the house dared a maid to touch her. The maid extended a plate of food toward the ghost. When the plate touched the spirit, it vanished and was never seen again. Unexplained noises upstairs and footsteps on the stairs continued to be heard.

What he did in life for forty years, the Christmas ghost of Emmitsburg continues to do as a ha'nt. Larry Dillman was the feckless son of Professor Henry Jasper Dillman, who taught music at St. Mary's College, and also led orchestras, composed marches for four Presidents of the United States, and wrote the well-loved hymn, "When glory lit the heavens." Larry, born in 1840, played several instruments but his talent lay with the banjo and minstrelsy. He operated a grocery store but his real career was sitting on the store's porch, chatting, flirting, and singing impromptu songs. As leader of the young people, he could be found at all dances, where he appeared in one of the amazing number of suits of clothes he owned—five! He had canes to match, cut from broomsticks, painted and decorated. After he married, his songs were of married love—for a while. Soon, his eye wandered; his wife, patience worn out, left him. He paid even less attention to business and drank more homemade wine. Altogether he was a disappointment to his father. Professor Dillman died in 1885. That Christmas, those who went to 5:30 a.m. mass heard a flute playing "Adeste fideles" and "When glory lit the heavens" in the cemetery on the hill. It was Larry Dillman playing at his father's grave. Every Christmas morning thereafter, he serenaded his father's grave similarly. In 1900, the congregation abandoned St. Mary's church to join St. Anthony's church, where the mass was at midnight Christmas Eve. Larry serenaded at midnight thereafter.

As he aged, when the weather was rough, his neighbors helped him get to and from the cemetery. The weather was good Christmas 1922. Larry was alone. At the church, the people heard the music falter and die away. Larry was unconscious when they reached him. He died that winter.

The flute still plays at midnight Christmas Eve in the Emmitsburg cemetery on the hill. If you are up that late, listen for it.

A Hempstead house has a ghost that has kept it empty for years. At the turn of the century, Rafe and Lena were caretakers of the house for a family traveling abroad. Rafe fancied squirrel for dinner, though hunting season had not begun and the game warden was active. Lena argued with him, begging him not to go hunting. He ignored her pleas, and bagged two squirrels. As he neared the back door with them, noises on the drive made him think "Game warden!" Hastily, he tossed squirrels through the open cellar door and the shotgun followed. It landed, butt first, and went off, killing Rafe. The owners returned to help Lena bury Rafe, but she was inconsolable and died within a few months.

Next fall, in the weeks before hunting season began, shotgun blasts were heard outside the house and noises of argument drifted through the windows, although no gunner or disputants were ever seen. Finally, the family sold the house and left. Jeremiah, Elizabeth and their eleven children were the new owners. They too heard the noise of a shotgun and the sound of argument. The next summer, a gypsy wagon stopped to ask for water and a place to camp. The water was given but a campsite farther away was suggested. Three times the gypsy woman tried to tell Jeremiah's fortune and was refused. "There is much you need to know," she said. Perhaps she cursed him before they drove on, but who knows? Shortly before hunting season, Jeremiah came in from the field with what he said was a migraine headache, went to his room, and killed himself with a shotgun. Elizabeth tried to continue living there but the noises and bad luck continued. When she moved the family, the eldest son drove backwards as they left the grounds to ensure their bad luck was left behind. The next purchaser also heard the sounds of argument. In hunting season, father and son went out together. When the father's shotgun accidentally caught in briers, and went off, the son was killed. That family too moved. The house was still standing empty when the story was recorded in 1972.

A Civil War period house in Harbaugh Valley is apparently haunted by several ghosts, one of whom was kindly disposed to the occupants as late as the 1980s. Douglas, Teresa and two small boys moved in with the aid of her mother and sister, who heard the chimes of a grandfather clock that was not visible. Neighbors later told Teresa, who had not yet heard the chimes, that they had often heard them. She heard them for the first time after another, and her first, spectral experience.

She was pregnant with a third child, and took afternoon naps. Awakening from such a nap, she found she was sharing her room with eight black women in long muslin dresses. They seemed to be planning the escape of another slave on the Underground Railroad. "I could see my furniture through them, and I could see their furniture too." A kerosene stove stood in their room; hers lacked one. When she mentioned what she had seen, her husband declared she must be sick...

Some nights later, Teresa awakened to hear a clock chiming. Remembering Douglas' disbelief, she lay still, saying nothing. Then Douglas growled, "I didn't hear a damn' thing."

When the baby, a boy, was born, a ghost became a kindly and efficient babysitter. The parents thought the baby unusually good and placid. They seldom found him uncovered. His pacifier was usually in his mouth. That this was not the child's normal behavior was recognized only the afternoon a summer storm blew up. Every one raced to shut open windows and to cover the baby who had been put to nap without even a sheet over him. When Douglas reached the child's room, he found the windows shut and the baby tucked under a light cover. Teresa and the two little boys denied having been to the baby's room at all.

Later that fall, Douglas' teen-aged sister, a tall girl with a dark-haired ponytail, babysat while the couple was out for the evening. Returning after midnight, the headlights of their car caught, briefly, the window of the upstairs room where the baby slept. Teresa saw a tall, dark-haired woman standing in it, patting the baby's back to put him to sleep. When they entered the house, the teenage girl was asleep on the sofa. Wakened, she said, "No, I haven't had to go upstairs since I put the boys to bed. The baby never wakened after I tucked him in." Upstairs, little Patrick was sweetly asleep, too neatly tucked in for it to have been done five hours earlier.

Shortly before the birth of their fourth child, a girl, an overnight visitor asked, "Who was that little blonde girl that tried to get in bed with me this morning? Is she a neighbor's child? You don't have any girls." After the fourth child arrived, the ghostly nursemaid stopped being helpful. "We've too many children now," Teresa believes.

With so many ghosts in Maryland—and there are more than are reported here—even unbelievers may see one unexpectedly. But do not expect to be frightened.

XII

Pow-Wow and Hex

Witches were among the first settlers of Maryland: Mary Less was hanged as a witch at sea en route to the colony in 1634. Witches are still here in the twenty-first century, if the silver screen tells the truth. However, for most Marylanders today, "bewitching" is a compliment, not the curse it once was, and "witch" a masquerade costume.

Perhaps fewer witches came to Maryland than to other colonies. One other Maryland witch was convicted: three years (1685) after the Salem, Mass., witchcraft trials, Rebecca Powell was hung at St. Mary's City for "witchcraft, ensorcellement and the fascination" of Frances Sandsbury. Three more trials for witchcraft were held in the next twenty-two years, with acquittal for all three defendants. A hundred years passed with no witchcraft prosecutions. Annapolis legislators, in 1810, took the laws off the books that made witchcraft a felony similar to murder, burglary, etc. Legislators thus allowed witches to practice their art, since they believed them to do little harm.

Those who lived beyond the Maryland mountains weren't as certain. Western Marylanders believed pretty much as did their former neighbors who had moved across the mountains into the Ohio country. The Reverend Joseph Doddridge, born and educated in Maryland, who preached in the upper Ohio valley, wrote of those beliefs in 1824:

> The belief in witchcraft was prevalent among the early settlers of the western country. To the witch was ascribed the tremendous power of inflicting strange and incurable diseases, particularly to children, of destroying cattle by shooting them with hair balls and a great variety of other means of destruction, of inflicting spells and curses on guns and other things, and lastly of changing men into horses, and often bridling and saddling them, riding them at full speed over hill and dale to their frolics and other places of rendezvous. More ample powers of mischief than these cannot be imagined.

Wizards were men supposed to possess the same mischievous powers as the witches; but these were seldom exercised for bad purposes. The powers of the wizards were exercised almost exclusively for the purpose of counteracting the malevolent influences of the witches of the other sex. I have known several of these witch masters, as they were called, who made a public profession of curing the diseases inflicted by the influences of witches.

The novelist Gath, in *Katy of Catoctin*, has a farmer's son in Washington County tell about a midnight ride with several wizards, a witch, and, perhaps, the devil himself:

Dot Shmoketown is an ole Shpooktown, py Jing! I come along tare one night purty trunk, riding a horse, and joost as I crossed a leetle stream dis side of Shmoketown an' begun to climb te mountain road dat comes dis way, and had got into de glen petween te Short Mountain an' te Plue Ridge, I see pefore me a black man with a white face like a chiny plate. I said to myself, "By Jing!, any company is petter dan none!' So I jined de black feller, and he was de nicest feller I ever did know: he was rale shentlemans.

Says he: "It's cold; we'll drink together!" He handed me a flask. When I got done trinkin', tere was another man riding with us.

As we come up te mountain through te chestnut forest, te moon shined on te road, and efery time we took another trink, tere was another man on horsepack, till, by Jing! I counted apout nine men, and de last man was a woman.

Te all seemed to know te black man with te white face: he was a rale shentlemans...

The first ting I knowed, we was at te steep edge of te mountain, and te captain rode right over. Down, down he went, and efery feller after him, and last of all, for my horse had stumpled—I was pitched off te horse joost pefore he jumped over, and I was fallin', too,—So down I went, hundreds of feet, and next mornin' tere I was found underneath te mountain.

The attitude toward witches changed in the middle of the nineteenth century. Joseph Barry, the historian of Harpers Ferry, described how the witchcraft he knew as a young man changed:

Starting from the railroad bridge at Harpers Ferry and running northwest, with the railroad track for six miles to Duffield's Station, is a region that has ever been the home of wizards, witches, and all kinds of adepts in occult lore...The construction of the railroad...was the first interruption to the dreams of magic, and, then, the civil war, with its very practical ideas, and, above all, perhaps, the subsequent introduction of free schools have completed the delivery of the worthy inhabitants from the very galling yoke of many practitioners of the black art—African and Caucasian—who profited in money and reputation by the fears they excited and the fees they received for cures or immunity. In justice, it must be stated that the whites, mostly of German origin, were generally of a benevolent character and that the practice of their art was always directed to counteract the malevolence of the negroes who seldom devoted their mystic knowledge to any good purpose, especially where any member of their own race was concerned.

Barry tells these stories about local witches. In Harpers Ferry, the slave Jesse Short wanted to "pay attention" to a girl of color working on the neighboring plantation of John Engle. Because Jesse had an unenviable reputation as a "disreputable scamp who enjoyed an immense reputation for powers of mischief," Engle forbade him to visit. One day, when Jesse was delivering a message from his master to Engle, five-year-old Margaret Engle brushed past Jesse and:

> the little girl screamed wildly as soon as his hand touched her and she showed the utmost horror of him. Her screams continued until she got into fits and the greatest difficulty was experienced in restoring her temporarily to her normal condition. But the little one was not the same from that time. Day by day she failed, lost appetite, and could not get natural sleep. In a month...hope of her recovery was almost abandoned...Somebody remembered that across the Potomac, in Maple Swamp, a place inhabited in a great measure by half-breeds descended from the Indians, lived a certain Mrs. Mullin, whose fame for occult knowledge was wide-spread...To her as a last resort the parents of the child appealed. The benevolent old lady responded at once, and crossed the Potomac on her mission of charity. She took the child on her knee, without the least repugnance on the part of the little girl. What mystic words or rites the old lady used, tradition does not say, but she took from her pocket a pair of scissors and with deliberation clipped the nails from the fingers of the child—from all but one finger—and herein lies the wonder, for the child at once began to improve.

She was still alive and hearty for more than seventy-five years with full use of all her limbs, except for the one finger whose nail was not clipped. That remained crooked, so Barry said.

A Frederick County woman remembered, in the 1990s, her mother or grandmother telling of a young mother and child coming into a Wolfsville store, where the store's clerk asked the child's name. Seeming to forget it, the clerk asked again, and a third time. When the family got home, the child became cranky, obstreperous and uncooperative, and remained so for several days, no matter what the distracted mother could do. "There's a hex on the baby," a neighbor said. "Try to break it. Write a prayer on a piece of paper, and make a pouch for the prayer out of a piece of muslin. But be sure you sew away from yourself when you make it. Then hang pouch and prayer around baby's neck." When this was done, the child again became its happy self. The next time the family visited the store, the clerk called the child by name and, at least three times offered the child a lick of candy. The mother refused to allow the child to have it. If the child had taken it, the spell would have returned.

In another incident, about 100 years ago, west of South Mountain, a previously healthy child was "fer hexed" into "Take-off." The Prayer Doctor consulted also put a written prayer into a pouch tied around the child's neck with string taken from between the leaves of a Bible. The parents were told to wait until the pouch came off on its own when the string broke. During this period, no one in the family was to lend or borrow anything. When the pouch came off, the child would be well and the witch would become as sick as the child had been. The child got well, as promised, and the step-grandmother became very sick, identifying her as the one who laid the hex.

Madeleine V. Dahlgren tells, in her *South Mountain Magic*, a number of stories of witchcraft practiced near South Mountain in the years after the Civil War. One is about a disgruntled landlord who was unable to evict a tenant from his property. He got a wizard to cast a spell that made the house so uncomfortable a place to live that the tenant moved. The wizard had to be recalled to remove the spell, or hex. He circled the house three times, muttering, and invoking the Three Holy Names (Father, Son, and Holy Ghost). After that, the landlord could move in.

Witches lay spells, country folk knew, on animals as well as people. When a herd of cows produced bloody milk, it was certainly the work of a witch. If a good milker suddenly went dry, a witch was calling the milk, possibly with a spell that brought the milk to her dishcloth that she wrung out over a basin.

Steps to break such spells were known, and sometimes also identified the witch if one watched. In Middle Catoctin Creek valley, one did it by putting milk in a skillet and making a cross in the milk with a silver knife, or by whipping the milk. Further west, in Flintstone, one boiled the milk and burst each bubble with a needle. This broke the spell and blinded the witch. Usually, they say, the witch came running to take the spell off before the first bubble appeared. If butter didn't come while churning, the first woman visitor must be turned away. She had spelled the cream. If the loan of a loaf of bread is asked during the humid dog days, refuse it, else the next baking will not rise. The loaned loaf gives the witch opportunity to lay a hex.

These identify neighbors laying hexes, but there are other ways:

A Negro discovered and killed a suspected witch. The husband pretended sleep. At midnight, the wife got out of bed, stood by the fireplace and shook herself. Her skin slipped off. She stepped out of it, and put it on a chair so it seemed she was sitting by the fire. Then she left the house. The husband got up and put salt in the skin. The wife returned about dawn and tried to put the skin back on. It wouldn't go more than half way up. She expired as the sun came up.

One could protect one's self against a witch even when no hex is anticipated. Are witches around? Scatter salt on all the sitting places in the house. Once a witch sits down, he or she cannot rise until released.

Keep a witch from entering by placing a broomstick in front of the door. All its straws must be counted before the witch can enter. A used horseshoe hung above house or stable door did the same trick; the witch must travel all the miles the shoe had traveled before entering. As no witch is able to count above three, brooms or horseshoes were effective bars. Negroes, with such protection in place, reported hearing witches counting all night long, "One. two. Three. Oh, pshaw! One. Two. Three. Oh, pshaw!"

The witch was careful not to reveal how he or she cursed or cured. Spells were muttered, gestures or symbols unexplained. Only the three-times-repeated Three Holy Names were clearly pronounced and heard. *A Friend in Need*, the little book of spells Michael Zittle published, which came to light in the 1980s, was a hoarded book of reference for Maryland witches.

A retired teacher remembered telling her class in Sabillasville, in the 1970s, about this book. One of the class said her family had such a book at home. When asked to bring it to show the class, the child replied, "Oh, I couldn't! It's dirty!" The teacher also heard a farmer had a book of spells which he kept on a shelf in the closet under the stairs. When he realized his adolescent boys had discovered the hiding place, the book disappeared. His wife and daughter thought he burned it.

Zittle's book, published in 1846, was a translation from an unnamed German book of 1824, which may have been a second edition of John George Hohman's *Pow-Wows, or, The Long-lost Friend* (published in 1819 at Rosenthal near Reading, Pennsylvania.). Madeleine V. Dahlgren had a spell book in German in her hands, briefly; she did not remember the title.

How to become a witch? By a spell and the devil. Both Dahlgren and Gath tell very similar stories of South Mountain girls seeking to be a witch. This is Dahhgren's:

> Sallie S—s, a rattling young girl, who lived on the hills between South-Mountain-House and Myersville, took a fancy in her foolish young nodule that it would be "great fun" to be a witch. Thereupon she went to Granny H—and said to her,
>
> "Granny, I've come to have you make me a witch."
>
> "Now, Sallie, do you really want to be a witch, for sure and certain?"
>
> "Yes, Granny, for sure and certain."
>
> "Well, then, you must wait till Friday. Then, when you get up, don't wash your face, but come to me by high noon, and I promise you, you shall see the old gentlemen."...
>
> These injunctions were carefully complied with, and the unwashed, unkempt damsel presented herself at midday at the hut of Granny H—.
>
> Soon after she got there a little old man came in and at once accosted the young girl.
>
> "So you want to have a trade with me, eh?"
>
> Somewhat frightened at his brusque manner, she timidly answered, "Yes."
>
> Then he said, "Sit down on the floor, put one hand on the top of your head and the other hand on the soles of your feet, and say—'All that is between my two hands belongs to the Devil.'"
>
> So the girl sat down on the floor, did as she was bid, and said, "All that is between my two hands belongs to God."
>
> At this unexpected termination the old man gave a hideous howl, like the bark of a dog, and vanished. But he left the room so filled with sickening gases that the poor child swooned away; and the old witch, being very angry, picked her up, and threw her, insensible as she was, out in the yard in front of the house. Here the open air revived her...Never has she since then ever had any wish to become a witch.

Pow-wows or "pau-waus" were, in western Maryland, what a witch did when healing. Family and friends observed them enough to record them, especially for children's ailments, for which they were frequently sought.

A baby who stayed awake till midnight every night would be taken for pow-wowing, or "try-for" as it was also called. The baby was stripped and measured with the witch's string. (This was often red, and was usually kept between the pages of the Bible.) Words were spoken over him, and the parents were told to take a strand of the baby's hair and place it under the hoop of a barrel and fasten the hoop tight. The child went to sleep naturally in the early evenings thereafter.

Thrush (a sore and congested throat) could usually be cured by pow-wow. The observed action of one cure was bending a straw of rye into three sides of a triangle and placing it on the child's tongue. Another was blowing on the tongue and throat through the straw.

Curing "take-off" was less certain. A child with "take-off" lacks energy, droops, cannot or will not eat, and eventually dies. One such recorded "try-for" required the mother to get flour from the witch, who said a secret pow-wow over it, and to make bread with it. The child and the loaf of warm bread were brought to the witch, who took a piece of the bread, said a spell over it, and had the child swallow it. Cure should follow in a few days. If it didn't, a second try-for had the witch take her string and measure the child's hands and feet. The string was carried home to be hung on the knob of the house door most often used. A cross was marked over every other door and window. This was supposed to remove a devil from the child and prevent its return.

The Frederick County Historical Society files record another pow-wow. A boy from Myersville was taken, in the 1880s, to a witch to try-for his crossed eyes. She mumbled over him, turned him around three times, gave him a buffet on the back, and assured him he was cured. And he was. The record says so, reading, "At times he could see better than others."

Perhaps this try-for was not as successful as it should have been, because the witch accepted a fee for services. The wizard Michael Zittle did not—at least, he did not, until he was aged and living with his son. Mrs. Dahlgren commented that accepting fees for his spells may have contributed to his ill health.

Besides using string in try-fors, hot coals sometimes had a place. A shovel full of glowing coals from the fire might be passed above and around the patient's body in a series of moves. In another try-for, the patient might step or jump over the red-hot coals.

Some healing could be accomplished for one's self, but worked better if a witch pow-wowed first. A potato carried in the pocket prevented rheumatism, but cured it if the witch had spelled the potato. Stepping with a bare foot on a nail required hanging a strip of bacon on the offending nail to ward off inflammation, but a witch's spell upon the bacon assured quicker healing.

Witch powers, as western Marylanders understood it, could be passed on, but only when the craft was transferred to a person of the opposite gender. A male witch could pass power only to a woman, and a woman only to a man.

In the first half of the twentieth century, a few witches remained. An indignant physician in the Catoctins, writing to the Baltimore Sun in 1909, said he had been called to treat a child scalded in a home accident, a week after the accident. Although he was one of two physicians within two miles of the family, the parents had called on a fire blower to treat the child. The treatment was unsuccessful. His efforts, because he had been called so late, failed to save the child.

Grant Conway, in his notes on local oral history, recorded that Lee Daniels, who lived on Herr's Island at Harpers Ferry in the first quarter of the twentieth century, was a witch. She cut off the tops of the high button shoes women then wore to eliminate the thirteenth button. She never washed. Her face was so black with soot, her unpainted lips appeared bright red by contrast. But nothing is recorded of what she did as a witch.

Henry Magin, a miller of Carroll County, resented being called a witch. Sometime in this same period, he called on a lawyer in Westminster with the request the lawyer act for him in a suit against Alice Carr for defamation of character. "There suddenly appeared nailed high on a number of trees leading to the water mill conducted by Magin, shingles on which were rudely lettered 'Hen Magin is a hex.'" Magin said Carr had put the signs up and that "hex" was German for a witch. He was not a witch, he declared, and defied Carr to prove he was. The lawyer hemmed and hawed, finding a number of reasons he could not enter the suit. Magin left much incensed that he couldn't get legal satisfaction.

One spell or hex from the past is remembered enough to appear occasionally on the puzzle pages as a curiosity. It is:

SATOR
ARETO
TASET
ORETA
ROTAS

This spell offers protection against fire or lightning, but unfortunately we do not have all the instructions.

At a May 1995 meeting, the Senior Citizens Luncheon Group of Wolfsville discussed superstitions and witchcraft. This story was told: In a mill where a number of men were playing cards for stakes higher than usual, a cat appeared late in the evening on the sill outside a partially open window, where it sat and stared balefully at one particular man. Stared and yowled. Nor would it be shooed away. Enraged at the yowls, and the further attempt of the cat to crawl through the window, the man slammed the window down on the cat's front paws. The cat vanished and the game went on. When the man came home he found his wife in bed, moaning with pain from the broken fingers of both hands. She was a witch and had been trying to stop her husband from gambling away their money.

A number of other witchcraft stories were told, but all were about events that happened to their parents or grandparents, or to a neighbor of those generations. It is clear witches no longer live in the hills and valleys of western Maryland.

Only this story came from recent years. Only a few years ago a confused young woman, remembering something about a broom and witches, refused to cross a porch on which a broom was lying until her hostess had removed it. She said she didn't want to be thought a witch!

Witches have left the valleys and mountains of western Maryland, although a movie popular as the millennium turned is supposedly laid on South Mountain. It describes witch powers no Maryland witch has had for 400 years. There is, however, some evidence witches have moved into the cities of Baltimore, Annapolis and Washington as followers of Wicca and the practitioners of the New Age feminism. But that's a story for some one else to write.

XIII

"Most Horrid Murder and Arson"

…read the headline over the first news of the murder of a family of six. The search for the murderer, his trial, and execution attracted so much public interest in 1831 that its memory lingers in western Maryland even today.

Lawyers recall the Newey murder trial as the first in Maryland to convict on circumstantial evidence alone. The public knows it as a ghost story. Some older families in the Sabillasville region have their own version of the murder, based, almost certainly, on long-forgotten arguments, gossip, or prejudice.

The murder of John Newey, his pregnant wife, their two small children, her father, and an apprentice boy, by Newey's nephew, John Markley, was reported by the newspapers of Baltimore, Frederick and Hagerstown. A pamphlet carrying the full trial record was published a short time after the execution,

Together, these accounts open an unusually wide window into the everyday life of western Maryland at that time. I have used the words and spelling of the various writers as I found them, though making small abridgements. The shifts, in the trial records, between first and third person may be confusing but they reflect a time when memory and rapid writing, rather than tape recorders, created official records. My own comments are in italics.

MOST HORRID MURDER AND ARSON*(1)*
Jan. 7 and 14, 1831 papers

One of the most inhuman murders we have ever recorded was committed on the persons of Mr. John Newey and family living near Sabillasville in Harbaugh's Valley in this county. On Thursday morning last (before day)/*December 30, 1830*/the house of Mr. Newey was discovered to be on fire by the neighbors. The fire was got under control before the house was entirely consumed, when six human skeletons were found; one with the skull broken in. They were ascertained to be the remains of Mr. Newey, his wife, and two children, his father-in-law, and an apprentice.

A jury of inquest…returned a verdict of murder by some person or persons unknown. Suspicion rests on a fellow by the name of John Markley, who has recently been liberated from the Penitentiary, and who has…been seen in the county. Some of our fellow citizens will recollect that about five years since a **robbery** was committed on Mr. Newey by this same Markley…convicted on the testimony of Mr. Newey…was sent to the Penitentiary for five years…His term of imprisonment expired sometime in November last. It is supposed that he has in revenge perpetrated the horrid crimes…His accomplice in the robbery, who was with him in the Penitentiary is in the county, and had warned the family of Mr. Newey before the murder of the designs of Markley. He states…he had heard Markley threaten that "when liberated he would kill Mr. Newey and burn him up in the flames of his dwelling." (2)

Mr. Newey was lying upon the floor dead, with his rifle under him, and a large hole in the side of his head; Mr. Tressler and the bound boy were also lying dead in different parts of the lower floor; Mrs. Newey was in her bed, which with the garments she wore, were completely saturated with blood!—The two children were also dead in their bed. The bodies of all were soon consumed by the raging flames with the exception of that of Mrs. Newey, part of which the falling of the wall, and the quantity of blood, prevented from being entirely consumed. Two stabs were discovered in her body; and it is stated, the sculls of all were cleft. Mrs. Newey was far advanced in pregnancy!

…Mr. Newey was known to have had a considerable sum of money in his house (some say 1000 and others between 4 & 500 dollars) which the wretches no doubt secured before they set fire to the house. (3)

ARREST
Jan. 14 and 28, 1831 papers

John Markley…on whom suspicion rested as being concerned in the late murder in Harbaugh's Valley—was last evening/*Jan.13*/apprehended in this city/*Baltimore*/by **Mr. W. Walker** and two or three of our citizens, and after an examination of James Blair, esq., was committed for further examination…He denied having ever been either in a Gaol, or State-prison, but on entering our prison was immediately recognized by one of the keepers of the Penitentiary, who happened to be there, as the same Markley described by the Frederick Citizen. On Friday night he slept in Westminster…and on the following day arrived in Baltimore.

The account he gave of himself since the murder...was contradictory throughout. It is hoped that those citizens of Frederick who can furnish evidence of the case will not fail to attend the examination on Saturday next. Markley is a powerful, broad-shouldered, athletic man, and answers the description heretofore given of him. There was found upon him a $10 Chambersburg note and a quantity of new clothing. (4)

We have conversed with Mr. King, the gentleman who went to Baltimore to attend the examination of Markley, which took place on Saturday last, and his statements would induce a belief that Markley is one of the party which committed the murders. Mr. King has known Markley for a long time, and was one of the witnesses on whose testimony he was sentenced to five years in the Penitentiary—but on being confronted with Mr. K. he pretended that he did not know him or Mr. Newey, and said he had not been in Frederick County for ten years.

Among the clothing of Mr. Newey, there was a pair of pantaloons of a peculiar make, of velvet, that were too short for him, and which had been torn or ripped on one side near the pocket, and sewed up, with **white thread**.—This pair of pantaloons Mr. King had seen Mr. Newey frequently wear, and had often joked with him on their singular appearance: and at one time was about purchasing them. On being asked by the magistrate if he recollected Mr. Newey's clothing, he described correctly the pantaloons above mentioned, and on examining Markley's bundle, a pair of pantaloons of precisely the same materials, etc., were discovered! which Mr. King made oath **were Mr. Newey's property.** In Markley's bundle were other articles of clothing, which Mr. King thinks will be identified by the neighbors, as belonging to Mr. Newey's family. (5)

THE TRIAL

The judge was John Buchanan. Mr. Dixon was the prosecuting attorney. Mr. Ross and Mr. Palmer were counsel for the defense.

Mr. Dixon said he would proceed methodically, first proving the corpus delicti, or murder.

The first witness, George Flaut, being sworn—Shall I state the first discovery of fire?

Mr. Dixon—Yes, the whole matter!

Witness—In the morning I called up my boys early, a few hours before day.—When my wife arose from bed she looked out of the window, and remarked that there was a great smoke over toward Newey's—One of my boys ran down and returned upon one of Newey's horses & told us the house was on fire and he saw no one about it. I went down—the house was all on fire—we had a good view of all the inside of the house and saw Newey lying on the floor with his feet towards the bed and his head towards the door—the hair was burnt off his head and the skull and skin appeared quite white, and on the right side of his head there was a hole—it appeared to have been done with an axe. The skull was broken in—there were small cracks from the main wound like the cracks of an egg shell. I examined it particularly, as I expected I would have to testify on the subject.

The joists above where he lay were yet up!

As the house was yet burning, I sent my son to collect the neighbors. I also blew a horn but it did not bring them together directly. By the time the neighbors came up the head of Newey was entirely burnt to ashes.

I did see Mrs. Newey after the neighbors came up—she lay in the bed downstairs—her head was burnt off—she was otherwise much burnt—old Mr. Tressler was burnt up entirely—the infants were less burnt—the bound boy was entirely consumed.

I saw the linen of Mrs. Newey which had three holes in it as if made with a knife. (Here defense counsel objected the trial was for the murder of Newey, not his wife. "It cannot be shewn that one person was murdered, for the purpose of showing by inference that another was murdered." The prosecutor said the question was to prove a link in the chain of circumstance that proved a murder, not an accident. The judge ruled the question was, "Whether Newey was murdered? Any circumstances may be admitted which will throw light on that question...The question is...admissible...but only for the purpose of shewing that Newey came to his death by undue means.")

—The linen was all bloody—I examined the stabs on the body but particularly one about the abdomen—the rent in the linen was crosswise and seemed to have been cut—We applied the linen to the body and the holes in the linen corresponded with the wound in the body.

Under cross-examination, Flaut said:

I thought that the family was murdered, and I would have to give evidence as a witness. I discovered the fire on Thursday the 30th Dec. There was a report in the neighborhood about Markley. I heard that Mr. Newey was warned to be on his guard—for his house was to be burnt down.

Yes, the roof had burnt and fallen in—the crack in his skull was about an inch...I thought the hole in the skull was caused by an axe—it was not a round hole: it was about two inches one way and longer another. There was much clothing in the room—it was all on fire: there was not much smoke in the room—I saw Newey distinctly. I was within 18 feet. He had no clothes on. There was blood on the floor where he lay. There was no wood near him where I saw him lay...The wound could not have been caused by a stick.

The smoke escaped through the opening above—there was none about the body—When we burn brush, there is smoke enough in the clouds, but none about the flame.

John Flaut was the second witness—Saw the wound in Newey's head and thought the flesh was burnt off of it; saw the hole in the head—It seemed to have been broken in—It was light as it is now—had a distinct view of the floor through the blaze of the fire—saw no blood—the floor was burnt away between me and where Newey lay—the floor above was also considerably burnt...was there 15 minutes before my father. Took one of Newey's horses and went home—the house seemed to be set on fire at top and bottom at the same time...from the manner in which it was burning...floor lay very close to the ground and in different parts of the house, it was burnt into coal.

Jonas Mannahan, Daniel Benchoof, and James Mannahan who had disinterred Mrs. Newey's body for investigation as the only one to survive the fire, testified.

There were three stabs in her body—the linen in which she was killed was put upon her and the cuts in it corresponded with the wounds in the body—she was disinterred 2d day after burial—the body was still in a condition to show the nature of the wounds—one of them was a clear cut through which parts of her entrails issued out—first saw the body in the house—lying on its face—the linen was burnt off that part of the body exposed to the fire—the part cut was under, and so protected from the fire—the wounds were all very deep. The cuts in the linen fitted the wound exactly—they were clear cuts across the threads—strong linen, not torn but cut. To be sure wound corresponded with the cuts, put my finger into two of the wounds—found them clear smooth cuts and very deep.

Markley's conviction for theft in 1825 and the sentence to the penitentiary was proven.

John King testified he heard Markley say in the courthouse after sentence was pronounced he would "have revenge." John Williams was at the jail that day and heard Markley say the judge and state's attorney were no better than Newey and his witnesses or they would not have believed them and (swearing very hard to it), "If I ever get out, I will have satisfaction if I have to kill and burn the whole of them!" Witness said to him, 5 years is a long time and you'll forget it—He said he never would forget it.

The testimony on Markley's movements before and after the crime gives us a picture of how most people traveled that time.

John Black, who lived on the Emmitsburg-Waynesboro turnpike, said Markley, calling himself John Markell, came to his house on December 21,

1830, asking for supper and lodging. Talking by the stove, I said the Penitentiary law was a bad one (not knowing that Markley had been there), he agreed and said that thieves ought to be hung instead of going to the Penitentiary. Markley staid till after breakfast next morning—had no bundle of any kind—after breakfast, he went off without paying his bill or saying anything about it—he told me he had resided in Middletown Valley and was then going to Hagerstown—that he had been in Baltimore with sheep and hogs—15 or 20 minutes after he left my house, I mounted my horse and followed him 2 miles—saw nothing of him. From my house to Newey's is 7½ miles. When pursuing Markley, I met several persons & inquired of them and also at the houses; could hear nothing of him—he must have left the road. Markley wore at that time a yellow flannel or coating "warmuss"—saw in the grand jury room a yellow "warmuss" like that worn by Markley in my house, but it now seems cleaner. *(The dictionary defines "warmuss" as an Indian hunting shirt.)*

Bernard W. Wright (of Smith's Town, Washington County)

—The first Friday after Newey's murder/Dec.31/about sunset, Markley came to my house, 7 miles from Newey's, another man was with him...Markley had a knapsack, roughly sewed up and well filled with clothing—he gave it to me to keep—they took supper, and both seemed very hungry—told me they came from Huntingdon County, Pa.—Newey's murder was then known...After these men went to bed, and myself also, I reflected that they might be the murderers; I became alarmed, got up and set up all night—they arose before day. Markley pulled out his purse, containing perhaps 7 or $8 in silver. I noticed Markley's purse particularly, and **thought it was the very purse that I saw Newey have at the house about two weeks before**. When they left my house they said they were going down the New Cut Road towards Frederick. Spoke of stopping at Jacobs' tavern on that road.

Joshua Kelley of Baltimore—On the 2d of January last (Sunday), Markley arrived at my tavern in Baltimore. I was not at home myself—did not see Markley until next morning about day light, when I went into the bar room and found him there. He asked for his bitters; drank; pulled out 4 or $5 to pay the bill (62½ cents); asked the price of board by the week—said his feet were sore from travelling...offered to pay a week's board in advance ($2.50) and insisted on paying me. I took it. There was large bundle in the bar which he said was his—took it—got out 8 or 9 pieces to send to wash—asked for a scourer saying he had a coat he wanted to get scoured—took out a blue coat which he carried in the direction of the scourer's. On Wednesday he brought it back, and I observed that the skirts had been taken off—It was made into a coatee—that day I asked him his name, for the first time he paused—I asked him the second time, he paused again for some time and finally said, "My name is **John Mockley.**" Same evening he bought from me a ticket to the Circus Lottery—sent it to the drawing by one of the boarders, who put the name on the back of it by Markley's direction, **John Mockley**. On the next Friday morning appeared in the newspaper the account of Newey's murder—Markley with the rest of the boarders spoke of it as horrid—next morning a description of John Markley—I read it in his presence. I did not then suspect him—Sunday evening after tea Markley went out and was arrested—never returned to my house—the bundle remained in my possession—saw in his possession a $10 note of the Chambersburg bank.

John W. Walker, who made the arrest, described it and the places at which Markley claimed to have stayed from December 29 to January. He refused to say where he was the night of the murder, and he also denied he had ever been in the penitentiary. When brought to the jail, a turnkey there, who had been a turnkey in the penitentiary, recognized him. Markley then confessed he had been there, and appealed to him to say he had behaved well. When the bundle left in Kelley's tavern was produced in the magistrate's court, Markley asked for, and got, tobacco out of it.

The examining magistrate in Baltimore, John Blair, testified Markley said he had been in Chambersburg the night of the murder and in Westminster the night after it. At the final examination, when King, a nephew of Newey, appeared, both King and Newey manifested great emotion; Markley's countenance underwent great change. The bundle was produced—

King described a pair of pantaloons belonging to Newey—the bundle was opened and they were produced, corresponding exactly to his description. Markley denied it was Newey's clothing—to several of my questions he was silent.

King examined the whole bundle, swore the pantaloons were Newey's, and identified one or two other articles he **thought** were his.

Judge Shriver and two others testified on the magistrate's examination in Frederick—I asked him to account for himself from the time he was released from the penitentiary up to the time of the murder. He appeared willing to do so. He stated that immediately after his release, he went to Philadelphia where he remained 5 or 6 weeks working at his trade…that he was in the neighborhood of Chambersburg on Monday, previous to the murder, and at Westminster on Friday after that event. But did not account for himself from the Tuesday prior to the murder. I said it was important for him that he should account from the Tuesday prior to the murder, until after that time, and particularly where he was on that night: he pondered—I pressed him—he answered, if I must tell the truth, I was on "a spree" from the Tuesday previous to the murder until the Friday after, and can't tell where I was. I then asked him why it was that many articles of his clothing were too small for him—he could not account for it. But said he had purchased some in Baltimore and some in Pennsylvania.

The testimony of twelve neighbors, relatives and friends of Newey identifying clothing found in Markley's possession show even a prosperous family had a limited supply of clothing and used it a long time. It also extended the trial into a second day.

John King—He knew a pair of Newey's pantaloons made of velvet; they were among the clothing found in Markleys' bundle—On the night of Newey's wedding he was present, but not having pantaloons of his own suitable for such an occasion he mentioned the fact to Newey, and Newey said he had a pair which he, King, might use for the night if he, King, was not too proud—he, King, accepted the offer of Newey. That the pantaloons had a rent in them, which the mother of King, who was also present, sewed it up with **white thread**. That the rent and the sewing on the pantaloons found in Markley's bundle, corresponded with that he knew to be on the pantaloons belonging to Newey—further, he knew the pantaloons because he saw them on Newey about 2 years after his marriage, and at that time recognized the rent and the sewing and stated to Newey that his pantaloons had the same rent and sewing on them that they had on the night of his wedding—which caused some laughter between them.

Sally Mannahan knew one of the handkerchiefs in Markley's possession to be the property of Newey. She had seen it often in the family, that she had it several times at the house to wash, and that she knew it by a **yellow patch**—and that she had seen it at Newey's 5 or 6 weeks previous to the murder.

Mr. Henshaw also knew the handkerchief with a yellow patch, saw it in Newey's hand about 2 weeks before the murder at Neweys. Mrs. Newey wrapt it around a sieve which he was about to take home to protect it from the rain—that he took it home with him and kept it several days and then returned it.

Mr. Mannahan recognized both pantaloons and handkerchief, and last saw the handkerchief at Newey's at last harvest.

Mr. Tresler, Mrs. Newey's brother, stated the boy who was murdered wore a vest corresponding with the one found among Markley's clothing—was positive the velvet pantaloons were like those frequently seen on Newey. The calico found among Markley's clothing corresponded with that he had seen Mrs. Newey wear.

Mr. Nichols knew two vests of Newey's, which he purchased while the witness lived with him about 5 years ago. He recognized the razor, razor strop, and shaving box as like Newey's, as were the pantaloons.

Mr. Oyster stated that he lived with Newey. He knew the razor, the razor strop, and shaving box, and that many articles of clothing in Markley's bundle was the property of Newey. He knew the razor strop and box from their general appearance, but he knew the razor from a mark it had on its handle—it being somewhat scaled. Counsel for the petitioner took the razor, kept it for a few minutes and returned it, asking him if that was Newey's razor. Oyster looked at it for some time and stated that it appeared to be the same; but that he did not see the mark & therefore thought it was not his. The court then told the witness to take the razor to the light. Witness did so and then discovered the scale, and said that it had the mark and was positive it was Newey's. He knew the pantaloons by the rent and white sewing; a handkerchief by the yellow patch, and one of the vests from its color, and one of the buttons being pulled out. Counsel then called his attention to a coat among the clothing, and asked him if it was Newey's...Newey was a stout man. He was asked whether Newey was as large a man as Markley—he replied he was not. Counsel then asked Markley to put the coat on; it appeared to fit him tolerably well but was a little too large.

John Bender then testified the clothing was Newey's.

Hiram Boyd—I sold Mr. Newey a piece of calico like that, about a year ago—I have in my possession a remnant of the same piece (here the remnant was produced which proved to be about an inch under). The selvage is torn off from the piece; this accounts for its being shorter than the remnant—they were both of the same quality...I am a merchant and somewhat a judge of the quality of goods.—Mr. Newey was in the habit of dealing with me. I had in my store sometime ago goods like the jacket.

There is generally a quantity of the same kind of goods imported—the figures are alike, but the quality of the different pieces are different—There were 28 yards in the piece from which this remnant of calico was cut—It appeared to have been a whole piece being finished at both ends.

Sara King, Newey's sister, testified.—These black pantaloons belonged to my brother, Mr Newey.—I mended them for him about six years ago, about the time he was married—I used this white thread because I had no other in the house. I sew with my right hand...

Elizabeth Jordan who lived with the Neweys for several weeks at a time over the last five years—It was nine months before the murder that I was last at Newey's. I was then there for two or three days. I have washed this jacket and these pantaloons at Newey's—they belonged to him—I know also this handkerchief by the patch. It was Newey's. I knew the pantaloons from their general appearance and this piece put in the back of them. It was 2 years since I washed them—I know the jacket from the pattern and the cut and make of it—it is double-breasted.

David Filson—I lived three quarters of a mile from Newey's. I was intimately acquainted with Newey—These pantaloons belonged to him. I owed Newey 15 dollars then for which he called upon me. He said he had been robbed of all his money and clothes, but these pantaloons. They were on Newey in May 1825. I observed them particularly because Newey said they were the best he had…they were not new then. Newey was married in March 1825.

Examination on the part of the state closed.

A juror examined D.W. Wright.—Markley was perfectly sober when he came to our house on Friday in Smithstown about sun down. I am bar-keeper there—it was raining at the time—It is between 6 and 7 miles from Newey's to Smithstown—I think it was Friday, because the next day was **lawday**. I did not write it down—I could not if I had tried.

Jacob Schriner examined by the defense—I saw the prisoner in Westminster on Saturday morning about 6 or 7 o'clock after the burning—I am positive that the prisoner is the man—He said he had been playing husslecap for a watch the evening before, and was then talking about it. I never saw him before or since until now—I breakfasted at the same table with him—there was a small man in company with him.

Mr. Blair, recalled, said the handkerchief around the bundle in Baltimore was different in color from that which Mr. Shriner said was around Markley's bundle in Westminster.

Mr. Wright, recalled, testified the handkerchief around the bundle Markley had at Smithstown was different in color from that described by the former witnesses.

After the closing of the argument, the jury retired, and in about half an hour returned with a verdict of "GUILTY OF MURDER OF THE FIRST DEGREE."

Judge Buchanan pronounced sentence two days later. His speech takes two full pages of the trial pamphlet and includes the fact that John Markley, like John King, was a nephew of the murdered man.

THE EXECUTION*(1)*
June 29 and 30, 1831 papers

A short account from the Frederick paper and a more detailed one from the Hagerstown paper are combined here. The unfavorable comment of both papers on the presence of women at the execution is an interesting comment on women's social position.

…about noon on Thursday, the 23d., crowds of people began to enter the city and by 8 o'clock P.M. the taverns were generally crowded to over-flowing. The morning of Friday presented a continuation of the busy scene, persons on horseback, in gigs, barouches, wagons, carts, &etc., all hasten-ing to the field…Age upon its crutch, youth in its bouyance, infancy in its helplessness, and we are sorry to say females in the attire of ladies, also hurrying to and fro to gaze upon the harrowing spectacle about to be presented—pity in the eyes of women, levity upon the feature of others, and curiosity in the aspect of all. (6)

John Markley was executed at 11 o'clock according to his sentence in a field adjoining "The Barracks" in the suburbs of the city. He was carried from the Jail to the place of execution in a carryall, which also contained the Sheriff of the county, and the Rev. Mr. Shaeffer, who has most zealously acted as his spiritual guide from the time of his conviction. Having arrived at the gallows, the criminal ascended the ladder which led to the platform, with a firm and undaunted step. After a hymn had been sung, the Reverend Mr. Shaeffer feelingly addressed the immense crowd which had assembled on the destructive consequences of crime and the Rev. Mr. Clark of the Methodist Church invoked the pardon of God for the wretched criminal, and the deliverance of mankind from their besetting sins.

The religious services having been concluded, Mr. Shaeffer, in the most earnest and solemn manner, entreated Markley…if he had any knowledge of the murder either directly or indirectly, to divulge the circumstances as the last duty he could render mankind, and for the relief of his own conscience.—But to these entreaties he protested as he has again and again that he did not **murder Newey and his family, and was entirely ignorant by whom the crime was perpetrated**. In a short time thereafter, the criminal was placed on the drop, the fatal noose adjusted, and the cap drawn over his face—and while in this situation he was again solicited to divulge the circumstances of his crimes; but he reiterated his innocence and was then launched into eternity. His struggles were brief—the rising of one leg, and the quick heaving of the chest being the only indication of agony.

It is for…God…to judge of the sincerity…of Markley, but we are grieved to say that his conduct since his conviction has caused but little evidence that he was in a contrite state, or duly sensible for the horrid character of the crime…and, but a few minutes before his execution, he alleged ignorance as to where he was on the night of the murder, or how the clothes of Newey came into his possession. Neither did he satisfactorily explain a single circumstance in that mysterious chain which pointed to him as the undoubted author of the deed.

We are happy to say…the crowd behaved with much decorum and that no accidents occurred—but we must express our indignation that some females so far unsexed themselves as to appear on the ground, and among them mothers with infants at the breast. We hope society will mark their conduct with decided reprobation…for we would as readily expect to find humanity in the bosom of a famished wolf, as to hope for tender and endearing sentiments in those females who crowd to see a fellow creature die.

Markley has left a narrative of his life, partly in his own handwriting, which will be published…

If such a narrative was published, a copy has not survived in western Maryland libraries.

The people of Harbaugh Valley and Sabbillasville were not entirely happy with the sentence, as a ghost story and opinions expressed as late as this century, indicate. Some evidence given at the trial suggest Markley had a companion with him before and after the murders, though nothing in the record suggests it was the same individual. The companion or accomplice was not sought for. That local people thought he should have been sought is indicated by the figure or figures (the number varies with the teller) in old-fashioned clothing which has been seen in the cold dusk of December lurking in the bushes that grew up around the site of the Newey dwelling, figures that fade if the passer-by approaches...Sometimes the story adds that one of the figures is the man who, years after Markley's execution, in far-off Ohio told those around his death bed that he was with Markley that night in December 1830(7).

Members of some of the old families in the region have their own tale, which some told as late as the 1960s. The true murderer was George Flaut, not John Markley. That belief apparently goes back to a long-forgotten grievance, or to religious prejudice. The Flauts were Roman Catholic, in a neighborhood thoroughly German Protestant.

XIV

Jack and the Cat's Paw

"I'm lookin' for work 'n' I kin do most anything," the young fellow with the bundle and dusty shoes told the shopkeeper at Foxtown crossroads.

The storekeeper thought a bit, then nodded. "Maybe there's a job up at Old Man DeLauter's. If you go 'long this road a piece, then take the lane between the church and the school," he gave more directions.

"Thank ee, sir." The young fellow shouldered his bundle and set off. "For sure, I'll say you sent me."

Down the road, up a lane, over the hill, and part way into the next valley, he trudged. Then there was the house, some bigger than the others along the way, with a barn behind. He stopped at the gate. "Hello, the house!" he called in mannerly fashion. He waited a bit, then opened the gate and came through.

The house door opened, and a man came out. "Young fellow, what do you want? I'm Mr. DeLauter." Jack told him. "Come in and we'll talk. What's your name?"

"My name's Jack, an' I can do most anything. The man in the store down at Foxtown said you might need help."

"Well, Jack, that I do. I got a mill on down the hill on the crick. It's the only one in these parts but it ain't running. I got no time to tend it myself what with one thing and another." He didn't say one of the things was the new wife he'd got this spring.

"I've helped Pa at the mill. I reckon I could run yours."

"I better tell you the whole of it before you decide, Jack. I've hired a couple of men already to run it. Each of them worked just one day because next morning they was dead. Looked like they'd been poisoned, but we couldn't tell how."

Jack nodded. "Maybe we better walk down and look things over first." So they did.

110

The house for the miller was a little off from the mill. It was a one-room log house, with the fireplace opposite the door. Everything was fixed so a man could eat and sleep there comfortably. Up under the eaves were four little windows, one on each side; they had no glass in them.

Jack looked things over. "It's right good. I'll run the mill for you."

"Good," said Mr. DeLauter. "I'll get word out the mill's open again. You get half of what you take in—and I'll give you enough victuals to keep you going this week. That right with you?"

"Right fair," Jack said. "I'll start grinding soon as anybody comes!" It wasn't long before work came, and kept coming. Jack was busy until the sun was behind the blue mountain. He had just shut the race off, and was sweeping up when an old man on a tired old nag came up. He had a little bag of grain.

"Looks like maybe I'm too late and you're shutting down for the night. The old horse don't go as fast as it used to. I sure need this grain ground. Would you grind it for me, Jack?"

"Sure, it won't take long—But how did you know my name is Jack?"

"I knowed it as soon as I seen you," was all the old man would say. Jack opened the race, got the wheels and the stones turning, and ground the wheat. He shut the mill down again, and found the old man still waiting.

"Jack, you're the first man who done me right at this mill. I want to thank you with a present." And he took a silver knife out of his pocket and gave it to Jack. Jack thanked him. The old man rode off in the deepening twilight, the old nag going perhaps a little faster than it had come.

Jack went into the house and lit a fire in the fireplace. There was no lamp, but with the fire and a full moon bright outside, he had plenty of light to cut up his meat and get out the skillet.

As he cooked, of a sudden it got pretty dark. He looked up. In each window was a big cat, black against the sky. At the open door was another cat. It came pacing in, tail erect like a ramrod but with a kink at the end pointing forward. The cat was all black in the firelight. The green eyes of all five cats fixed on Jack.

Jack wasn't scared, not even much surprised, at least not enough to stop cooking. Jack kept busy; the cats just sat, tail wrapped around paws, four in the windows, one by the fireplace. The meat popped in the skillet, and was about ready to turn. The cat stood up, put out a paw toward the skillet. "Sop paw," it growled deep in its throat.

Jack reached out and pushed the paw back. "Better not put your paw in the meat or you'll be sorry."

The cat jerked back and stared, green-eyed, at Jack. The other cats never moved, just kept staring.

Once more the black cat reached for the skillet, growling, "S-o-p-p-p p-p-p-a-w-w-w!"

Jack swung hand and knife again. "Told you not to sop your paw in my dish. Try again and I'll cut it off."

The cat drew back; its tail twitched. The other cats stirred. One meowed. Jack went on cooking his meat and making his gravy.

Quick as lightning, the black cat had its paw out and into the skillet. "Sop paw!" it gloated.

Jack was just as quick. The silver knife flashed out and cut that paw right off into the gravy. The old cat jumped for the door. The four cats yowled— And all were gone from there.

Gone even from sight when Jack went to the door. He came back to the fireplace and started to throw the meat into the fire, but stopped. There was a woman's hand, with a ring on it, not a cat's paw, in the gravy. He took the hand and wrapped it in a bit of paper and put it on the shelf. Then he emptied the skillet, washed and scoured it good, and put some more meat on to cook. After he had his dinner, he went to sleep.

Next morning, up the hill, old man DeLauter got up. "Old woman," he said to his wife. (She wasn't that old either.) "Get up and get me breakfast. I got to go down to the mill and take care of burying that young fellow."

She turned over. "I ain't getting up just yet. I don't feel so good. You can get your own breakfast." So DeLauter did. After all, he hadn't been married to her for many months.

He heard the mill running as he got near. Jack was grinding for a customer. DeLauter hollered over the noise, "Good to find you alive. Thought I'd have to bury you."

Jack hollered back, "I'm glad you don't have to do that."

"Shut the mill down when you finish that lot. I got to talk to you," DeLauter hollered. So Jack did, and it was quiet enough to talk. Now, Jack, tell me what happened that you're still here, while the other men were poisoned."

Jack told him about the five cats, maybe all black, but the one by the fireplace black for certain. He also told him about the silver knife gifted him by the old man. "Ya," said DeLauter, "I see it now. Those were witch familiars come to get the house ready for a meeting. They must have poisoned the meat in the skillet the other times."

"That's what I thought," said Jack. "That's why I scoured out the skillet real good, and cooked more meat. But that ain't all. When I looked to clean the skillet, there wasn't any paw. 'Stead there was a woman's hand. You might not believe me, but I can show you." He got the hand off the shelf.

DeLauter unwrapped it and looked it over careful. "I'd never have thought it! Those cats were the witches! It's a good thing you had that silver knife. You can't harm a witch with a knife or a bullet less it be of silver."

"I knowed that," said Jack.

"Let's go back to the house. We got things to settle there," said DeLauter.

When they got to the house, Mrs. DeLauter was still in bed, but four neighbor women were sitting with her visiting. Old woman DeLauter was moaning and crying. DeLauter pushed right through the visitors and said to his wife, "Give me your hand!"

She stuck out her hand. "That's your left hand, old woman, I want to see your right hand."

She wiggled and twisted under the covers and thrust out a hand. It was the left again. This time he grabbed her rough like and pulled out the other arm. There was no hand at the end of it.

"Jack," said DeLauter, "I'd guessed there might be a gang of witches hereabouts, but I never thought my own wife was the chiefest witch. Let's get away from them."

Jack and DeLauter pushed out, with the neighbor women still fussing over the woman in the bed. Jack asked, as they went out the house door, "Are you sure she's the boss witch?"

"Soon as I saw that ring on the hand, I knew it must be her." DeLauter slammed the house door and locked it. "This has got to be taken care of." And he set the house afire.

Not one of the witches escaped. And that was the last of witches in the Foxtown settlement. The story doesn't say how long Jack kept running that mill. Not long, I'd guess, Jack had a wandering foot...

XV

Was it Treason?

Almost fifty farmers and tradesmen of western Maryland were arrested in the last weeks of June 1781 for plotting against the Maryland government. Seven of them were tried for treason in July, and were sentenced to the ancient, and bloody, English punishment of hanging, drawing and quartering. Three of them were executed three weeks later in August. The executions carried out the full gory rite, according to a descendant of one of the victims; a Frederick historian says the criminals were merely hanged. Which is right? What happened to the four other men convicted? to those not tried?

The story is convoluted, beginning several years in the past, reaching crisis in the summer of 1781, and fading to an end fifteen years later, before being forgotten

SETTING THE STAGE

The Amercian Revolution began in New England but western Maryland was quick to send troops north to General Washington. There were probably more Maryland families loyal to England east of the Great Falls of the Potomac than there were west of it, but that is not to say western Maryland was not a divided society. It was.

Its divisions were between English speakers and German speakers, between pacifist and weapon bearer. On both sides of South Mountain, English and German were commonly used, though speakers of one language did not always understand the other. The English speakers belonged to a spectrum of religions, but the German speakers, as a whole, belonged to German Protestant sects, some of which had very strict beliefs: that oaths might be made only to God, that weapons could not be carried. Some families of the Brethren or Dunkard Church did not even own a "table gun" for killing animals for food. When the colonies rebelled and militia companies formed, the young men of these faiths often joined their neighbors in the militia, while their stiff-necked fathers refused the oath of allegiance to Maryland, even while providing supplies or services such as transport to the new state. Although most German settlers supported independence (an historian says there were fewer Loyalists among that ethnic group than others), some refused to provide supplies and paid heavy fines instead, just as the openly Loyalist families of Tidewater Maryland did.

One of the German settlers prominent at that time was Christian Orendorff II (also written as Orndorff). He had immigrated to Lancaster, Pennsylvanaia, with his father; he later, in 1762, bought land on Little Antietam Creek setting up a mill. Mills and roads were so important to each other at that time that a miller often had a secondary career as innkeeper. Christian Orendorff II did not keep an inn, but his reputation for hospitality to travelers was so widely known, an historian writing a hundred years later mentions it. An important businessman, Orendorff II was a member of the Committee of Correspondence in 1774 and of the Committee of Observation that replaced it in 1775 to handle the functions of local government until the organization of Maryland state government.

In these posts, Orendorff was involved with two events that had reverbera-tions in 1781. The first was the plot of Dr. John Connolly. The British offered him 25,000 acres of land in the Ohio country to go out to Detroit, then a British wilderness fort, and recruit an army of Indians and frontiersmen to capture first Pittsburgh and then Cumberland, before proceeding down the Potomac to meet the British Navy in Chesapeake Bay, and thereby cut the rebellious colonies in two. On their westward trip from the Chesapeake, the behavior of Connolly's party roused suspicion in Frederick but they evaded capture. Their arrest was made on the banks of the Conococheague, with assistance of Washington County authorities, which probably included Orendorff II.

Orendorff's second involvement began in December 1775, when a John Parkes (usually written Parks) of Hagerstown purchased a chest of tea. Some chicanery was involved because the Committee of Observation forced him to burn the tea publicly "with his hat off, and a lit torch." Evidently some mem-bers of the public felt this was insufficient punishment because they smashed his windows. In 1776, when rugs and blankets were being collected for the troops, Parkes contributed. Some time thereafter, Parkes removed to Baltimore, where we will meet him again.

Christian Orendorff II had a son, also named Christian Orendorff, and sev-eral daughters, one the beautiful Mary Magdalena, who married Jonathan

Hager, Jr., after a one-day courtship. Christian Orendorff III entered, as Second Lieutenant, the Maryland battalion that marched to Massachusetts to join Washington's Flying Camp. They fought in the Long Island campaign, surrendering at the Battle of Harlem Heights in 1778. Lt. Orendorff spent the next couple of years in a British prison ship lying off New York City. Just when he was exchanged is not clear but he was back in Maryland with the rank of Captain in January 1781. And the events that led directly to the trial for treason began.

PLOTTERS AND PLOTS

Now, meet the three "traitors." Another German settler was Peter Sueman (the family today spell it Suman, and a country road near his former farm is Suemanville Road). He owned a farm north of Burkittsville which he and his eleven children farmed, although a descendant today says he owned three farms. Be that as it may, Sueman also shared work occasionally with a fellow farmer, Peter Arnold. Sueman attended the Broad Run Church of the Brethren which has services even today. One of his sons, Allen Ellsworth, was serving with Francis Marion, the "Swamp Fox" in the Carolinas in 1780–81; his descendant says he joined as a drummer boy.

Yost Plecker (who appears in the records variously as Pleger, Blecker, and Bleachy) was a Mennonite German living in Washington County. He too had a son of the same name. No genealogist has clarified which Plecker, senior or junior, was part of this story.

In Frederick, John Caspar Frietchie (also spelled Fritchie) had three daughters and a son (also named John Caspar Frietchie) born in the town before 1780. Local tradition says Frietchie was a leather worker who repaired harness for the British officers; trial records only say he was a "skin-dresser." Dorothy Quynn, the historian who has studied the records most carefully, found some evidence Frietchie and family were in New York City in 1779, needing financial assistance which was sought from the British occupying the city. He could have been recruited to return to Frederick to organize Loyalists there to aid the British army. (The British Commander-in-Chief, Sir Henry Clinton, in New York had appointed a board of American Loyalists to do just that: supervise other Loyalists in recruiting aid to British forces.) Certainly, Frietchie was in Frederick in the spring of 1781.

There were also seven hundred Hessian prisoners of war in the stone barracks at the edge of Frederick and almost six thousand imprisoned at Fort Frederick up the Potomac. There were also about seven hundred German officers who were prisoners of war but in looser confinement because of their higher social status. The officers' public behavior offended local sensibilities, and the total number of prisoners was large enough to cause fears of a mass escape. (The 1790 Census for Frederick County counted only 7000 men over 16 years, Washington County had just 3500. The number in 1780 would have been somewhat smaller. Some fear was justified.)

In that uneasy spring, Captain Christian Orendorff III joined the Sixth Maryland Militia Company. We know this from the Maryland State Archives, which carry the only surviving record of plotting and trial. The minutes of June 8, 1781, of the Maryland State Council granted him thirty-four gallons of rum and 136 pounds of sugar, presumably for the troops, and "Cloth and Trimmings for a suit of Cloaths and Linen for four shirts" for himself. The cloth may have been a payment for activity preceding and causing another item on the Council's agenda for the day: an order to the lieutenants of Frederick and Washington counties to arrest Henry Newcomer and a Bleachy of Washington County, and a Fritchy, Kelly and Tinckles of Frederick County as "Disaffected and Dangerous Persons whose going at Large may be Detrimental to the State."

Filed with the June 17 Council minutes is an undated, unsigned memorandum headed "Christ. Orendorff. Information abt. the conspiracy in Washington and Frederick county." Several pages long, written without punctuation, it tells what Captain Orendorff and these local men had been up to that spring. Some minor changes (punctuation and initials added) have been made to make the text more quickly understood.

Henry Newcomer who lived "within five or six miles of Hager's town" called Orendorff "out of his father's house and asked what he thought of these times?"

> C.O. The king would over-come this Country.
> H.N We have raised a body of men for the Service of King and we thought proper to make appln. to you to go to N. York for a fleet.
> C.O How many men have they raised?
> H.N. Upwards of 6000.
> C.O Who the commanding officer of the party?
> H.N. One Fritchy of Fred.Town a Dutch man. Don't know his Christian Name. Go to his House and he would shew him.

They went by horseback to Frederick but did not go to Freitchie's house…Newcomer informed him Fritchy would meet him ten Miles from

Town. He met him and then took him aside and said he understood Orendorf was "let in to a Matter that was carrying on now."

C.O.   I understand you are the Commanding Officer.
C.F.said He was, and told Orendorf the Name of the Man in Virginia from whom he received instruction to recruit. (Here Orendorff said he forgot the name.)
C.O.   Why they pitched on him.
C.F.   He had been in N. York so long they thought he was the fittest Person if he would undertake it—though they were not quite ready for a Thing of that sort."

Orendorff asked for names of the group. Freitchie promised to furnish them later, adding: "Some of his officers were so violent for it that he was afraid it would be made public. One Kelly a Lawyer & an Irishman who lives in the mountains about twelve or fourteen miles from Fred. Town."

After parting, Newcomer and Orendorff rode for several miles before Newcomer said: "Orendorff, you look so dead I'm afraid you ruin the matter." Orendorff replied, "Not at all, sir."

Newcomer continued: "Keep it a Secret whatever you do, for we will soon give these Fellows a damn Threshing. As we are not ready, I must send my Boy up to the South Mountain and let them know We are not ready yet. Our Boys are so violent we can scarcely keep them in—He sent an Express last week to Lancaster to hush them a little longer." After slapping Orendorff on the shoulder, he went on, "I am so glad as if I had 10,000 we have got you, Orendorff, for they could not get one so proper for the Expedition as you are—We have consulted one another a great while and were afraid to mention the Matter on your Father's Account as we knew him to be a violent Rebel."

From this distance in time, two things occur to the reader: Orendorff had a remarkable memory for conversation if nothing else. Also, Orendorff seems an unlikely person to recruit for a project which sought recruits to support or fight in the British army. Quynn wrote : "We get the impression Orendorff undoubtedly caught Frietchie and others in mischief of some kind, but it looks as if he may have exaggerated the magnitude of the plot in order to get credit for saving his country from perpetrators of high treason." Or, to do more than his father did in the earlier affairs?

Orendorff's testimony says that, a few days later after that first meeting, "Bleachey, one of the Captains," came to him. In the conversation, Plecker said he had fifty men, and "He had applied to twenty who refused him."

In another section of the Maryland State Archives there is a June 17, 1781, letter from the County Lieutenant of Hagerstown to the State Council in which he says that he had arrested Henry Newcomer and Yost Plecker and:

> A great No. are concerned/with the conspiracy revealed by Orendorff/in this Cty, Many in Virga., some in Fredk.Couty. There is about 30 in Gaol, and expect the Guards every moment that are detach'd for 50 or 60 more. Of those in prison, their/sic/are 5 or 6 that Acknowledge themselves to be Captains, that they have Inlisted and Admin'd the Oath of Allegiance to many persons, one of them to the Amot. of 42.

On the next page, also dated June 17, is the deposition of one Philip Reploge, who said, first of all, that Dr. John Hose had administered an oath to Reploge not to bear arms against the British and to supply the British with provisions and a horse and wagon. Hose told him "John Parks of Baltimore was one of the Head men and Fritchie in Frederick was Colonel." Reploge also reported that a few days later, he was told that, if the Potomac were not so high, "The people from the South Branch would Come down and rescue the prisoners from the Fort and Take them to the English; there was Two or three thousand that had sworn in. That the Head man at the South Branch wears a long Beard but does not remember his name." Reploge also named another fourteen men (all with English names) as sworn in also.

Some people living in the South Branch valley of the Potomac were indeed disaffected though the number was nearer a hundred than a thousand. That spring, a number of men had refused to pay Virginia taxes or to furnish men for the militia. The Hampshire County sheriff sent Colonel Vanmeter and a troop of 30 soldiers. They met 30 armed Tories. Both groups were reluctant to begin a fight. In the parley, Vanmeter urged the Tories to go home and abide by the law. His troop then departed, believing all was settled. Not so, the Tories grew more confident and formed their own company, commanded by Captain John Claypole, with the intention of marching to join the British. When Brigadier-General Daniel Morgan heard of this, he collected 400 militia and marched into the South Branch valley. In the resulting skirmish, Claypole was taken prisoner, one man was killed and another wounded. Two days later, Morgan departed, leaving a pacified valley. The historians of the county, writing a hundred years later, remarked that later many of the so-called Tories joined the American forces.

THE TRIAL

Another June 17 action of the Maryland State Council was to appoint a special court of oyer and terminer to look into the western Maryland conspiracy. They were well-known, capable men, all favorable to the American cause. One was Alexander Countee Hanson, son of John Hanson who was soon (November 1781) to be elected President of the Continental Congress; he was a lawyer of distinction in his own right. Another was Upton Sheredine, equally able and respected; a Frederick resident, he was elected to Congress by Baltimore voters in the 1790s. The third member was Col. James Johnson, commander of the militia in Frederick County; he had commanded the Maryland militia that quelled the 1778 disturbance in Carlisle, Pennsylvania, caused by Tories, deserters, and Indians.

The court moved quickly, with trial of seven men set for July. There being no Maryland laws as yet, the trial followed English laws, and the sentence was the sentence for treason Britain had used since the Middle Ages. The records of that trial have not been found and may not exist; what survives is the court's letter transmitting the verdict to Annapolis. Upton Sheredine and Col. James Johnson wrote, "To be so minute as to give circumstantial detail of all the facts related by the witnesses upon the different trials, would be exceedingly prolix and tedious." Testimony was "so full and so pointed, as to not to leave the smallest doubt of their guilt."

Orendorff's deposition gives reason for trying Caspar Freitchie, and Yost Plecker. The court's transmittal of the verdict says the trial proved all the defendants had administered an oath or affirmation to give allegiance to King George III, to support him, to obey his officers when called on, and to keep trust. Two witnesses, and three corroborating witnesses appeared against Freitchie, one of these being Orendorff. The same number of witnesses and corroborating witnesses (again one being Orendorff) appeared against Plecker. Against Sueman, there were only three witnesses, with Dr. Philip Thomas a supporting witness. Why the other four men were included in this trial is unclear today. They were evidently young men, and were described, after the trial, as having "want of Education and Experience." Henry Shell (who signed his name Schell) had married in April 1780. The other three were Nicholas Andrews, Adam Graves and John George Graves. Against the Graves brothers, three witnesses appeared, and one corroborating witness for each. Andrews and Shell had three witnesses appear against them, but had no corroborating witness. (Incidentally, all witnesses were given unconditional pardons.)

The warrants of execution prepared by the court adds these details: Freitchie administered the oath of allegiance to George III to Henry Nicodemus and Jacob Cost; Sueman to David Dingle. It also names the twelve jurors who sat on the case of each of the seven accused. When one checks the names of jurors against the accused, it appears each juror was responsible for deciding two cases: George Scott was a juror for Sueman and Freitchie; John Bruner for Sueman and Plecker; John Jacob Schley for Plecker and Fritchie, etc. If judges could combine trials and juries today, it might make for crowded jury boxes, but think how trials would be speeded up! Also notice the pace of justice then: the crime discovered in June; the trial in July, punishment in August.

> You cannot, ought not to look for Pardon...You shall be carried to the gaol of Fredericktown, and be hanged therein; you shall be cut down to the earth alive, and your entrails shall be taken out and burnt while you are yet alive. Your heads shall be cut off, your body shall be divided into four parts, and your heads and quarters shall be placed where his excellency the Governor shall appoint. So Lord have mercy upon your poor souls.

Alexander Countee Hanson, the senior justice of the three man special court, read the sentence to seven farmers and businessmen of Frederick and Washington counties on July 25, 1781. Their crime, high treason against the State of Maryland.

In reporting the verdict of guilty, and the passing of the sentence of death by hanging, drawing and quartering, the Frederick correspondent of the Maryland Journal (Baltimore) made this personal comment that no doubt reflected current public opinion:

> Your correspondent cannot help remarking that the Sentiment contained in the Charges and Sentence, bespeak a Maturity of Judgement, a Dignity of Soul, and a Harmony of the Heart, that would do Honor to any Court of Justice in the Universe.

Col. Johnson, writing August 6, believed a "considerable number of gentlemen of Rank and Distinction and known friends to our proud Cause" respected the sentence of execution.

THE EXECUTION

Two weeks later, a Baltimore paper laconically reported:

> On Friday the 17th Instant, Caspar Fritchie, Peter Sueman, and Yost
> Plecker, suffered Death in Frederick Town for High Treason.

Luther Martin, Maryland's Secretary of State, who was then in Frederick,
wrote Governor Lee on August 6:

> I have no doubt your Excellency will think it necessary to hasten the
> Execution...But I would submit it to your Excellency and the Council
> whether it/be/a safeguard to Humanity: and whether...real advantages will
> not be equally obtained by simply hanging them by the Neck until dead as
> in the case of the Torries.

Lee did hasten the execution. Eleven days later, on August 17, Freitchie,
Plecker and Sueman were executed. How—by simple hanging as Martin
urged, or by the full sentence?

The descendant of Peter Sueman (through his son Allen Ellsworth, who
fought in South Carolina) thinks the full gory sentence was carried out. He
wrote me about his evidence:

> Somewhere in my records there is a handed down account of the scream-
> ing sermon preached by a minister just before Suman and Fritchie were tor-
> tured. The mob cheered hysterically when the men were told they could not
> go to Heaven. Others sickened by the sight went to their homes.

The Reverend H. Austin Cooper, in his history of the church to which
Sueman belonged, says of Martin's suggestion:

> There is no record that this was accepted. There is no recording that the
> original court proceeding was not carried out. There are many traditional
> stories to attest to the fact that the original plan was carried out.

But Quynn, writing in 1945, saw documents in Maryland's Hall of Records
directing the sheriff to take the malefactors from prison on or before August
22, 1781, and:

> them safely convey to the Gallows in the County aforesaid the common
> Place of Execution of Malefactors...there...to hang by the Neck of the said

gallows until they are dead, forbearing to execute any other Part of the said sentence.

That this is what occurred is supported by Dr. Cooper's story that Mrs. Eleanor Sueman asked her neighbor, Peter Arnold, to beg her husband's body from the sheriff and to bring it by night to be buried in the Ausherman cemetery. A fieldstone was used to hide the identity of the one buried "lest his body be exhumed and the bones scattered to the dogs, as the threat came to Mrs. Sueman." Freitchie and Plecker were buried similarly in other cemeteries, Cooper says.

AFTERWARDS

The three widows, Susannah Fritchie, Elizabeth Plecker, and Eleanor Sueman, petitioned for their husbands' estates, but the state confiscated them. Dr. Cooper tells us that, in 1796, the properties were returned to the rightful owners. The Sueman farm, he said, had been badly used by the interim owners, but Eleanor Sueman was so good a businesswoman that, on her death in 1818, she left a sizable inheritance to be administered by her son, Allan Ellsworth.

If, even before the August 17 execution, officials felt the sentences were probably excessive, what about the four men still under sentence of death, and the several dozen others not yet tried?

As early as August 6, Col. Johnson was noting that Andrews and Shell showed signs of repentance. Even earlier, on July 30, he wrote of the several dozen men not yet tried. "Some of the men who are convicted of swearing allegiance to the king...are now desirous serving three years in the Maryland Line." He asked they be pardoned to give such naval service. Attached to his letter is a long list of names. One presumes they are those enrolled for such service because the same collection of manuscripts also contains an undated petition from Washington County residents asking clemency for the plotters because of "possibility of reform...may become serviceable members of the Community...We are of the opinion that they cannot return to their homes with Safety to themselves and Satisfaction to their well-effective Neighbors." Pardon them, but send them somewhere else!

Public opinion changed even more after the executions. On September 3, John Andrew Krug, minister to the Lutheran Congregation at Frederick, petitioned Governor Lee for clemency for the four men remaining under death sentence, as having been led astray by "ill-designing people" and their own "want of Education and Experience."

Nicholas Andrews, Adam Graves, and John George Graves signed acceptance of Governor Lee's pardon on September 10 and agreed to serve in the Maryland Navy.

Alexander Contee Hanson wrote Lee September 15 about the pardon. "Hardly a man in this County is Dissatisfied that their lives are spared" but there was dissatisfaction Shell was still under sentence. "There is really Nothing more than a vague report to warrant the Distinction between him and the other." That damaging testimony hinged on something done or said in Carolina, and it might not have been Shell after all. Shell had not been out of the state "above 2 or 3 weeks" at any time after his marriage April 1780. Shell signed his acceptance of Lee's pardon September 20 and agreed to Navy service.

A Lt. Smith received orders on September 22 to take the four men to Baltimore to deliver them to an appointed person. That is the last we know of Andrews and the two Graves.

Henry Shell reappears December 1781 in, of all places, Frederick. He is prosecuting witness in the court martial of an Ensign Karr of the Select Militia of Frederick, who was accused of having struck, while drunk, Private Henry Shell of that company with the hilt of his sword.

Henry Newcomer, Orendorff's first contact, was sentenced to a year's imprisonment and a fine of a thousand pounds on July 6, 1781. The fine was reduced to fifty pounds in January 1783 because he had completed his sentence and his wife and eleven children were in a state of beggary. Dr. John Hose, with wife and seven children, petitioned the court in October 1781 to be permitted to remove to Baltimore where he might be able to work to support them.

The only one of the accused men who denied the charges of them was the John Parkes whom we first met with "hat off and lit torch" burning a chest of tea in Hagerstown. Filed next to Orendorff's account of the conspiracy in the State Archives is Parkes' memorial to the Governor. He is a "Peacable and unmolested citizen," he goes on to say, indignantly:

> Since the late insurrection in Hagers Town, some Persons, divested and acting repugnant, to every Principle, that might actuate the Honest Man, have maliciously, and from designing motive of Falicy been induced to Propagate a report, intimating that your Memorialist, was interested, and accessory, to the Design, and Intentions of those Insurgents, which your Memorialist, conscious of the Line he always pursued, of Amity to America, totally disavows and deeming it repugnant, and odious to this Feelings, as a citizen, and a Friend to this Country.

He says that nothing subversive was found in his papers when he was arrested; nevertheless, he was remanded to prison in Baltimore and there he remained without trial. (A suggestion he be brought to Frederick for trial was ignored by the Special Court.) George Scott, a friend or business associate, wrote Parkes in the summer that the Frederick prisoners did not claim him to be associated with them. "Some person in Washington County had confessed something relating to it—but could not say what it was." (Did some one, perhaps Philip Reploge, carry a grudge against Parkes?) After three Baltimore men had each written the Governor about clemency, Parkes was released under bond August 18.

These Loyalists of western Maryland were ordinary men who were out of step with their neighbors. Whatever "insurrection" they planned or attempted to carry out will remain forever unknown. What the records remaining say they did, does not seem wicked enough today to justify the sentence given.

Tacitly, Maryland recognized that, fifteen years later when the confiscated properties were returned. Governor Lee's commutation of the gory two-thirds of the sentence allowed the whole event to fade into the background of history, though not quite out of legend.

XVI

A Contract with the Devil

Thomas Solvan contracted with the devil in 1771. In 1789, he regretted it.

How the contract was broken by five Protestant ministers was told by one of them, Johann Georg Schroeder, who claimed he had a Doctorate in Divinity but never named his school. He wrote in German; his account was translated into English by Pastor Larry M. Neff, Secretary of the Pennsylvania German Society. Here, his story is put in chronological order, somewhat abridged. Many speeches that Schroeder wrote indirectly have been put into first person, and are so indicated by an apostrophe, rather than the usual quotation mark, which is reserved for direct quotations from Schroeder's and Neff's text.

St. Peter's Church, near Leitersburg, Md., was central to the event. It was then, and is still occasionally, known as Beard's Church, because the first log church building was on the banks of the Antietam on land donated by Major Thomas Beard. The Evangelical Lutheran congregation was in existence by 1749 and, in forty years, had grown so a new building was needed, and was built in 1787 at its present location a couple of miles away from the first log building. (The 1787 structure was replaced in the mid-nineteenth century.) The program for a recent church anniversary listed the ministers who had served the congregation, reporting that from 1785–1787 the Reverend Daniel Schroeder was minister, followed by the Reverend J.H. Hale who served from 1789–1796.

In his account of struggle with the devil, Schroeder spoke of "my church elders and the deacon who was closest to me," which implies he was minister of St. Peter's Church, in whose parish he lived in 1789. Did the program get his name wrong? Did he serve as interim pastor between Daniel Schroeder and Mr. Hale? The Evangelical Lutheran Synod of Pennsylvania and adjacent states did not recognize him as a Lutheran pastor. The Synod's 1787 minutes show that Johann Georg Schroeder and Johann Georg Hehl (both from Germany) had presented themselves, claiming they had been ordained by the same man, and asking admission to the synod. Schroeder was entirely rejected because of "his impudence," Neff noted, but Hehl was permitted to baptize and preach until the next synod meeting (1788?). At that meeting, Hehl, too, was rejected because his essay on Mark 1:15 was "too poor for a common country schoolteacher." This story by Schroeder shows that both men continued to preach in Maryland, despite rejection by their church's governing body.

Many little points in Schroeder's tale of besting the devil are improbable to us entering the twenty-first century, but the eighteenth century was a very different world.

The man who signed the contract with the devil, Thomas Solvan, was one of nineteen children born to Thomas Solvan, a Roman Catholic, and his wife, Catherine Burck, who belonged to the High Church of England. There was "always conflict over religion and disunity" between the parents. The father "was a very bad man, given to all devilish evil work, and sunk very much in debt" before he abandoned home and family and "no one knows to this hour what became of him." An older brother, John, "also stood in an evil alliance" and disappeared from family knowledge in 1786. Our Thomas Solvan was not baptized as a child nor did he go to school. He was apprenticed twice, his first master dying when he was 11; his mother then apprenticed him to a Mennonite in Lancaster County, Pennsylvania, until he was 21. This master sent him to school for four months to learn to read and write in German. He also presented Thomas to his Mennonite congregation, where at age 18 he received baptism on Easter Sunday 1771.

In July of that year, a stepsister was having a wedding and Thomas wanted a part in it so asked money from his master. It was refused. Nor was he allowed to attend. "Solvan was a great lover of all types of sinful goings on with cursing, swearing, playing, dancing, and other evil works of the devil" and he was "much angered over his master who had constrained him already so often from celebrating, and said he wanted money to celebrate, "if he had to get it from the devil."

That night cattle broke into the yard, and Solvan got out of bed at 11 o'clock to chase the cattle. He was still angry, still swearing, and calling to the devil to bring money to him, if the devil had any.

Suddenly the devil came in the form of a man, saying, "If you give me your baptized and family name, I will give you money."

"I have no ink, pen or paper."

"I will find some for you. You must give me your name written in your own blood."

Thomas took his small penknife and opened an artery on his right thumb, took of his own blood, and signed with it his baptized and surname and gave it to the devil." He was given a little money, which he did not recognize and threw it on the ground. Seeing it gleamed there, he picked it up and found it was a silver thaler.

Solvan realized the man might be the devil when he asked, "Would you like to go with me? When shall I come for you?" Solvan answered with totally cross words, "You need not come for me for eighteen years." The devil nodded with satisfaction and they parted.

Solvan soon discovered that "in no way could he use this thaler for something good, for as soon as he bought anything, and wanted to pay for it, he didn't have the thaler." He could use it "for only evil works of the devil, as drinking, gambling, dancing, and that sort of thing, and when he had spent it, it always came back to him, and he could not get rid of it."

For the next few years, he lived "such a godless evil life" that "his poor old mother...sent to him and urged him with a totally upset heart, pleaded, exhorted, reprimanded him with tears."

"If you continue such a godless, evil life, and do not improve, then you are a child of the devil, and cursed by the Lord."

"If I be cursed, so are you" and he "refuted all his old mother's talk, and went on in his evil, devilish life." He made a special point of scorning preachers and the holy sacraments, and poked fun at preachers and their sermons.

This continued until 1789, when he went to work as a linen weaver in Franklin County, Pennsylvania, with one Peter Breimbrecht.

On June 25th in the evening at approximately 6 he went out of the house into the grain fields under an apple tree all alone to lie down in the shade. There came the devil to him again, all dressed in green. The man asked,

"Do you know me?"

"No."

"But I know you."

"It's no concern of mine, whether you know me or not."

"Take this," and the devil handed Solvan a playing card.

As "he took the card...he saw his/the devil's/feet and noticed that he had a cloved foot; then he thought it was the devil; at last he looked at his hands and noticed his own bloody handwriting in the devil's hands." The devil said, "I own you."

"Go, by Beelzebub, Belial and Satan, go! I have nothing to do with you."

"Time is up for you in eighteen days, July 8. The time you asked is past then. I will come for you."

"Whereupon Solvan...went into the house again, but said nothing to any one about what he had encountered. Rather laid his cards, which he had received from the devil at the window and by the time he had turned around again, they were gone."

For a while, he did his work quietly, but on the third day, "his conscience awakened, and he looked for help and deliverance." He first went to a minister in Hagerstown "but had no strength to lament his oppressed condition and went away again with the matter unresolved." He came to Jacob Metz's wife who "was frightened by his dreadful recital, and took him and directed him to the Rev. Joh. Georg Schroeder, Evangelical Lutheran preacher at St. Peter's Church in Washington County, Maryland" and explained "his whole condition" to Schroeder. Schroeder wrote that Mrs. Metz was in tears, and that Solvan "started to weep deeply, so that the tears flowed down on his cheeks" and he could scarcely talk. He hung his head, refusing to look at Schroeder most of the time. He said "his time would be past" on July 8 "and he was afraid the devil would then come to get him, and perhaps even earlier; with which he had no peace, and the devil laid so many claims on him, that he should have taken his life." He pleaded for prayers so that he might be saved.

Schroeder assured him, "You may be delivered if you have heartfelt desire of it, but it is a task I cannot perform alone. I need more preachers, and such a thing must take place publicly in church, so that Christian hearts may call upon the Lord and thereby deprive the devil of his gain."

Solvan sobbed, "No, everyone will look at me, wherever I walk and stand. I must have their mockery as long as I live."

"No, you will not be put to shame, rather the devil; you will be spared and God will thereby be praised and lauded. You will escape his clutches. Only believe in Christ."

"Cannot this take place in the home of Joachim Luther?"

"No, it must be in a consecrated church. You must confess your sin before the entire congregation, to the spite of the devil, and the honor of God." Here Schroeder reported: "I had a sharp battle with the devil, until I got Thomas Solvan to the point where he gave his will to me."

Assuring Solvan he should believe the word of God before the devil's, he suggested they meet next day with more witnesses present.

Jacob Metz, his wife, and Solvan came next day. Schroeder had asked the attendance of the church elder, Andreas Stephen, who "was very much afraid to go into the house, since he led a Christian life with his household"; he had to be reassured he would see nothing of evil. Nikolaus Barth came as did "one that did not please me, and I could not tell him to go away." So did

Schroeder's wife, bringing with her Mrs. Oswald and her two children, and Mr. B.B.'s maid. Hymns were sung. "The poor sinner could not sing but rather sighed and wept." After a prayer, Solvan was asked three times to tell his story and speak the truth, but he said no more than the day before.

Schroeder "presented the whole thing to him and started to make a fantasy or dream out of the whole thing." In response, Solvan cried, "As true as God is God! That is the way it is!" He asked for prayer and deliverance. After reading aloud Psalm 42, Schroeder asked seven questions of Solvan's religious beliefs. The answers satisfying the preacher, he consecrated Solvan and forbade the devil in the name of the Father, Son and Holy Ghost to do him harm. He did this three times. Solvan was adjured to remain in prayer and entreaty with good Christians until the appointed day.

He returned to Jacob Metz's home where he took a book of sermons from the shelf and read it "with so many tears, that the pages became so wet that they had to be dried in the sun." Schroeder added, "thereafter, he went...in company with good friends and acquaintances, but always with a heavy heart, until the other day (so he says) God appeared in his heart with a bright light, whereby he found a soothing of his anxiety."

The following Tuesday afternoon, July 7, the Reverend J.G. Hehl came to Schroeder "completely distraught...for the people had come to him with all kinds of untruth" about what was going on involving Solvan and the devil. To reassure Hehl they met with Solvan at Nikolaus Barth's house where "Mr. Hehl spoke so comfortingly and powerfully to him that he at last became tired and in order to regain strength stopped for a while." The small assembly sang hymns and said prayers until night, when the group broke up. Schroeder and Hehl had a "long discourse in my room" that night about what they would do next day, when the devil was to call for Solvan.

People were gathering at Nikolaus Barth's house and at the church by 7:30 next morning (July 8). When the two preachers and the "poor sinner" went to church at 9, they had to wait for the deacon to bring the key and unlock the building. Schroeder took the opportunity to address the crowd:

> Many people have come here to see the devil. You will not see him. If you came with that intention, you should not go into the church. If you wish to go away damaged, you should not blame me. If, however, you are here to call on the Lord with prayer and supplications, that he receive the poor sinner and deliver him from the devil's hold, so they would. All the angels in heaven rejoice over one sinner who repents.

He spoke more, but he, too, had tears running down his cheeks, as did his audience. Mr. Hehl and a Mennonite minister Schroeder did not know also prayed there, at the church door.

When they entered the church, Solvan was placed in the parson's chair, which is at the front of the church but to one side. There he could be seen by all. After Schroeder and Hehl gave each other absolution and communion, Schroeder made an introductory address to the assembly, in which he pointed out the poor sinner, hoped for his delivery:

> through the tearing up of the handwriting which the devil had against him. Hereto came three more preachers, a reformed named/Ulrich/Heuninger and two English Baptists/Absolom and Peter Bambridge/. Today we looked at no one on the basis of his religion, rather let the poor sinner take part in all Christian prayers and supplication, so that the devil, who has shattered Christians into many sects and factions, also here find no power and might in us.

After a hymn, Schroeder began the morning sermon, using the text 1 John 3:8, "He that commits sin is of the devil, for the devil sinned from the beginning." During the sermon, whose main points he gives, he said Solvan began to be "full of fear and trembling, and cried loudly, shook and trembled, and the anxiety sweat was on him so strongly he could not stay in the Church, but had to be led out-of-doors." This did not interrupt Schroeder's sermon. About noon, Schroeder, Hehl and Solvan "took a little food for the strengthening of our bodies" at Nikolaus Barth's before returning to church.

This time, Hehl preached from Luke 14:2, "This man received sinners and eats with them." During the sermon, Solvan and a Reformed Lutheran preacher began to talk together, so loudly that the congregation listened to them, rather than to Hehl. Schroeder nudged the preacher. "The devil is attempting by this to take power from the preacher." They stopped speaking. Schroeder was also disturbed because more people wanting to see the devil were gathering outside, and they were taking "bread, spice cakes, and also strong drink" right in front of the church door.

When Hehl concluded his sermon, the audience was promised a sermon in English in half an hour, after the five ministers had examined Solvan about his life and also how he made pact with the devil. However, the crowd kept growing so that Absolom Bambridge was sent to preach "so that the English people also, who were there, could have some edification." The examination given Solvan was recorded in both German and English, was signed by "Thomas

Solvan, a poor sinner," and attested to by the five preachers. It has been summarized above.

When preachers and Solvan returned to the church, the confession was read aloud in both languages. Solvan was brought from the pastor's chair to stand in front of the altar and there he admitted his sins and the pact with the devil. He pleaded with the people to keep themselves from such frightful sins. "There was hardly a person that heard it that could keep himself from weeping: indeed, even the small children wept."

"A powerful prayer" followed. Next, thirteen questions to be answered "yes" or "no" were put to Solvan. Following this, he was given absolution and communion. Peter Bambridge then preached an English sermon. Schroeder commented that, during this sermon, "I had never seen him/Solvan/so free with his head held up. O! how he looked the preacher in the eyes, desiring as a hungry man the Word of God."

The sermon ended, the five preachers took Solvan to Johann Barth's house, where dinner was to be served them, the crowd following them into the house. Several efforts were made to clear the room, with limited success. Schroeder wrote, "I must say that I have not seen the likes in my life of what power the devil has even among well-intentioned people, and here I saw how the devil can disguise himself in the form of an angel of light; the woman pushed into the room with might and prepared the table, and so room was made." Solvan, he said, ate little more than chicken soup with rice for "the inward fear and fright was gone, but the outward fear of the people was great."

The plan for the evening was that Hehl was to preach again in German, with Schroeder following, but it was changed. "The unrest of the people became so great" and "Various messages came to me, that we should beware: there was a mob before the door, they wanted to kill either the preachers or the poor sinner."

Hehl went alone to preach, while Schroeder remained behind to explain the situation to Solvan. Schroeder considered climbing out the bedroom window but decided it wouldn't do. For one thing, the window was shut tightly; for another, uproar and suspicion would follow if they were seen. Eventually, they simply walked out the door and went to the spring to freshen up...There they climbed over the fence and crossed the meadow to Schroeder's house. It was then after 9 p.m.

Leaving Solvan with his wife and a couple of friends of his wife, Schroeder returned to the church to pick up his hymnal and Bible, and tell Hehl what he was doing. He found the church so full no one could go in or out the door. The Bambridge brothers were outside, unable to enter. "I will bring you in," and he led them to the side of the building, where he asked the people by the window nearest the parson's chair to move away. He stepped in, helped the English preachers in, got his things from the altar, while making a sign to Hehl all was well and that he was going back to the poor sinner.

He had not been long at home before three people came to the door, wanting to talk to Solvan. They were told, "No one speaks to him except I and the other preachers."

"Where is he?"

"He is well preserved from his enemy. The devil will have no power over him."

They left, and his wife's friends went to church, with instructions to give Schroeder notice of any incipient riot. This left Solvan sitting behind the stove, alone with Schroeder, his wife, and two small children.

> Every moment I looked at my clock to see whether it was 11 o'clock. Because this was the hour at which I expected the greatest tribulation...The outward fear of wicked men was so great that I was sufficiently occupied giving comfort.
>
> As soon as it was 11 o'clock, a large crowd approached my house. I would not have known how many if I had not found out afterwards, that it was 19 or 20 men, who had agreed amongst themselves to kill me or the poor sinner and they all had clubs and big rods in their hands. I stood behind the door with a stick in my hand, and my wife at the window. Then they came and I heard them say, in English: This is the house. They knocked at the door and asked who the proprietor was, but they received no answer. They asked a second time and also a third, but no one gave them an answer. Then they became restless and said if no one would open the door they would break it down: whereupon my wife made a sound next to the window, so they all fled from the door to the window.

"What do you want?" she asked.

"Where's your husband?"

"I believe that he is in church, for I have not seen him since sunset."

"Where's Solvan?"

"I don't know, but I can say he is at a good place."

"Aren't you afraid the devil will come get your husband or Solvan tonight?"

"I'm not at all afraid of the devil getting my husband or Mr. Solvan. You should beware that the devil does not get you. If you carry on so and do not repent as that poor sinner has, I am concerned the devil will get all of you."

One of them grabbed for her hair, but she pulled her head back, grabbed a rod, and said, "If you don't all soon go, and let me and the children rest, I will beat in all of your heads."

They ran away, with Schroeder's wife crying after them, "I'll get a writ next day for each of you."

Mrs. Schroeder's voice was not strong enough protection for Solvan: he went first to the kitchen and then to the steps to the attic. The din surrounding the house could still be heard there. Schroeder then took him up into the attic and gave him a sack of wool on which to rest, before going back to the kitchen. The uproar continued. Solvan began to make a hole in the gable, which Mrs. Schroeder heard and reported, "The poor sinner wants to break through the roof." Schroeder found Solvan trying to crawl through the hole he had made, grabbed him, and would not allow him to consider going into the woods to hide. "You are not to get out of my sight until tomorrow morning. Lie down again. It is already 11:30 and when it gets to be 12, everything will be past, for this is the hour when the wicked one will try his power." Solvan lay down. "As soon as 12 o'clock was past, everything was quiet."

Schroeder's story now abandons Solvan, three preachers, and all the pious or impious people present that day and evening. We may believe Solvan no longer feared being carried off by the devil but we will never know his final fate. Schroeder does tell us Hehl "experienced great tribulation inwardly and outwardly. He is still a young preacher, and has not yet experienced such things, but has read and heard much about such occurrences." Schroeder felt that, after this experience, Hehl had learned much that would benefit his congregations. He also wished more Lutheran preachers could have shared their experience of the "power of the pure Lutheran teaching." Neff noted that Schroeder and Hehl were, as late as 1795, still seeking admission to the synod.

Schroeder's account of victory over the devil may not have influenced synod ministers in his favor, but it demonstrates to readers two hundred years later what the depth of religious feeling was then, and how strong the presence of the devil.

Rituals were important. Three adjurations using either the three Holy Names or names of three devils were required. The magical numbers, seven and thirteen, were also used.

The size of the population is hard to realize. A large crowd was 19 or 20 people!

Note, too, the relative importance of men and women in the eyes of Schroeder and, possibly, the church. Every man who appears in the story is given his full Christian names and surname, but the women are only "Jacob

Metz's wife," "my wife," "Mr. Oswald's wife," "Mr. B.B.'s maid" and "the woman" who pushed through the crowd to set a table. Observe how the preacher allows his wife, as daughter of sinful Eve, to tell the lies that rout the mob.

Did the mob really intend to kill Schroeder and Solvan? Perhaps Schroeder was a coward?

We will never know.

Why did Solvan believe he had a pact with the devil? We will never know. Solvan and Schroeder believed in a real devil, a real pact; perhaps we should believe as well.

XVII

Blackberry Theft

One of the pioneer histories tells this story:

There's no full blood Indians in these parts nowadays. The last may have been the Susquehannocks that lived on one of the Pipe Creeks. They were there when my folks came down from Lancaster town before I was born. They were around for a few years more and went away so quietly it seemed they vanished overnight. Indian blood—yes. Take the farm we just passed, the Lohman place. Until a couple years ago, half breed George Lohman owned it. His mother lives there still, she must be near ninety. No, she's not a squaw; she's white.

Yes, there's a story to tell. It began near Lancaster town when a family from the Palatinate came over. Where they settled, English speakers surrounded them, so they called themselves "Carpenter," the English for their German name. After a few years, the cheap land being offered on the Monocacy (only ten shillings rent a year) made them move down. They bought the Cochran's one room cabin on Flat Run. By then, they had several boys and one girl, Mary, maybe 8 or 10.

Those were the years of the Indian and French troubles up north and out on the Ohio. Most of the folk who had gone out as far as Shawnee Old Town or Will's Fort came back over the mountains. So did some from the Conococheague, Opequon and Antietam areas. People here didn't worry.

During harvest, Herr Zimmerman—they'd gone back to their familiar name, with all the Germans and Dutch and Swiss about—Zimmerman and his boys helped the neighbors harvest. The day I talk of Frau Zimmerman had butter to make and was busy at the churn most of the day. She sent Mary out to pick the ripening blackberries to put by for winter. The butter came, and the made up crocks went into the spring. Other tasks, and a fretful baby, kept Frau Zimmerman busy.

It was late in the afternoon; she thought Mary ought to be back, and went out to call her. No answer. After calling several times without a reply, she walked as far from the house as she dared leaving the baby alone. She didn't see Mary. When the men of the house came in near sunset, they made a wider search. One of the boys found the half-filled pail of berries under a tree. No Mary.

With the fall of darkness, search had to be suspended, and the neighbors called to help look next morning.

It was mid-morning when some one asked the lackwit if he had seen Mary the day before. "Ja, she went with the Indian." He waved generally north.

Careful questioning revealed a small party of Indians had traveled past him in the morning. Later he had seen Mary walking with them, chattering happily. No, he had not thought anything was wrong.

Pursuit proved valueless. So did inquiry of friendly Indians or of traders. No one saw Mary Zimmerman. She was gone for good.

Years passed. There were frontier troubles again with the Six Nations after the Wyoming massacre. Somewhere up in Pennsylvania or New York, some militia skirmished with a small band of warriors and killed most of them. In a blackberry patch, the militia caught up with the squaws and children the braves had been protecting, and took them prisoner.

One of the squaws—she had a small baby on a papoose board—had light brown hair and blue eyes, but spoke only Indian. All the prisoners were brought, or exchanged, to Shamokin where there were interpreters. The blue-eyed squaw said her name was "Mary" but did not understand or speak English. As the days passed, she seemed to understand a little of what she heard. Finally a German-speaking militia man spoke to her in German, and she replied, "I am Mary—Mary Carpenter or Mary Zimmerman, I think."

She remembered picking berries and meeting friendly Indians. One of them said she looked like his daughter. Would she like to come with him and visit? She went. His daughter had died recently, and she was adopted in her place. She lived there happily, married a young warrior, and had a baby son.

Mary was returned to her family in Maryland, taking the baby with her. In a year or two, she married George Lohman and built that farm I mentioned a while ago. He adopted Mary's boy, gave him his own name, and raised him as his eldest, though he and Mary had two sons and some daughters of their own.

When the senior George Lohman died in 1800, Mary had dower rights in the farm, and she lives there still, as I said. He left a quarter of his property, mostly the farm, to the half-breed George, who farmed it. When he died— only a few years ago, in 1818, I think—he was still a bachelor, and the farm then went to his half-brothers and sisters. He's buried in the family cemetery beside his father. Mary Lohman says she'll be buried there as well.

XVIII

Rosaline and the Indian

So you go to Belinda Springs? Come sit here with me; it will be a while before the men finish fixing the harness. Then they'll talk horses a while, before you go.

It's not like the Big Spring up the valley, is Belinda Spring. Big Spring is sweet and cold, and always flows, winter, summer, drouth. The old Indian roads and our white men's all go there for the water, from over Shenandoah Mountain and up from the Potowmeck.

Belinda Spring? It's the other spring everybody knows in the Antie Eatam valley, but it's not like the Big Spring. Its water is strong and warm, though not as hot as the Warm Spring a couple days' journey down the Great Valley. It's a healing spring. The Indians knew about it and nobody was an enemy there. We whites—traders or settlers—didn't know about it at first. Not till Rosaline went there. By rights, it should be Rosaline's Spring. She got well there.

Ja, there's a story to tell. My grossfader heard it after he brought his family to the Antie Eatam valley. It had happened not too many years before. It's been told so many times that maybe some of the details have been prettied up. But it's a true tale.

> The Frenchman Orlando and his wife Laurette were among the first to settle here. That was on Red Hill. They just had two children still living, young Thomas and the older Rosaline. Her hair, yellow it was, was still down her back though maybe it should have been put up; she looked old enough to be married. Orlando—nobody remembers was that his Christian name or his last—was more a hunter and trapper than farmer, but most men were back then. It was the women and childer who put in the garden and any crops, and tended what animals they brought with them. And the women and girls did the spinning and weaving as well. There was no time to sit and talk as we're doing, leastwise for the women.

They put up a log cabin just like the old ones you still see hereabouts—one room, a door, maybe a hole in the roof to let the smoke out. It was on Red Hill, at the north end of the Elk Mountain. Wasn't anybody else near?

That was the year of the big battle between the Delaware and the Catawba Indians: some say it was 1728, others a year or two later. They say two big parties of young braves met near the mouth of the Auntie Eatam and got to fighting. It wasn't the way the English fight with everybody in line and shooting all to once when some one yells "Fire!" They fought the woods way—slipping into the enemy's camp in the dark hours before dawn with tomahawk and scalping knife, hiding in ambush in a thicket or behind a log and rising to shoot the last enemy in line on the trail, and then stealing away to another ambush. One or two Indians stalked another one or two and maybe were stalked in turn…Surprise and skill with gun or tomahawk makes for small, scattered battles. They went on all over the valley for days. It was a dangerous time for others to be about.

Orlando took his family up to the Blue Mountain where the trees are big and the slopes rocky and steep. Somewhere, they found a sort of cave under a ledge and stayed there for three or four days. It wasn't safe to have a fire unless it was foggy or raining, so mostly they hid cold. The women and boy weren't so used to being out in the woods all the time and they took ill.

When the sound of guns hadn't been heard for a couple of days, they went back to their cabin. It hadn't been harmed. Some food was gone from the rafters and an animal or two was gone but they had enough to do with. The family went to their work, and Orlando went scouting to see what had happened.

All but one of the Delawares had been killed; that one had escaped and fled toward his home in the north. Several Catawba Indians had survived, and all had taken a scalp or two—all but one. That one was tracking the fleeing Delaware north.

Agues and fevers were the lot of the three at the cabin. The boy Thomas was weakest. His mother nursed him and Rosaline day and night, though she herself was ill. The boy died, maybe even before Orlando returned from his scouting. Laurette tried to keep going, the way mothers do, but she, too, died pretty soon. Rosaline got over the ague but she still had a cough and was weak.

When she didn't get stronger, she went to the medicinal spring. How she knew about it, the story don't say; only that she was the first white person to go for healing. Maybe Orlando found it. Maybe an Indian told him about it. They were always friendly to us whites and had much to say about the paths and the land around.

Rosaline stayed at the spring a while. She probably used one of those hunting shelters the Indians built along the paths they traveled. Our men make them, too, now. Four cut saplings stuck in the ground, and four more saplings tied on top to make a roof. They covered the roof with sheets of bark from near-by trees. Sometimes they made walls for three sides of branches leaned against the frame. More sheets of bark made dry sleeping on the ground. It only takes an hour or so to make a shelter, and Indians—our men, too—left them standing when they went on. The next traveler to pass would use the shelter, maybe improve it a little—but always turning the bark on the ground over to be sure no snakes sheltered there. Build a fire at the open side, and you sleep comfortable, men say.

Rosaline stayed at the spring a while—maybe a week or more. It was a place of peace so, no doubt, Indians came and went while she was there. They may have exchanged news of the day, and offered meat from their hunting. Indians are generous that way. Any road, Rosaline got well.

At the cabin, she put up her yellow hair as a grown woman does, despite her pa's grunted objections. And she did all the work around the cabin, even the spinning Laurette used to do.

It wasn't long before Orlando noticed that some one was watching the cabin from a distance. The sign told him it was an Indian, a Catawba. Some folks say it was a Catawba chief; others that it was the brave that went after the fleeing Delaware and killed him on the banks of the Susquehanna up near Wright's Ferry. Any road, Orlando told another settler or two about the watching, when he met them elsewhere. He didn't mention it to Rosaline. Maybe she never noticed the watcher—but she ought to have. People watched for trouble those days, though mostly it never came.

Orlando took to sitting in his door with his rifle by, especially when Rosaline was about her outside work. One day soon, an Indian came walking right up to Orlando, carrying a big piece of elk or buffalo which he gifted to Orlando.

The two of them sat and smoked a pipe together and talked a while, about the weather and hunting and all the little things men talk about while edging toward what they really want to say. Presently the Indian got to that. Rosaline was a fine strong woman but she didn't have a man. He, the Indian, was a good hunter bringing meat home every day like the haunch he'd brought to Orlando. He was a brave warrior as the recent scalp he carried showed. He could provide well for Rosaline and give her strong children. Would Orlando give her to him?

Orlando didn't like the idea at all. Give his daughter to an Indian warrior? No! It was all right to marry an Indian squaw, the way Martin Chartiers over at the mouth of the Munkazy had. No! Rosaline was needed right there, doing for him in his cabin.

The Indian went away. Orlando told his grievance about the proposal when he met other settlers, but he never said what Rosaline thought about it. Like other women, she was too busy at the cabin to visit round. The settlers suspected an Indian was still in the neighborhood, but Orlando never said, only that he wanted Rosaline at home.

Then some one came to the cabin on Red Hill—most likely because a many turkey buzzards was circling toward it from all over and that wasn't natural. Orlando was lying in the cabin door, shot through the heart, with rifle by him. He wasn't scalped. It wasn't an enemy then. Inside the cabin, there weren't many women things to be seen. Rosaline was gone.

No one ever saw her again. Some folk said she went willingly. Who's to know?

(This story told in the words of a 19th century traveler.)

XIX

Murder in Monokassy?

The earthlings had a fragile peace with the natives of the alien planet, whose languages and customs they only partially understood, and who were more powerful than they. Then a hasty blow caused the death of an important native, and the men from earth feared war. How to defuse the situation?

A familiar situation in science fiction, true. But it really happened when western Maryland was unknown territory into which traders from the two colonies that claimed the mountains and valleys around the Monacacy River, ventured to seek furs from the Indians of the powerful League of Five Nations. As in science fiction, the major characters, heroes or villains, are European, and the natives, with their strange, hard to pronounce names, are in the background. The account we have, preserved in documents of the colonies, if read carefully, tells us much about the life of that time, so very few changes have been made here—except to make it easier to follow.

In the winter of 1721–22, the poorly defined area of the Monokassy (it lay west of the Great Falls of the Potomac, south of the fords of the Susquehanna at Conestoga but its other boundaries were known only by the Indians) was inhabited only by Indian hunters and visited by traders from the Lancaster area of Pennsylvania or by the few who came up the Potomac.

Empty as the country was, word of the death of an important man of the Seneca Nation at the hand of the Quaker traders, John and Edmund Cartlidge, spread rapidly. The traders drew back to safer territory fearing trouble from the Indians. When they reached the frontier fort Maryland had located in the Sugarlands west of the Great Falls, its commanding officer, Major John Bradford, sent a letter of warning to his superiors in Annapolis, that the death:

> seems very much to threaten this our province with an Indian war...All the
> Frontiers are in the greatest want of Powder and Ball to defend ourselves.

The day that letter reached Annapolis (February 26, 1721–22), Charles Calvert, Governor of the province, wrote Pennsylvania's Governor, Baron William Keith:

> I thought it my duty for the preservation of public safety to acquaint you with it/the death/and earnestly desire you will use your endeavours that the Indians may be satisfied in order to prevent the ill Consequences of such a rash action.

Sir William had already heard of the incident from "sundry persons of credit near Conestogoe" and "near Perquayomen." His Council agreed on the "absolute necessity" to take measures "upon so extraordinary an occasion for the preserving the peace of the Province."

Two "persons of Integrity, Reputation and Ability" were selected to go at once to Conestoga "to make Inquiry into this matter…to assure the publick Safety and Tranquillity of the government." They were Colonel John French, a member of the Council, and its Secretary, James Logan, whom the Dictionary of American Biography calls a Colonial statesman and scholar, and adds he was "always successful in his relations with the Indians."

Having sent the High Sheriff of Chester County ahead, French and Logan set out on March 7, 1721, with a signed commission and other instructions in hand, and with the knowledge the Provincial Assembly, then in session, had passed a resolution that said in part:

> The House will cheerfully defray the necessary Charge that shall arise…

The seriousness with which the government viewed the situation is emphasized by that word "cheerfully." How often does that adverb appear in an appropriations measure?

When the commissioners arrived in Conestoga the afternoon of March 9, they found John Cartlidge at home, with the High Sheriff:

> Edmund Cartlidge was then over the River Susquehannah waiting with a Gang of Horses…for his Brother to joyn him to proceed on their Business of Trade toward Patowmeck; but on our informing John of the Necessity there was of our seeing his Brother, he was prevailed upon to send for him the next day, and accordingly he came.

A messenger was sent thirty-six miles up the Susquehanna to get a translator, Peter Bizaillon. Bizaillon owned no horses, and had no near neighbor from whom to borrow, so he did not get to Conestoga until the afternoon of March 13.

The official inquiry began next morning. A number of important Indians had been invited to attend: Civility, a Susquehannock chief whose name appears frequently in the records of the time; Tannacharoe, Gunnehatorooja, and Toweena, Conestoga Indians; Savannah, chief of the Shawnee; Winjack, chief of the Gawanese; Tekaachroon, a Cayuga; Oweeyekanowa and Noshtarghkamen, Delawares or Lenni Lenape. The prospect of an unusual event drew "other old men of the Conestogoe Indians" and "divers English & Indians," the commissioners' report of the inquiry noted.

Sentence by sentence, the proceedings were translated from English into the Delaware language by Bizaillon, and from Delaware into the three other Indian languages by Captain Civility and "Smith the Gawanese who excels in the skill of those languages." The slow pace of translation must have added to the entertainment of the audience.

In Indian fashion, the commissioners opened the proceedings by laying a belt of wampum before the chiefs. James Logan recalled William Penn's league of friendship and brotherhood with the Indians, its renewal, and its observation for "near forty years past." Now the governor had received "by Report only…of an act of violence resulting in the death of one of our Brethren." The commissioners had been sent, Logan said, to condole with the Indians, and "to inquire how the matter came to pass, that justice may be done and Satisfaction be made."

Then, in the English tradition of law, the commission to investigate had to be read and the case to be investigated established:

> Question: When did Civility and the other Indians of Conestogoe first hear of the Death of the man, and by whom?
> Answer: They heard of it by several Indians much about the same time. The fact was done, they understood, about forty Days ago.
> Q: Where was it done?
> A: At Manakassy, a branch of Patowmeck River.
> Q: What was the Man's Name, his Nation, and Rank among his own people?
> A: His name was Sawantaeny of the Tsanondowaroonas or Sinnekaes, a Warriour, a civil man of very few Words.
> Q: What was his Business there?
> A: He was hunting, being used to hunt in that place.
> Q: Who, do you understand, was present besides the English at the Commission of the fact?
> A: The Man had been hunting there alone, with a Squaw that kept his Cabin, until John Cartlidge and his people came thither to trade with him

for his skins.

John and Edmund Cartlidge's people included two servants, William Wilkins and Jonathan Swindal, and the guide, Ayaquachan, of the Gawanese tribe. Two Shawnee "lads," Acquittanachke and Metheegueyta, came to the cabin about the same time. The squaw, Weynepreewayta, a cousin of the Shawnee chief, Savannah, remained in the cabin.

The tribal chiefs, Winjack and Savannah, now instructed the four Indian witnesses to speak the truth impartially and without "Malice and Hatred, Favour or Affection." The commissioners asked the three Shawnee to withdraw out of hearing, while the Gawanese gave his evidence, in the English tradition of keeping witnesses apart. The Indians thought this unnecessary but cooperated.

The Indian guide, who was about thirty years old, said the Cartlidge party arrived at Sawantaeny's cabin in the evening. Three times during the evening John Cartlidge gave the Seneca small quantities of rum and punch; after these gifts, he sold him a quantity of rum. Sawantaeny and Ayaquachan sat up all night drinking. In the morning, the Seneca said he had not received all the rum he had paid for and he wanted more. When he demanded it of Cartlidge, he was refused. Cartlidge took the pot Sawantaeny was holding to be filled and threw it aside. Sawantaeny then said Cartlidge should not be angry because he only asked for what was due, and he again pressed the claim. Cartlidge then pushed him away so hard that:

> he fell with his Neck cross a faln tree, where he lay for some time, and then rising walk'd up to his Cabin.

Ayaquachan was sitting at the fire, which he estimated to be thirty or forty paces from the cabin (later witnesses made it about one hundred paces). He saw John Cartlidge stripping off his clothes near the fire. Then the guide got up and went toward the cabin with:

> saw the Sinneka sitting on the ground with the Blood running down his Neck, and that John Cartlidge when he came kick'd him on the forehead with his Foot.

He admitted "the Deponent was in Liquor at the time and knows no more." Asked if he saw any gun, he replied, "None."

Next to be questioned was the older of the two Shawnee "lads," Aquannachke, aged about twenty-two. He confirmed that the Seneca "had

Liquor over night" and had sat up all night drinking. He himself had gone to sleep. He confirmed the beginning of the argument, the fall "cross a Tree," and the victim's going to his cabin.

Giving new testimony, he said the servant William Wilkins followed the Seneca and met Sawantaeny coming out of the cabin with his gun.

> Wilkins laid hold of him & the Gun and they both struggled, but not much; That Edmund Cartlidge coming up forced the Gun from the Indian, struck him three Blows on the Head with it, with which it broke. He struck him also on the Collar Bone. That John Cartlidge being at the Fire there stript off his Clothes, and coming up kick'd the Indian on the side and broke two of his Ribs; that the man then bled at the Mouth and Nose and was unable to speak, but rattled in the Throat...That the Sinneka in the mean time went into his Cabin where these Shawanese Lads left him.

After the kicking, the Cartlidge company packed up their belongings and left. The two Shawnee followed so they could trade with the Cartlidges. A final question placed the fight about nine in the morning, which agreed with John Cartlidge's statement that he had left the cabin at ten by his watch.

Metheequeyta, the younger Shawnee, repeated what his friend had said but would add nothing more.

Here the commissioners digress to comment on the "Pains" and "Endeavours" they used to get confirming, independent accounts from the three witnesses, in accordance with English law. The Indians, having another tradition of witnessing, could not be convinced, "Alleging it was to no purpose to repeat what others had already declared." Only "by many leading Questions that Aquannachke was induced to mention any part of what the Gawanese had said before."

The woman who had kept the cabin for Sawantaeny was the next witness. Weynepreeuayta said she was in the cabin when her husband came for the gun. "She shrieked out, and endeavoured to hinder him from carrying it out, but could not." So she followed, and saw Wilkins, then near by, try unsuccessfully to take the gun. Then Edmund Cartlidge forced the gun out of Sawantaeny's hands and "struck him first on the Shoulder, and then thrice upon the Head, and broke the gun with the Blows." She agreed that John Cartlidge "stript off his Clothes" at the fire (but why? No explanation is given) before coming up to find the Seneca sitting. "He then gave him one kick, in the side with his foot, and struck him with his fist." Sawantaeny spoke once more, but only after he got back into the cabin. He said, "His friends had killed him." There he bled so much that the blood clotted on the bearskin. "His Mouth and Nose were full of Blood."

He died the next morning about the same hour in which he had been wounded. Being alone, she left the body in the cabin and went to get help to bury him. She was gone several days, and she reported that two passers-by "coming thither by accident and finding him dead buried him in the Cabin, and were gone from thence before she returned." She said she met them on the way, and was told of the burial.

The passers-by were "an Indian woman, wife to Passalty of Conestogoe, with the Hermaphrodite of the same place." (Writing today, the commissioners would have said "transvestite" rather than "hermaphrodite." The Indians accepted with equanimity the males who dressed and behaved as women.)

In their testimony, they said a Cayuga Indian, Kannannowach, found the body before them. He hired them (perhaps burying the dead was women's work?) to bury it "lest the Fowle should eat him." It was then about seven days after his death, they judged, because the "Body then Stunk." Yes, there were three wounds in the head. When they washed away the blood, the brains appeared. Two of his ribs were broken, and "his Side on that part was very black."

Concluding the record of the Indian testimony, the commissioners remark that, despite making the examination with all the "Exactness" and "Impartiality" in their power, they were dissatisfied with the testimony of the three Shawnee. "They seem all to have agreed on their story before hand, especially in the particular of the man's Ribs being broke."

The belt of wampum was again displayed, and the Indian chiefs were told Sir William wished it to be sent to the Seneca Indians with his message about the accident. Would they decide on a proper person to carry message and belt? Their decision would be received at a meeting next morning, "the day being far spent, and the Company tired (for we sate on the Business near Eight hours)."

With little entertainment in prospect for observers, only the commissioners, the Indian chiefs and the translators attended the March 15 meeting. The presents to be sent the Senecas were agreed on: a belt of wampum and two "Stroud coats." Selecting a messenger took time. Only the promise of six bushels of corn, a new Stroud coat, a new gun, six pounds of lead and three of powder got the agreement of Skatcheetcho, a Cayuga Indian living in Conestoga, to make the trip. (The commissioners record the scrounging necessary: local German settlers provided the corn; John Cartlidge the gun and lead: and Peter

Bizallion promised to deliver the powder and the coat when the messenger passed his house near Paxton.)

The chiefs were urged to send their own message north with the commissioner's but they hedged. "They could not joyn any Words of theirs to our Present, for no such thing was ever practiced by the Indians, and they had no Belt ready of their own." Logan had had the forethought to bring a second belt of wampum with him, so Colonel French told Captain Civility quietly that the Indians might take it as their own. They agreed to have a council next day to send the belt in their own name to the Senecas with their own account of the proceedings.

While Logan and French waited for this meeting, word came that "the five Nations had sent down a large Belt of Wampum with the figure of a Runlet and an Hatchet on it to the Indians settled upwards on the Susquehannah with orders to stave all the Rum they met with."

This Prohibition Act by the Five Nations prompted the commissioners to send with Skatcheetcho a public order to all traders, reminding them carrying liquor to Indians was against the law, and to take no action if the Indians broke their kegs.

Skatcheetcho expected to leave the morning of March 17th, reach the Finger Lakes in eight days, and return in thirty. He and Civility would then come to Philadelphia to report on the delivery.

During the investigation, the Cartlidge brothers had been in the custody of the High Sheriff of Chester or his deputies.

> We then very much pressed John Cartlidge (Edmd. being gone before with an officer to his own House almost in our way) to hasten and go along with us. His Wife grieved almost to Distraction/was she an Indian?/, and would force herself and her child with him, but was at length prevailed with to stay; This caused us some Loss of Time. The woman's sorrows being loud the Indians went in to comfort her, and so we departed.

On March 20 in Philadelphia, the two Cartlidges and "the Lad Jonathan who was present at the fact" were committed to the custody of the High Sheriff of Philadelphia..."William Wilkins was one hundred and fifty miles up the Susquehannah trading for his master, and therefor too far out of our reach."

The commissioners told the Council that "Suspicion of Killing" was the most serious charge that could be brought against the prisoners. The killing could not be proved because:

the body of the Indian supposed to be killed had been buried about six weeks before their arrival at Conestogoe, in a solitary uninhabited wilderness, three Days Journey from thence: So that it was not only out of time to have a satisfactory view taken of the same, but also it was then impractable for them to get such a number of Christians to undertake this Journey as would constitute a legal Jury.

The brothers' petition to the Council said they were "heartily sorry for the Death of the Indian (if he be really dead)." They had no intention to hurt or injure him but did what they did "in their own Defense and for preservation of their own lives."

Five hundred pounds bail was set for each brother, and levies placed on their goods of two hundred fifty pounds each. John Cartlidge's name was struck from the Chester County Commission of Peace. A month later the Attorney General agreed with John Cartlidge's appeal and dismissed the charge because of lack of further evidence. The brothers returned to trading.

On May 4, Sir William Keith and the Pennsylvania Council received the messenger Skatcheetcho, the chief Civility, and three Conestoga Indians. The Iroquois League had accepted the investigation; war was averted. (Cost to Pennsylvania: forty-one pounds, 18 shillings, and nine pence. This included twenty shillings a day travel allowance to each commissioner.)

James Logan, Captain Civility, and even Edmund Cartlidge reappear in history. John Cartlidge does not, because he died a few years later. Edmund's next reappearance was ten years later when another Governor asked him to come to Philadelphia to tell what he knew about the French at Fort Duquesne. He replied, December 5, 1731:

> I have a large interest in ye woods and if I should leave my winter's Trade, which may Bee done for not being up in time, would Entirely ruin ye whole and quite Disable me from making returns to my Creditors to whom I am Deeply Engaged.

Two days later, he gave to a justice of the peace of Lancaster County, a sworn statement of his observations of the relations on the Allegheny River between the Indians and the French trader Cavalier. In his judgment, Cavalier was "a respectable, reasonable man" who made annual trips to buy furs. In another few years, Edmund was settled in western Maryland and was a justice of the peace, before he passes from history.

If the colonies and, later, the states had continued to deal with Indian tribes as was done in this trial, what might have been the result?

XX

In-Comers in Four Colors

Americans are always moving on.
It's an old Spanish custom gone astray,
A sort of English fever, I believe,
Or just a mere desire to take French leave,
I couldn't say. I couldn't really say.
Stephen Vincent Benet "Western Star"

The opening lines of an epic on the British colonization of America are also descriptive of how the culture and society of Maryland west of the fall line began...Between 1700 and 1800, four different groups of emigrants came into the region.

THE RED

The red man was first, having been in the Americas for a dozen millennia. He had been in all parts of Maryland much of that time, but were Indians in western Maryland in numbers in 1700?

Probably no more than a very few.

Indians of the Middle and Late Woodland period, with some connection to the Adena-Hopewell cultures further west, had erected burial mounds on Antietam Creek. Others had sheltered in Bushey's Cave as early as the Late Archaic period and as recently as the mid-sixteenth century. Fish weirs at various places along the Potomac River were there long before the white man fished the river. Village sites of the pre-European period have been explored by archaeologists, but only two were dated as active in 1711, one being King Opessa's town . This was occupied by Shawnees who had come south from the Susquehanna region. Captain John Smith's map of the Chesapeake, published in 1621, showed the course of the upper Potomac, and the names of three Indian tribes who dwelled in the region—the Mannahoacs, the

Monacans, the Massawomeck. Who were they? Perhaps these names were ones only the Chesapeake shore Indians used. Perhaps their information on Indian tribes of the upper Potomac was no more accurate than that showing the river's course. Perhaps, they were correct in identifying the tribes but in the eighty years since the map was made, the Massawomeck, Monocans, and Mannahoacs had moved away or died. So many tribes were decimated between 1500 and 1820, as white man's diseases for which they had little immunity spread. All that is certain is what Captain Richard Brightwell reported in 1698 after he had completed his exploratory circuit from New Scotland at the Little Falls of the Potomac west along the river and then north to the Patapsco River. He found no Indians, only "old Cabins and Tents" in the "barrens back of the River."

Williams, in his histories of Frederick and Washington counties, described western Maryland as a hunting area for tribes to the north and the south. And this is what it seems to have been at the time the next map was made: Philemon Lloyd's "Potowmeck above ye Inhabitants." That map, dated 1722, showed King Opessa's town (later, Shawneee Old Town; now simply Oldtown) on the North Branch of the Potomac a few miles above its confluence with the South Branch, and a village of Tuscaroras at the mouth of the Monocacy.

Local tradition, which both Scharf and Williams recorded, report two battles along the Potomac between Indians from southern and northern tribes. Both are dated variously between 1720 and 1732. The accounts may even be two versions of the same incident. One has a party of Lenape or Delaware Indians from Pennsylvania fighting near the mouth of Antietam Creek with a similar size band of Catawba Indians. All but one Delaware was killed; he escaped north but was followed by a single Catawba who caught and killed him near the Susquehanna River. In the second account, the opponents are the same, but the battleground was the Conococheague Creek. A Delaware survivor took refuge in the cabin of fur trader Israel Friend.

The presence of hunting and trapping Indians in the valleys and mountains north of the Potomac attracted white fur traders as early as 1721, when the "Murder in Muncazy" incident threatened a war between the Iroquois League and the colonies of Pennsylvania and Maryland. Israel Friend had been commissioned by the provincial governor of Maryland in 1728 as ambassador to the Indians, though the majority of traders seem to have come from frontier villages along the Susquehanna in Pennsylvania.

The entrepreneurial fur traders soon set up permanent bases. The Frenchman Martin Chartier had a cabin near the mouth of the Monocacy as well as a Tuscarora wife. John Hance Steelman and a son of the same name settled on Big Pipe Creek. The trader Charles Anderson was first heard of as living on the Monocacy but, within a year or two, was at "Sprigg's Delight" on the Antietam, and, ten years later, was living above Will's Creek in what is now West Virginia. Charles Pike settled on Little Tonolaway Creek in 1734, to be visited by the young George Washington in 1747.

Some of the traders with a permanent post also acquired land patents. Israel Friend signed a treaty that gave him a large tract of land on the Potomac north of Antietam Creek. Seven Indian "Kings and Rulers of Five Nations" were the signatories. One of them was "Sivillitie" of the Susquehannocks, whose name appears several times in one spelling or another in the history of the period.

Close on the heels of the traders came settlers. The first settler on Antietam Creek, a German from Pennsylvania, was as early as 1726. Another purchased land from the Indians and, later, confirmed his ownership by buying a patent from the province of Maryland.

By the mid 1730s, resident Indians were moving away. Shawnee Old Town was abandoned by 1732. Most of the Tuscaroras went north to New York. As had Charles Anderson, the traders followed furs and Indians to the west. Not all the Indians left, however.

A Moravian missionary, Michael Slatter, noted in 1748 of the Conococheague Valley:

> In this neighborhood there are still many Indians who are well disposed and very obliging, and are not disinclined toward Christians, when they are not made drunk by strong drink.

Another missionary described the local Indians:

> The men are tall, well made and active, not strong, but very dextrous with a rifle-barrelled gun, and their tomahawk, which they will throw with great certainty at any mark and at a great distance. The women are not so tall as the men, but well made and have many children, but had many more before spirits were introduced to them. They paint themselves in an odd manner, red, yellow, and black intermixed, and the men have the outer rim of their ears cut, which only hangs a bit, top and bottom, and have a tuft of hair left at the top of their head which is dressed with feathers. Their match coat is their chief clothing, which is a thick blanket thrown all around them, and they wear moccasins instead of shoes, which are deer-skin thrown all around the ankle and foot...In the day they were in our camp and in the night they go into their own, where they dance and make a most horrible noise.

All during the first half of the century, Indians lived:

> at peace with the settlers in the western part of the county and committed
> no depradations upon their property other than now and then appropriating
> to their own use, when they were on the war path, cattle and hogs which
> they encountered on their march.

This behavior was proper manners between Indian groups.

Change came when General Braddock's march over South Mountain and along Nemacolin's Path toward Fort Duquesne and his death near what is now Uniontown. Just how much changed is hard to tell. Williams writes, in both his county histories:

> Almost the first news of the defeat of Braddock our settlements had was
> the onslaught of the Indians who kept up a warfare upon the settle-
> ments...for a period of eleven years. The war upon the defenceless settlers
> of this county was so ferocious that for a time scarcely a white person was
> left west of South Mountain. All had fled to the older settlements for safe-
> ty and were pursued by parties of Indians within thirty miles of Baltimore.

Later, he uses "slaughtered," "driven away," "their homes in ashes" as he recounts in detail raids and atrocities that occurred—all at a considerable distance from western Maryland. He does not mention a single incident in Washington or Frederick counties. A recent writer, Schildknecht, also reported savage raids, but tempered his remarks with:

> few Indian raids in the lower Catoctin and Monocacy valleys, but some
> toward the north and in the mountains.

The single such raid he identified was more a kidnapping than a raid, which is expanded here as "Blackberry Theft." The Traceys, father and daughter, in their compilation:

> I am also to inform your Excellency that one William Roberts, who is an
> esteemed man of credit, was with me yesterday and says that he came
> through South Mountain Thursday last, this side of which he saw houses
> burnt about four miles from Major Ogle's and that a message came to him
> yesterday morning to give him an account that four men were killed the
> same day he came through the mountains and at the same gap he passed,
> which is about 60 miles from this place.

Some atrocities did occur but, by and large, Maryland historians of the French and Indian War period have given the Indians a bad press.

After 1770, Indians disappear from formal histories of the state. It is almost as if the Delawares, the Susquehannocks, the Shawnee and Tuscaroras had slipped into the same dark as the Massowomeck, the Mannahoak and the Monocan. They didn't—quite. But we must go to local historians.

Such a historian of Carroll County mentions a Susquehannock village of fifty or seventy people that "vanished" over a short period. Another tells of a group of Indians who moved away leaving behind an old man to die, with a younger man to nurse him. The next day, the young brave killed and buried the old man and followed the tribe. The letter written in Burkittsville, supposedly by the Confederate soldier Benjamin Prather (which is challenged as having been written in the early twentieth century), does contain much authentic material of local history; in it, he wrote:

> Six of us was sent to check on the Maryland Home cavalry to see if they was on the prowl out of Berlin. On the mountain Road toward Knoxville we came on the strangest site. We met an ancient old Indian who had snow white hairs. We fed him and drank him. He said his squaw and all his family was dead and buried on the Indian graveyard on top of South Mountain.

Joseph Barry, discussing pre-Civil War health and medicine in the Harpers Ferry region, mentions a half-Indian woman who practiced herbal medicine—and some witchcraft.

Absent or present, the Indians had considerable influence on western Maryland men for seventy-five years after 1770. A favorite item of men's every day dress was the "warmuss" or "vomis." It was a garment of leather or cloth made like the hunting shirt of the Indians. Josie Dixon of Elk Garden wore it well after the Civil War, a biographer noted. (Something similar but with another name has appeared, in recent years, as an outdoors garment)

WHITE

For two centuries after the first settlement in Maryland, its population centered on the Chesapeake Bay. Population density faded into almost nothing once the fall line of its river was passed. This continued to be true for the first third of the eighteenth century.

Although trading posts were established in the Monocacy and Antietam valleys and land patents were granted provincial politicians and their friends, comparatively few left the comfortably settled parts of Maryland for the frontier. But the river valleys of the western lands saw white men passing through. Immigrants, landing at Philadelphia, went through southeastern Pennsylvania and the valleys of the Monocacy and Antietam into the valley of Virginia without stopping. Only after Maryland's provincial government offered immigrants a financial inducement did serious settlement begin on both sides of South Mountain. Once begun, it went quickly. Frederick town and county were established in 1748, and Elizabethtown (now Hagerstown) was laid out four years later. West of North Mountain in what is now Allegany and Garrett counties, settlement was slower to begin. Although the Ohio Company built a storehouse at Wills' Creek as early as 1749–50, Cumberland was not laid out until 1780 and real settlement of those counties began only after 1770.

Who were the settlers of western Maryland? Many came from Britain. It is difficult to determine how many because no records were kept of the migration of British citizens to British colonies. A considerable number of men from northern Ireland came, because the Scotch-Irish there faced the end of the hundred-year leases made when Scots were settled there to reduce trouble in Ireland. This first great Irish migration was largely from the Scotch-Irish population, though "Irish" was the common appellation.

A great many, some say the majority, immigrants came from the Rhineland, the Palatinate, and the German-speaking areas of Switzerland. They came, perhaps, for religious reasons: their Protestant beliefs were not in full accord with the Protestant beliefs of the larger churches of their homeland. They emigrated in groups of eight to ten families. Some settled for a time in Lancaster County before moving south; others came directly from the ports: Annapolis, Alexandria or Philadelphia. They brought their language and their religion with them. The first church built in western Maryland was the log church near Creagerstown on the Monocacy, built 1732 or 1733. It conducted services in German and was the second church to do so in all the colonies. So many other churches were built that one local historian said the story of settlement was the story of the churches. On both sides of South Mountain, up until the middle of the nineteenth century, German was so commonly spoken that newspapers, almanacs, and books were published in the language.

Perhaps court records of naturalizations in Washington County in its first ten years of being a separate county give us as good a picture as any of the homelands of the new settlers. Between 1776 and 1781 the minutes of the Washington County Court recorded 156 completed naturalizations. Of these 93 came from German-speaking areas (89 from one of the several German states, the rest from the Netherlands, Denmark and Switzerland). 56 came from the British Isles, of whom 42 were identified as "Irish." The other seven were from France, with one of them stating firmly he was a "subject of Napoleon." An interesting side light noted was that many of the German-speakers chose to be naturalized under Anglicized names (as Adams, Cooper, Baker).

Not all the German-speakers came as voluntary immigrants. During the Revolutionary War, Hessian troops captured at Saratoga and at Yorktown were interned in Frederick and Fort Frederick. While public fear of these prisoners contributed to the Frederick treason trials, en masse escape did not materialize. Single escapes occurred frequently. One Hessian regiment, which had entered Maryland with 450 men, had so many desertions that only fifty men remained when the regiment was to be sent home. These deserters frequently re-appeared as help on local farms; many of those were reluctant to leave when the imprisoned troops were released to go home.

When, in 1781, Congress gave prisoners of war the right to remain in this country for the payment of 80 Spanish dollars, many Hessians ransomed themselves. Those who could not raise the money could accept an advance from an American and repay the sum by labor. A recent study lists several hundred men who remained in Maryland and farmed, either by buying a farm with savings or by marrying the farmer's daughter.

This repayment of a loan by labor was similar to the indentures accepted by many European immigrants in the seventeenth and eighteenth centuries. A ship captain bargained with would-be immigrants to bring them from the port in Europe to the colonies without charge. On arrival, the captain sold, for a certain period of years, the labor of the immigrants to colonists needing help. During his time of service, the "redemptioner" had little more legal rights than a slave, because the purchaser could resell his labor. However, those with skills in a trade or with education enough to teach were always in demand. After the time of indenture was over, the redemptioner faded into general society, many becoming leading members of the community and proud of their achievements. A number of respected western Marylanders began thus.

The first homes of the settlers were one- or two-room log cabins, with bark roofs. The French traveler Bayard described one such:

> A narrow cabin built of logs rough hewn with the chinks filled with clay, was the dwelling place of the man who has just subjected the land to the yoke of agriculture. A few fences, laid out in a zigzag manner, surrounded the "manor house" whose only openings were a door, and a square hole covered by a sheet of oil-soaked paper.

In a few years, when sawmills were established, and a second house, also of logs but with two stories, was built, the cabins became "henneries" until they collapsed from age. Some second houses still stand, although the logs are hidden by siding.

The commandant of the seamen accompanying General Braddock described early Frederick in a description which probably fit all the new towns:

> The town has not been settled above 7 years; there are...houses... Churches; the inhabitants chiefly Dutch; Industrious but imposing people: Provisions & Forage in Plenty.

Bayard commented, in 1791, that in Frederick "nearly all the houses are of brick."

Barns built early, even before the larger farmhouses went up. Also very early were the rail fences. Later, as fields were cleared of stone for easier plowing, came the building of the limestone fences which are seen today. By 1748, the missionary Michael Slatter commented on the farm:

> very fruitful fields for grain and pasture; they produce Turkish corn almost without any manure, among which are stalks ten feet and more high, and the grass is exceedingly fine.

Most early settlers in western Maryland had large families, and did not require, at least for the first few years, much additional labor. By the end of the eighteenth century, farmers in the older counties often had one or two German or Irish redemptioners as well as their family. There were also some slaves, no one knows how many. The far western counties in those years resembled what the more easterly counties had been fifty years earlier. The white race had settled in.

BLACK

The arrival of black men and women was unremarked in the first century of settling the five western counties of Maryland. Probably the majority were slaves. Only a few studies of black history in western Maryland have been done, so this summarizes what is known up to emancipation in 1864.

In the first half of the eighteenth century, slave holding tended to be precarious. When Indian settlements were to the west, an unhappy slave or redemptioner could be sure of welcome there. Shawnese felt no obligation to restore strayed property.

Historians agree that the number of slaves increased in the last years of the eighteenth century because indentures for European immigrants became uncommon and wheat farming, which could use slave labor effectively, increased. The 1790 census gave Frederick County a total population of 20,791, of whom 7000 were white males 16 years and older, and 3600 were slaves; Washington County's population was 15,822, with 3700 white males and 1286 slaves. The figures may be misleading: were both sexes counted or only male slaves?

By 1820, the slave population was at its highest point in the region, beginning a continuing decline to 1860, when that census showed there was one slave to every thirteen white men in Frederick County, and one slave to every twenty white men in Washington County. (The researcher who cited these figures added his interpretation that only one family in sixty-four had slaves.) Another writer warned against such statistics because a few slaveholders had large numbers of slaves.

The Dunkard and Mennonite churches, which did not approve of slavery, were strong in the region; most of their members did not hold slaves. Some even bought slaves for the purpose of freeing them. One Philip Thomas, M.D., bought four slaves from as many owners for the purpose of freeing them on Christmas Day 1779; he freed at least three other slaves at other times.

Members of other churches had uneasy feelings about slavery. A Carroll County woman was instructed by her father's will to free the family slaves at her death. She did so. Her slave, Betty Frantz, got her personal property and a farm with the proviso the farm be maintained or it would revert to the local Catholic church. The former slave rented it out to white farmers who so mishandled it that the farm was taken by the church, and the Orphans' Court took over her care. Other slaves bought their freedom: the black ferryman at Harpers Ferry paid $100 for his freedom at the settlement of Robert Harper's estate—a lordly sum for that date. The Reverend John Baptist Snow of Westminster bought his freedom; he also taught himself to read and write.

As property, slaves had value. One black historian found an 1803 tax valuation that gave the value of a slave as chattel property; a male slave between 17 and 45 years was valued at 45–50 pounds; a female slave of childbearing years (14–36 years) at 20–30 pounds. These valuations probably increased when slaves were raised for sale to southern plantations, as did some Maryland owners after importing slaves from Africa became illegal.

There were no plantation gangs of slaves in western Maryland; very often, the black farm hands worked side by side with their white farmer. Most slaves in western Maryland were house servants or farm hands. A percentage worked in industry. Leigh Masters operated his iron furnace with slaves. So did Launcelot Jacques. Slaves dug iron ore, loaded it into barges that they poled up river to Antietam Furnace, where white men and blacks (who may have been free, the records are unclear) worked the furnaces and produced finished metal products. Libby, who studied the workers of this furnace, called these men "an elite group of ironworkers just as their cultural forebears had been in Africa." Slaves operated the ferries at Harpers Ferry until bridges were built, and also at the Shepherdstown ferry, where they worked with little supervision from their master at Ferry Hill Plantation. He even gave them money to buy their own blankets and clothing.

Local black historians say the slaves lived in their masters' houses or might have their own cabins. One such cabin, probably located in the Monocacy valley, was seen by Bayard, in his 1791 trip through the state:

> I made an inventory of the household goods of a family of slaves.
> A box-like frame made of boards barely roughed over, upheld by stakes, constituted the marital couch. Some wheat straw and cornstalks, on which was spread a very short-napped woollen blanket that was burned in several/places/...An old pot, tilted on some pieces of brick, was still white with *Hominy*. A few rags soaked in water, were hanging in one of the corners of the fireplace. An old pipe, very short, and a knife blade, which were sticking in the wall were the only effects I found in the dwelling.

This is not unlike the first homes of settlers.

The history of blacks in the early days of the region is closely tied to the history of their churches, a Carroll County black historian said. Slave owners both encouraged and feared churches that served blacks: encouraged them because religion provided another control, and feared them because slaves were in contact with free blacks who were also church members. In western Maryland, some churches permitted slaves to attend services with their masters—but in a separate section of the building. Other churches were all white or all black. Some interesting histories have been written of a few segregated congregations.

Slaves were not always pacific. Williams, in his history of Washington County, wrote:

Slaves were generally unprofitable, and appear to have been a somewhat unruly class, for the papers are filled with complaints of gatherings of noisy crowds of negroes in the Market House/of Hagerstown/and elsewhere, drinking, gambling and carousing, pitching cents, playing cards and other unlawful games in stables. The town's statutes books were full of ordinances prohibiting the gatherings, but apparently they brought no good results.

That slaveholders punished their slaves was taken for granted and not recorded. Both Bayard and Doddridge report witnessing the beating of a female slave for some offence. Their horror and revulsion at the two incidents suggest it was not a common sight.

Slaves in Maryland and other border states feared with mortal terror being sold to the cotton fields. The threat of such a sale always produced results, Williams said. Sometimes, the drastic results were not expected by the owner: the slave mutilated himself (a hand cut off, for instance), or committed suicide. Reaction to such a threat was suspected as cause for murder of an owner by his slave or slaves. There were, Williams reports, maybe half a dozen such murders over a century and a half in the two counties he studied. He also reported slaves received trials for the crimes. Slaves took action against their owners for other reasons: a female slave in Emmitsburg burnt down her master's house in town because she was to be sent back to his farm for impertinence or a similar fault.

The proximity of Pennsylvania, where slavery did not exist, was reason enough for two related phenomena—the Underground Railroad and slavecatchers.

Until the Dred Scott decision in 1850, reaching Pennsylvania was sufficient to free the slave, and all through the first half of the nineteenth century, slaves made their way north, some from adjacent Maryland, others from many miles further south. After 1850, the Quakers and other abolitionists set up the Underground Railroad that carried escaped slaves safely through the northern states into Canada. Even more quietly, the Underground Railroad also functioned south of the Mason-Dixon Line, using the homes and churches of white sympathizers and the homes of free blacks.

The Underground Railroad in western Maryland is less known than its routes on the Eastern Shore of Maryland. It is certain that slaves crossed the Potomac at fords or on ferries, if they had a coin or two and were dressed well enough to discourage suspicion. A slave who escaped from Virginia in 1847 reported his ferry trip:

I seated myself with a colored man and a white man./After paying the five
cents fare./ The colored man asked me: "Are you a free man?" It staggered
me at first to think that a colored man should ask me that question. The
white man reproved him: "What the devil do you ask that question for? do
you think a man dressed like him could be a runaway?" I got across safely.

Another slave narrative (all were collected in the 1930s by WPA historians)
tells of walking the C&O Canal towpath from somewhere in Montgomery
County to Williamsport, sleeping outdoors one night and spending another in
the home of a colored man beside the canal. He, too, felt he was under suspicion but the white man met on the way did not act on the suspicion. He continued to Hagerstown and into Pennsylvania.

Escaping slaves could usually depend on help from the free blacks, and
from white sympathizers. The farm of Big Sam Williams near Four Locks on
the C&O Canal is known to have harbored escaping slaves. "Shockey's,"
which was the house belonging to Dr. D.M. Wantz, in Rohrersville is believed
to have been a station on the Underground Railway. So was Ebenezer
Methodist Episcopal Church in Hagerstown. A homeowner in the Harbaugh
Valley showed me a trapdoor, easily covered by a rug, in front of the parlor
fireplace that opened into an underground room reached only by the trapdoor;
she thought it might have been built to hide escaping slaves.

Lacking local geographic knowledge, escaping slaves followed natural features, including the ridge tops. *Katy of Catoctin*, by Gath, has a scene at one of
the gaps on South Mountain. A pair of runaway slaves dodges out of the
woods to cross the road in front of hero and heroine; they were following the
ridgeline much as the Appalachian Trail does today. A few pages later we find
the pair of escapees in the hands of a slave-catcher.

The slave-catcher, often called "paddarolle," found it profitable to work out
of Hagerstown, Emmitsburg or Westminster. Here, escaping slaves usually
ignorant of where the state line was became less cautious. Virginia slaveholders regularly advertised in Maryland papers offering rewards for the capture of
the fleeing slave from $10 up to several hundred dollars.

40 dollars reward

Ran away from the subscriber…a negro man, named OVERTON PARKER,
about 21 years of age, 5 feet 10 inches high, tolerably black, well made,
down look when spoken to, three fingers believed to be on the right hand
bent towards the palm of the hand by a severe burn…Had on when he went
away a blue frock coat, blue cloth pantaloons and waistcoat, white fur hat,

and coarse shoes. The above reward will be given if taken out of the state of Maryland, or $20 if taken in the state—and secured so that I get him again, and all reasonable expenses if brought home. ANTHONY ROWE.

Hagerstown jail was often so full of escaped slaves to be returned to their owners that there was no room for criminals. The town had its own slave market because recaptured slaves might be sold south if not reclaimed or if their owner was vengeful. Although Emmitsburg had its slave-catchers. "A few/slaves/were arrested in the town; as a general rule, they gained freedom when they reached there," the town historian wrote. Free blacks there were loud in denouncing slave-catchers. On one occasion, when the paddarolles attempted to carry off Ned Crummel, the free negro who was town barber, free blacks and white men alike almost lynched the two slave-catchers.

If escaping slaves banded together, as some did, they carried clubs and similar weapons, and were dangerous to attack. Nor did all captured escapers remain captured as two advertisements in the Hagerstown papers indicate:

RUNAWAY

Was committed to the jail of Washington County, as a runaway, on the 2nd instant, a negro man who calls himself JOSEPH QUINN…Also committed…on the 5th instant, a negro man who calls himself WILLIAM HARRIS…He says he was raised by John Walkman of Loudoun County, Virginia, and was sold by said Walkman to William Conrad, who sold him to a Southern trader…He has a pass in the name of Charles Binns, Clerk of Loudoun County, with the County Seal on it, but which no doubt is a forgery. The owner of said negro is requested to come forward, prove property, pay charges, and take him away, otherwise he will be released according to law. ALEX'R NEILL, Sheriff.

$40 Reward

Broke jail on the night of the 26th of April, the Negroes who were lately committed as runaways, names JOSEPH QUINN & W'M HARRIS, a description of which may be seen by reference to my advertisement, now in the Torch Light and Maryland Herald. The above reward will be given for the apprehension and delivery of said Negroes in Washington county jail, or $20 for either of them. ALEX'R NEILL, Sh'ff.

Uneasy doubts about slavery and race were felt early. A news item of May 22, 1831, in a Hagerstown newspaper announced the organization of a

Washington County Colonization Society, as an auxiliary of the Baltimore Society. Its purpose was to encourage "colonizing the free people of color of the state of Maryland, with their own consent, on the west coast of Africa." Launcelot Jacques, the iron furnace owner, was one of the charter members.

Free blacks existed in small numbers. (The four major towns of Washington County, in 1820, had a population of 4017 white men and women, 473 slaves, and 222 free blacks) throughout the period. They had their own farms and small businesses (barber shops in both Emmmitsburg and Westminster, blacksmith shops in several towns) or worked with others. (We know of black waggoners on the National Pike, a black mate on a C&O canal barge.) They had sufficient wealth to be potential customers of public entertainments; an 1831 advertisement for the Hagerstown performance of the play, "Tom and Jerry" says:

> No money received at the door. No lady admitted unless accompanied by a gentleman. N.B. A place is appropriated for people of color.

Williams has this comment on the term "people of color" which re-echoes today:

> It is a curious fact that the term negro was seldom used. The name was very offensive to these people and so considerate were people here of the sensibilities of their slaves that they were nearly always spoken of as "people of color." Such tender regard has long since passed away.

The Civil War made life more difficult for both free blacks and slaves in Maryland. Over 8000 blacks (presumably free blacks) served in the Union armies during the war, but no record has been found of where their homes were. The businesses of free blacks as well as whites suffered from visits alternately by Confederate and Yankee troops, who took goods without payment or damaged the property. Then, in November 1864, Maryland freed all slaves within its borders, without compensating the owners for the loss or making provision for the future of the slaves. Some light on how the war and the transition from slavery affected slaves and owner is found in the diary of Otho Nesbitt, who lived near Clear Spring:

Sept.9, 1861. Free negroes taken by the army...

June 17, 1863. I sent the rest of the blacks and the horses to the mountains to save from the Rebels...

June 4, 1864. Miss Kate Fingley here nearly all day teaching the negroes...

June 24. Rebels took Mary Jane and her mother...

Oct.30. The negroes had a meeting today for the first time in their new log church towards the Big Spring.

Nov.1. The negroes all set free in Maryland without compensation to their owners.

Nov.2. Told the negroes that I had nothing more to do with them. It was now near winter and they had no house, no home, and probably could get no work this time of year, and if they cared to work on as they had been doing till spring, they might do so, that I wouldn't pay a whole family of negroes to cook a little victuals for me after all that I had lost to both armies. They said it was so and they would work on until spring as they had been...

Dec.22, 1864. Frances Gillis left for Harrisburg. Her Father took her as far as Hagerstown in my sleigh...

Oct.27, 1868. Nance, Frances and Sal Gillis all moved into my little house...Nance cooked my victuals for many a long year, but she has probably left the old kitchen for ever. Mary, Liz, Ellen and Charles comes back often...

Sept.14, 1872. Old Nance here today, making peach preserves. Likes to come back when she is able to make a little money. Came last week and baked me six loaves of bread.

GREEN

Green immigrants came unobtrusively, unnoticed, with the white and the black immigrants. Their arrival in western Maryland, as it was in the rest of the continent, made changes that only a few botanists and ecologists recognize as having occurred.

Seed for familiar crops, saplings to start fruit orchards came with the settlers. Wives brought potherbs for cooking and home remedies, and starts of flowers to remind them of home. Wheat, oats, rye were so domesticated they seldom escaped the plowed field. Other plants took joyfully and quickly to the wild. Tansy and peppermint grow as happily by a woodland spring as in a garden. Soapwort, or Bouncing Bet, prefers the roadside.

Plant-wise Indians immediately saw the desirability of fruit trees and appropriated them. In 1777, when General Sullivan ravaged the Finger Lakes villages of the Iroquois Nation, he commented on the number and maturity of the fruit trees there. Some time in the late eighteenth century, the princess tree (Pawlonia) was brought to the East Coast to be a garden exotic: it soon escaped to the woodlands along the Potomac.

Plants were also stowaways. Burdock, thistles, dandelion, bedstraw came without conscious help from mankind. Came and flourished so well that the Indians called the broad-leaved plantain "the white man's foot."

Thanks to a Carroll County collector of local history, we know how one plant—the small English daisy—came to Carroll and adjacent counties. Soon after Leigh Masters settled at his Furnace Hill Plantation, he sent to England for red clover seed. When planted, it was found seeds of the daisy had come with it. The daisy spread quickly to other fields, both Masters' and beyond. Masters is two hundred years dead; the daisy still blooms each year.

Man or plant, "Americans are always moving on."

XXI

Wilderness Maryland

Was western Maryland a wilderness when in-comers began to record its history? Just what did it look like?

A full picture will never be possible, because the in-comers were too much like ourselves. We do not, nor did they, report on what was familiar to them. Although very few records remain from the first quarter of the eighteenth century, later reports and interpretations of related evidence give a general idea of what Maryland west of the fall line and the mountains must have been like in 1700.

Certainly the valleys and mountains were wild, but they were not primeval. For too many centuries, Indians had left their mark—by their travels and by their accidental and intentional use of fire.

The trails created by Indian travel have been studied enough that they give a base for picturing what western Maryland was like when major changes began. Any male Indian was considered a warrior, and it was Indian men who went visiting, or hunting, or, occasionally, to war, along their trails so the white in-comers called them "Indian war roads" or "tracts." The north-south paths of the Indians are best known because they sometimes limited the westward expansion of European settlement or, as in western Maryland, were a route the settlers followed.

The earliest map showing Indian trails was "Potowmeck above ye inhabitants" made in Annapolis in 1721; it showed the "Great Warr Road" coming up the Shenandoah Valley to pass near what is now Indian Spring and Clear Spring before continuing northeast to the important Indian town of Shamokin (now Sunbury) on the Susquehanna. Two Seneca Indians stopped in Annapolis on their way back from negotiating for the Iroquois with tribes in southwest Virginia, and met with Philemon Lloyd, secretary of the Provincial Council. He showed them the map and:

Ye fellows were pleased to see their Warr Road or Great Tract in ye
Southwards laid down by double Prickt Lines wch of themselves they took
Notice of & as well as they could make me to Understand that it was their
Tract where they went to Warr unto the Southeast Indians & wondered how
I came to know anything about it.

Several other major northeast-southwest-trending trails are known. The
most easterly of these is recorded only in Virginia records: it ran east of the
Blue Ridge, to cross the Potomac at Noland's Ferry. Further west other trails
crossed the Potomac at King Opessa's Town (now Oldtown) and Will's Creek
(Cumberland) and were sometimes known as the Tuscarora and Catawba
paths, respectively. Another Catawba path connected the site of Uniontown,
Pennsylvania, with the Cheat River region of West Virginia. For all of these
trails, we have only the general direction of route between known points
(often the river crossings or destinations), not mile-by-mile description.

The trail known to settlers coming from Pennsylvania first to the
Shenandoah Valley and, later, to Maryland's Catoctin and Antietam valleys
was the Monocacy Path, which was used earlier by Tuscarora Indians moving
north to New York. For the Europeans, the path began at the town of
Conestoga east of the Susquehanna, then the boundary beyond which
European settlement was forbidden by the treaty of Lancaster. For Indians, the
path began at Canojohela west of the Susquehanna. All three names,
Conestoga, Canojohela, and Monocacy, have been given to the trail that
passed the sites of the present Hanover and Littlestown, Pennsylvania, and
Taneytown, Maryland, to the fords of Big and Little Pipe Creek. It is still a
matter for argument where the Monocacy Path went after that point—was it
down the Monocacy River? Did it go closer to South Mountain? Did it cross
one of the gaps, or go around the end of South Mountain? Schildknecht, a
recent student of the ancient records, believes there were two branches of the
Monocacy Path after the Pipe Creek fords—the Main Monocacy Path down
the Monocacy River, and the German Monocacy Path which went closer to
South Mountain.

So many travelers had used the trail by 1730 that Pennsylvania widened it
for wagons as far south as the probable province boundary. Maryland widened
its portion of the Monocacy Path in 1749. There is no certainty, however, that
either improvement followed the original Indian trail. Continued heavy travel
made macadamization necessary as early as 1808. Pennsylvania's and
Maryland's State route 194 still follows the 1808 route.

East-west trails from tidewater to the mountains existed, but their names
are much less remembered. William B. Marye searched old deeds to describe

"the old Indian road" from a point on the Gunpowder River west to Big Pipe Creek and the Monocacy Path. Other local historians cite traditions of Indian trails running from Montgomery County to the Sugarlands on the Potomac, or into the mid-Monocacy valley. One or two modern roads, such as Md. 28 west of Rockville, are said to follow an Indian trail.

The limited number of Indian trails suggests a similar limit in number of Indians to create and use them and confirms the opinion Williams expressed in his histories that western Maryland was, at the time of white settlement, a "hunting ground for the Indians." The Indians set fires to improve grazing for game and this also affected the creation of accepted trail routes. Walkers, when their destination is visible and obstacles few, tend to go their individual ways, creating no single path. The uncertainty over the route of the Monocacy Path after the Pipe Creek fords speaks for an open, grassy landscape in that part of Maryland.

"Barrens back of the River" were reported as early as 1698 by the ranger, Capt. Richard Brightwell. Dr. Charles Carroll (he died in 1755) wrote an undated letter from Annapolis to his son in London that described, thirty miles from navigable water:

> a range of barren dry land without timber about nine miles wide which keeps course about northeast and southwest through this province, Virginia, and Pennsylvania, but between that and the mountain the lands mend and are very good in such parts.

The size of these barrens is in question. Several other bits of evidence tell us that the valleys on both sides of South Mountain, and some of the narrower valleys further west were open and grassy: the speed with which productive farms came into existence after settlement; the existence of bison; the comments of a few travelers; even some tax records.

In his Washington County history, Williams quotes from the unsigned obituary of a man who settled in the county in 1771. The writer said the deceased once told him that:

> the beautiful lots of timber which are now seen in Washington County grew up in his lifetime. When he first came here many acres now covered with tall oaks were overgrown with hazel bushes. The buildings of those days were of humble character, and the Indians' paths served as roads.

The Moravian preacher, Michael Slatter, wrote, about 1748, that his fellow religionists settled near the mouth of the Conococheague because there was timber near from which to build houses. Everywhere else in the region were "scrub oaks" and "hazle bushes."

The admiring descriptions of the farms around Frederick and of the prosperous look of that ten-year-old town by one of General Braddock's officers and by another Moravian minister indicate the settlers had far fewer trees to clear off their acres than did my direct ancestor who settled on 400 acres above the Ohio River in 1777. Court records show he had, after twelve years of work, only fifteen acres cleared.

Foote's description of the Shenandoah Valley, written in the 1750s, is quoted by a geographer of this century (Maxwell) as saying settlers had only young growth to clear because of the constant burning of the valley by Indians for game. The valley was prairie-like, with scattered trees growing along the watercourses. That prairie extended a distance of 150 miles and covered more than one thousand square miles.

Buffalo roamed there, and also in Maryland, as surviving place names tell us. The geographer quoted thought that, by the eighteenth century, the bison herd was declining. The last buffalo known to be killed in Maryland were two bulls killed in a glade in Garrett County before 1743; two cows with them escaped.

The Maryland General Assembly levied a land tax on all counties in 1783; the schedules for Montgomery County land tax were studied in detail recently. According to the tax schedules, all Montgomery County land, except in the southeast corner of the county, had at that time few or no trees. The description used for what grew on the lands was "saplings," indicating brush or small trash trees, whereas timbered land was identified with an adjective, "good" or "strong." The author of this study lays the existence of "sapling" tracts to Indian burnings several decades in the past. Earlier geographers agree that Indians regularly burned land to provide better forage for the game they hunted; they also tended to leave campfires burning untended. Burnings, sufficiently repeated, produce open landscapes.

Beside the wide valleys near the Blue Ridge, the narrower valleys of the Appalachians contained glades that may have had similar origin. Meshach Browning described them, as he remembered them from his youth in 1790:

> The glades are, or then were, clear, level meadows with high grass, which was altogether different from what is there produced now being of a much better character, growing nearly as high as rye, with a blue tassel at the top. The blade was set very thick, on the stalk, to the height of three or four feet.
>
> There were hundreds, if not thousands, of acres of this grass growing where there is now nothing but bushes, and a rough and very inferior kind

of grass, which serves very well for early pasture, but is of very little worth for hay.

He added a memory of watching wild turkey poults, several dozen of them, dashing through glade grass in spring catching grasshoppers. He claimed the heavy pasturing by large numbers of cattle year round destroyed the original herbage. The state geologist, J.T. Ducatel, in 1841, was even more enthusiastic about the beauty of the glades:

> natural meadows of variable extent, with a deep mould for soil...which throws up a spontaneous growth of succulent grasses and plants that afford the finest and most abundant pasturage for cattle during a long portion of the year, and during the months of June and July present to the eye of the traveler who crosses them, a delightful parterre of flowers of all hues...

The valleys of western Maryland were more grass than woodland in 1700, due to burnings over many years. Hillside forests were also affected as Bayard, the French traveler, observed in his 1791 trip through western Maryland. East of Middletown, his party walked by the road because:

> The road had become so rough/from rocks carried by a torrent/that, for the sake of the horses and, for the safety of the travelers, we had to descend from the carriage. We walked at some distance from the road on a nice sod...Covered by the tree tops which protected us from the rays of a burning sun, we felt only the mild warmth of a beautiful spring day, although at the foot of the mountains, we felt the heat of the torrid zone.

After crossing the Middletown valley, their driver chose a shorter road over the mountains than the usual route to Hagerstown, and Bayard continues:

> This mixture of plains and mountains does not offer as yet sights agreeable to the traveler: but when the too monotonous mass of trees which conceals the pleasing variety of sites has been cut down, this region will be delightful. After having made a few miles, we found ourselves on the bare summit of a very high mountain.

The sod and easy walking of the first quotation and the bare summit of the second are indicative of forests that have seen fires.

Bayard names the honey-locust, stately oaks, and the hickory, but no other species. The first description I have seen of the woodlands of the western

Maryland was by the geologist Ducatel in 1841, describing a view from some mountaintop in Allegany County:

> The crests and flanks of the mountains are covered principally with pines and chestnuts...On the bottom lands are found nearly all of the most valuable forest trees: oaks, walnuts, poplar, locust, hickory, and Magnolia acuminata, or cucumber tree as it is here called, and the maples, among which is the sugar maple...The lime tree (Tilia glabra) here called the Linn. Among the flowering shrubbery are particularly noticed the mountain laurel (Rhododendron maximum), calico bush (Kalmia latifolia) and the wild honeysuckle (Azalea viscosa) of large size, bearing a cluster of white flowers that emits a delicious fragrance.

F.W. Besley, a state forester, wrote in 1922 of Washington County woodlands, which were of three types: the ridge-top (with the true chestnut and chestnut and scarlet oaks); the slope (with true chestnuts, black and white oaks on upper slopes, and white and red oaks, hickory, and tulip poplar on lower slopes), and bottom lands (carrying ash, elm, willow, sycamore, and some white and red oaks and hickory). For Ducatel and Besley, chestnuts were the major tree species.

Both Ducatel and Besley commented on the continuing destruction of the virgin forest. Besley said that, by 1922, almost all the woodlands remaining in Washington County were second and third growth, due to timbering which took out the valuable trees, and to the frequency of fires. The 1920–21 fire season in the county was typical: seventeen forest fires, over half due to arson. In that respect, the new inhabitants of Maryland were like the Indians that preceded them.

A 1937 report on Maryland geography has this comment:

> Only remains of the unbroken forest are left, and not until recently has serious effort been made to preserve areas for the safe abode of wild life, both animal and plant, that has survived the encroachment of civilization. In general, the native plants have survived better in the restricted habitats available to them than have the animals.

Wild animal life was abundant in Maryland in 1700, though perhaps reduced in the eastern, settled portions. A pamphlet, "A Relation of Maryland," published in London in 1635 writes enthusiastically:

> The woods are free from underwood, so that a man may travell on horseback almost any where. In the upper parts of the countrie there are bufaloes,

elkes, lions, bears, wolves, and deare there are in great store, on all the places that are not much frequented, as also beavers, foxes, otters and many other sorts of beastes. Of birds, there is the eagle, goshawk, falcon, lammer, sparrow-hawk, and merlin: also wild turkeys in great aboundance, whereof many weigh fifty pounds and upwards, and of partidge plenty.

This abundance lasted more than a century. Meshach Browning, a western Maryland man who hunted more than he farmed, judged that from the time he was eighteen (in 1799) to 1854, when he wrote his life story, he had killed between 1800 and 2000 deer, three or four hundred bears, 50 panthers, and about the same number of wolves and wild cats. He kept no count of otters or other animals trapped, or of birds killed.

As noted above, the bison the London pamphlet reported had been killed off before Browning's birth. Nor does he mention killing elk. The author of *Mammals of Maryland* (1969) believed they were extirpated in Maryland by the early nineteenth century, though they survived in Virginia until 1844. Browning certainly helped in killing off the gray wolf, which had once been common as far east as the barrier islands, and the mountain lion. The author of *Mammals of Maryland* thought the wolf was "exterminated in Maryland at a very early date, except for those in the more inaccessible parts of western Maryland." The late part of the nineteenth century was his probable date for the last Maryland wolf, and "sometime toward the end of the nineteenth century" for the last panther in the state.

Although the last passenger pigeon did not die until 1914, western Maryland saw its last great flocks of pigeons in the 1880s. A Frostburg man recorded the story his father told of those flocks, as they came over the tableland of Piney Mountain:

> We often saw great trains of wild pigeons that looked to be a mile wide and reached from the Savage Mountain west of us to the Blue Ridge in Virginia (a distance of twenty miles) which we could see plainly on a clear day.
>
> The spring migrations were usually from east to west during mid-April though the direction of flight was unpredictable. Smaller flocks might come from any direction when beech and birch buds were swelling. These buds seemed to be their favorite late winter or early spring food. We could see large groups of birds break away from the main flock and circle down in the hollows where beech and birch grew…the sun gleaming on their slate-blue wings. From where we stood the dense flock of birds looked almost like a blanket fluttering in the wind as they alighted on the trees in the valleys.

Frank Leslie's Illustrated Newspaper in the 1850s
portrayed flights of Passenger Pigeons.

Frank Leslie's Illustrated Newspaper in the 1850s
portrayed flights of the passenger pigeons

In the distance we could see some limbs bend and break under the weight of so many birds, causing a few dozen of them to take to their wings as the broken limbs dropped from under them. In about a quarter hour we would see that group of pigeons fly up into the mile-wide train of birds that still reached from mountain to mountain. Then another group would break away and descend to the valley. When summer came we could see many dead trees in the valley that had been stripped of their buds by the pigeons...

The roar of pigeon wings in that flight sounded like a strong wind in a barren March forest. The flyway was perhaps three miles from where we worked, and as the sun was sinking behind the mountain west of us, we saw the end of the great horde of birds. The roar diminished as the distance between us and the last of birds lengthened, but it was a full half hour until we could hear it no longer...

Around the middle of that June 1887 I learned what Uncle Sam meant by warning of their destructiveness. There was no long train of pigeons like we had seen in April, but out of the western sky came a dense flock of tens of thousands of hungry birds. They swooped down on our fields and ate the young stalks of corn down to the roots. They flew over the rail-fence into our rye field and ate every head and trampled the straw under their feet, leaving the field looking like it had been struck by a hailstorm. The men tried to scare them by shooting them with muzzle loading rifles, but all they got was a few dead pigeons. There was no way to scare them away as long as there was a stalk of corn or a head of grain left.

...They stripped every corn and grain field in the Porter Settlement and flew away as suddenly and mysteriously as they had come. In three days they ate the crops and left nothing but dung an inch deep on the fields. We couldn't walk on the field until the sun dried the gooey, sour smelling mess.

It was still early enough to plant buckwheat, which would give a saleable crop but:

within a week after the pigeons had raided the crops, news spread over the settlement that they were nesting on Wolfe Ridge, a distance of about four miles from where we lived. The farmers then began worrying about their buckwheat crops. But Uncle Sam said "Huckleberries will be ripe by the time the squabs are ready to fly; then they'll all leave together."

...the nesting area covered many acres of forest land...as many as sixty nests in a single large tree. Every fork or crotch held a crude, bowl shaped nest that had been carelessly built of sticks and straws and lined with a few big leaves spread out flat. The nests contained only one egg each.

The nesting area was a quiet place during the incubating period...at which time both male and female took turns setting on the egg. By the time the squabs were hatched the huckleberries on the ridge were ripe and the pigeons had a feast right in their own back yard. Whitish-purple excrement from the squabs ran down the limbs under the nests and dried on the tree trunks. The whole place had a foul scent...faintly of huckleberries.

The squabs grew fast and soon seemed to fill their nests. The parent pigeons fed their young by regurgitation, and when the squabs had enough so that they were quiet, the father and mother birds would cuddle up close together and "coo" on a limb near the nest.

When the squabs grew and fattened to half-feathered, weak legged, squatty creatures, pigeon hunters came by the hundreds with sacks, pack horses and wagons. With long poles they knocked the helpless squabs from their nests, sometimes breaking their necks or legs in the fall. Another blow on the head with a short club killed them, and they were put in sacks and hauled to towns where they were sold for a half dollar a dozen. Young squabs were delicious eating...

By the time the squabs would have grown wing feathers to fly, there were none left to fly away with the parent birds who hatched them.

The passenger pigeons are gone. Still with us, though in far fewer numbers than in the eighteenth century, are poisonous snakes. Meshach Browning described three varieties of rattlesnakes: one patterned in yellow diamonds which grew big (he had killed them as long as 5'6" and 10" in circumference); a smaller variety that was almost black in color; and a third, dusty brown in color like the color of the ground, which never grew to a large size "but is so very wicked it will run at a man and bite as soon as near enough to reach him." He said the larger variety was "not spiteful unless provoked"...

Rattlesnakes were frequently found in the grain and flax fields, because they ate rodents found there, as well as rabbits, squirrels and even groundhogs. As many as a dozen rattlers might be killed in a day. Browning recalled making hay in one glade where there were "hundreds of snakes," so many that he did not want to be there after dark. The chief danger from snakes in the grain fields came from their habit of hiding under the grain or hay left to dry in the sun after cutting: the person gathering the grain to make into sheaves might pick up the snake with the grain.

Rattlesnakes were killed on sight, the early writers Browning and Doddridge agreed; Browning said, "I have killed thousands." Their dens, when discovered, were also destroyed, often by fire in April and early May when the snakes were still in them. These efforts, and the frequent forest fires that burned through the woods in summer, had reduced the number of rattlesnakes substantially in Browning's lifetime. When he wrote his autobiography, he said "they are now rarely seen, except in a few locations difficult of access, or near their dens."

The other poisonous snake of western Maryland, the copperhead, was rare enough that Browning had never seen but two or three in his entire life.

Mountain Maryland, more open and grassy in its valleys than tidewater Maryland had been, was in the eighteenth century rich in plants and animal life, and a land that could adopt aliens from other environments and cultures. Some native plant and animal species would be lost in the process, but it would remain a welcoming land.

Sources and Gratitude

During the last months of working on this book, I lost my sight to macular degeneration and have depended on friends in the Potomac Appalachian Trail Club to complete the work I would otherwise have done. In particular I thank Jean Golightly for assuming all of the details in bringing this book to publication.

George Walters has skillfully portrayed the wildlife.

Photos of the C&O Canal are courtesy of the National Park Service.

The Hagerstown Almanack provided the photo of their almanac.

The photo of the passenger pigeons is from a Department of the Interior booklet called "A Passing in Cincinnati" printed in 1976.

As every one must, who is concerned with the history of western Maryland, I founded this book on three others:

Scharf, Thomas. *History of western Maryland.* 1882.

Williams, Thomas J.C. *History of Frederick County, Maryland, from its earliest establishment...*1910.

Williams, Thomas J.C. *History of Washington County, Maryland, from its earliest establishment...*1906.

No specific attribution can be given to their contributions to this work, so much has been absorbed. I gratefully acknowledge that generosity.

Other sources have added to that foundation: the town and county histories written in the twentieth century, many of them around the time of the nation's Bicentennial, and the two century and more family histories created by descendants of early settlers. Most useful of all are the crumbling clippings or faded manuscripts rescued from attics and wastebaskets over many years by many people, who collected, preserved, organized unique hoards of historical information about their own locality.

The past and continuing work of these patient workers, both amateur volunteers and paid professionals, provide sources for this and any other study of the mountain counties of Maryland. I appreciate and am grateful for all those who created and maintain these collections:

Allegany County Public Library, Local History Room

Allegany County Historical Society

Carroll County Public Library, Maryland Room

Carroll County Historical Society

Emmitsburg Public Library

B.F. Artz Memorial Library, Frederick, Maryland Room

Frederick County Historical Society

Garrett County Public Library, Local history files

Garrett County Historical Society

Maryland Historical Society

Montgomery County Public Library, Maryland collection

Montgomery County Historical Society

Washington County Free Library, Western Maryland Room

Washington County Historical Society

With few exceptions, usually identified, all the documents cited in the bibliographies that follow, were found in one or the other of these collections, although my erratic data-keeping may fail to identify which one it was.

Carroll and Montgomery counties are not usually thought of as western or mountain Maryland counties, yet much of each county lies west of the Falls of the Potomac, and their history and social climates have more in common with the mountain counties than they do with tidewater Maryland. For those reasons, I worked in these collections but, generally speaking, used only the sources that provided information similar to what had been found in the other counties, or which reported specific activities occurring west of Westminster in Carroll County or Damascus in Montgomery.

The limited use of material from Allegany and Garrett county collections is due, in part, to their being younger collections and therefore having less to offer and, in part, to the necessity of keeping the book a reasonable length.

Chapter I: A Walk in Spring

Audubon Naturalist Society. (Archives, boxes 3, 8, 30).

Blackburn, G.F. "The"Justice Douglas hike." *Appalachian Trailway News*, v.15 no.2, p. 22–3, May 1954.

Blackburn, Ruth. (Personal communication, March, 1954 and 1993).

Bookman, George. (Personal communication, April 14,1994, with copies of March 1954 dispatches to TIME).

C&O Canal folder, 1955–1964; C&O clipping envelope, 1959, C&O Canal pamphlets. (Washingtoniana Room, D.C. Public Library).

Chesapeake and Ohio Canal. (Vertical file, Western Maryland Room, Washington County Public Library).

Chick, J. Drew. Report of Justice Douglas, "Hiking trip along the Chesapeake and Ohio Canal," *Washington* Post, March 20–27, 1954.

Conway, Grant. "Cumberland to Washington on the C&O Canal." *Bulletin* of the Potomac Appalachian Trail Club, v.23, July 1954, p.90–6,105–7.

Douglas, William O. Papers, cartons 306, 312, 357, 370, 371, 502, 1774. (Manuscripts, Library of Congress).

Douglas hike news stories, March 1954. (William D. Richardson's collection of clippings from Cumberland and Washington, D.C. newspapers of March 1954).

Durham, Jack. "The C&O Canal hike." *The Living Wilderness*, no.48. Spring 1954, p.1–25.

Durham, Jack. Papers, Archives. (Chesapeake and Ohio Canal Association).

Estabrook, Robert. "The challenging creation of the C&O Canal." *Trailblazer* of the Rails to Trails Conservancy, v. 9 no.1, Jan-March, 1994, p.5.

Hauck, Paul E. (Personal communication, some recollections of the '54 hike, March, 1994).

Mackintosh, Barry. *The C&O Canal: the making of a park*. National Park Service. 1991.

Potomac Appalachian Trail Club, Council minutes, 1953–1954. Also, C&O Canal file, Archives 1950–1959, various issues of *Bulletin* of the P.A.T.C. 1953–1960.

Chapter II: A Modest Marathon

Burnside, Bruce. "The runaway 50 mile-hike." (Personal communication, March 1990, with program of 12th hike in 1974.)

Carey, Arthur B. Jr. "Twice a marathon, three times the pain." *Maryland Magazine*, Autumn 1977.

Cumberland Valley Athletic Club. Programs of John F. Kennedy 50-mile, 1962–1994.

Imhoff, Ernest. "The JFK 50-mile hike/run and the man behind it." *Baltimore Sun*, Oct. 28, 1987.

Jackman, Phil. "Competition and camaraderie on 50-mile JFK can warm heart of coldest runner." *Baltimore Sun*, Jan. 23, 1983.

JFK Hike-run. Vertical file (Hagerstown Public Library).

Sawyer, William J. (Personal communication, May 23,1990).

Chapter III: Spirits—Legal and Otherwise

Anderson, Elizabeth. (Personal communication, Feb. 26, 1990).

Bast, Douglas. *History of Boonsboro*. n.d. (MSS) (Western Maryland Room).

Bready, James. Maryland: "Whiskey, the nation's long-favorite—but now has let vanish." *Maryland Historical Magazine*, v. 85 no. 4, Winter 1990, p. 345–75.

Conway, Grant. Archives (Western Maryland Room).

Distillery exhibit records. (Washington County Historical Society).

Mathias, Charles McC. Letter to the editor. *Maryland Historical Magazine*, v.8, no 4, Winter, 1997, p. 359–60.

Michaels, Mary. *History of Boonsboro*. n.d. (MSS) (Western Maryland Room).

Nakhleh, Emile A. and Mary B. Nakhleh. *Emmitsburg: history and society*. 1976.

Pryor, James. Personal communication, April 1990.

Seabright, Thomas B. *The old pike: a history of the National Road*. Uniontown, Pa. 1894.

Shellman, Mary Bastwood. "The pioneers of the early days in Westminster." (Speech before Carroll County Historical Society) n.d.

Woodring, Frank. "Penal farm neighbors..." *Maryland Cracker Barrel*, v.27, no.5. Feb/Mar, 1999. (Penal Farm issue) p.5f.

Chapter IV: The Hagerstown Almanack

Gonz, Dietz. "John Gruber and his almanac." *Maryland Historical Magazine*, v.45 no.2. p.89–100, 1951.

Hagers-Town and Country Almanack. 1797–1995. (Western Maryland Room).

Hagerstown Almanack. (Vertical file, Washington County Free Library).

Oldenburg, Don. "Eye on the weather: the little almanac that makes the calls." *Washington Post,* Feb.28, 1994, p. B-5.

"On top of the weather." *Washington Post*, March 10,1994, Maryland p.2.

Chapter V: Game in Western Maryland

Brown, Stephen D. *Haunted houses of Harpers Ferry and regional ghost stories*. 2d. ed. 1977.

Cannon, Timothy L. and Nancy F. Whitmore. *Ghosts and legends of Frederick County*. 1980.

Chaplin, Gordon. "The grand bicentennial Washington Post POTOMAC magazine expedition to darkest Maryland in search of the monstrous snallygaster…" *Washington Post*, Oct.10, 1976.

Charninsky, Mark and Mark Opsasnick. A field guide to the monsters and mystery animals of Maryland. *Strange Magazine,* no.4.

Hooper, Anne B. *Braddock Heights: a glance backward*. 1974.

Hooper, Anne B. *Braddock Heights history*. 1978.

Opsasnick, Mark. "Do monsters roam the Alleghenies?" *Journal of the Alleghenies*, v.16, 1990, p.54.

Tufty, Barbar. "Mountain lion reportedly seen near Seneca." *Audubon Naturalist News*, May, 1997, p.15.

Chapter VI: Celebrations and Superstitions

Abel, Florence Harris. "Baetzel family lore." *Journal of the Alleghenies*, v.25, 1989, p.13–28.

Ackerman, Lonnelle. "Nature's healing arts: from medieval times to modern drugs." *National Geographic Society*, Jan.1977.

Baltimore Section. *Baltimore Sun*, Oct. 26, 1974.

Balyard, Elizabeth. "First footing." *Journal of the Alleghenies*, v.18, 1982 p.23.

Brown, Malcolm L. "Medical properties of plants as seen by early settlers." *Journal of the Alleghenies,* v.3, no.3–4, p.6–7.

Collen, Thomas C. "Early medicine in Maryland: an address." August 26, 1927 to the Medical and Chirugical Society of Maryland (Pamphlet) (Western Maryland Room).

Conway, Grant. Archives. (Western Maryland Room).

Cordts, Jeanne M. "Ginseng in the Alleghenies." *Journal of the Alleghenies,* v.2, 1966.

Cordts, Jeannn M. "Medical use of herbs." *Journal of the Alleghenies*, v.17, no.6.

Hagerstown lucky bean. *Maryland Cracker Barrel,* March, 1972.

"Harrison at Hagerstown and ball." *Maryland Cracker Barrel.* 1976.

Hay, David R. "Serenadings on "Bruders Thal." *Journal of the Alleghenies*, v.10, 1970, p.3–8.

Malcolm, Charles. "Christmas memories of 'Bell Snickeling' cherished by Keedysville resident." *Maryland Cracker Barrel*, v.23, no.4, 1994, p.11.

Marshall, Annett Hammell. "A visit from Belsnickels." *Journal of the Alleghenies*, v.2 nos.2–4, p.21, 1965.

Murray, Mary E. "Christmas in western Maryland." *Journal of the Alleghenies*, v.2, nos. 2–4, p. 16–17, 1965.

Nakhleh, Emil and Mary B. Nakhleh. *Emmitsburg: history and society.* 1974.

Schrock, Alta E. "Negro Mountain Belsnickel." *Journal of the Alleghenies,* v.2 nos.2–4, p. 22, 1965.

Scott, Harold L. Senio. "First footing in Vale Summit and Learstown." *Journal of the Alleghenies,* v. 27, p. 42–3, 1991.

Smith, Elmer K. "Shanghaiing: a custom of the past." *Journal of the Alleghenies,* v.2 nos. 2–4, p. 17–18, 1965.

Tamarack. pseud. "Sarah's signs and omens." *Journal of the Alleghenies,* v.17, p. 13–16, 1980.

Chapter VII: Balls, Bats, and Picnics

Bayard, Ferdinand Maria. *Travels of a Frenchman in Maryland and Virginia in 1791…tr.* by Ben G. McCary. 1950.

Bready, James. "Play ball! The legacy of nineteenth century Baltimore baseball." *Maryland Historical Magazine,* v 97, p. 27–40, 1997.

A hearthstone history of Washington County. Hagerstown Arts and Literary Club, Hagerstown Board of Education, n.d.

Hilman, James A. *History of Emmitsburg, Maryland.* 1909.

Little, Gina. (Personal communication on history of Frederick Keys Baseball Team, Oct. 2, 1995).

Nakhleh, Emil A. and Mary B. Nakhleh. *Emmitsburg: history and society.* 1976.

Maryland Cracker Barrel. Baseball edition. v.25 no.6, April–May, 1997.

Ross, Jean B. "The lady and the Fourth of July: popular culture in the early Maryland period." *Maryland Historical Magazine,* v.90 no.2, Summer 1995, p.18–3. (Reprint: *Columbia Historical Review,* v.10 1907, p. 86–226. Diary of Mrs. William Thurston).

Shullman, Mary Bestwood. *The pioneers of the early days in Westminster.* Carroll County Historical Society, n.d.

Chapter VIII: Frederick Occupied

Schaeffer, Anne R. Lute of Frederick County. Records of the past, 4–20 September, 1862, (MSS 1860 Box 2 of 6) (Maryland Historical Society).

Chapter IX: Three Flags in September

"Civil War Years." *Valley News Echo* (Reprint by Potomac Edison Corporation).

Douglas, Henry Kyd. *I rode with Stonewall.* University of North Carolina Press. 1941.

Rhoderick, George C. Junior. *Early history of Middletown, Maryland.* Middletown Valley Historical Society. 1989.

Smith, John. "Phileomon Reminiscences of Sharpsburg, Washington County, from July 2, 1730 to January 1, 1911." (MSS) (Western Maryland Room).

Valley News Echo. "Civil War Years" (Reprint by Potomac Edison Corporation).

Chapter X: Clara on the Battlefield

Barton, Clara. Manuscripts (Library of Congress).

Chapter XI: The Half Life of Ha'nts

Ankrum, France. *Maryland Pennsylvania history sketches.* Masontown, Pa. 1947.

Bach, Ellyn. "150-year-old house comes complete with ghost baby-sitter." *Hagerstown Daily Mail*, Dec. 19, 1981.

Cannon, Timothy L. and Nancy F. Whitmore. *Ghosts and legends of Frederick County.* 1980.

Dahlgren, Madeleine V. *South Mountain magic.* 1974.

Davidson, Amos. *Leigh Masters.* n.d. (MSS) (Carroll County Historical Society).

Glass, Jesse. *Ghosts and legends of Carroll County, Md.* Carroll County Public Library. 1982.

Hahn, Thomas. *The C&O Canal boatmen, 1892–1924*...American Canal and Transportation Center. 1980.

Harbaugh, Thomas. *Middletown in song and story.* 1910.

Leigh Masters, untitled clipping. *Democratic Advocate*, Jan. 14, 1937.

McKinsey, Folger. "Ghost stories of Burkittsville." *Baltimore Sun*, April 5, 1947.

McGrain, John W. "Haunted mill near Westminster." Clipping from unidentified newspaper dated only 1984. (Carroll County Public Library).

McNutly, Margaret. *Maryland folklore.* n.d. (MSS) (Western Maryland Room).

Miller, Doug. "Peddlers wagon: Boonsboro shop offers ghost tales, arts and crafts." *Hagerstown Daily Mail*, Oct. 30, 1985.

Sharp, Merily Bennet. "Ghost." *Carroll County Times*, May 4, 1971.

Shellman, Mary Bastwood. "The pioneers of the early days of Westminster." (Speech before the Carroll County Historical Society). n.d.

Singerwald, Joseph T. *The iron ores of Maryland.* Johns Hopkins University Press. 1921.

Warner, Nancy M., Ralph B. Levering, and Margaret Taylor. *Carroll County, Maryland: a history 1837–1977.* Carroll County Bicentennial Commission. 1976.

White, Larue A. *Account of black history in Carroll County from 1773 to 1900.* n.d. (MSS) (Carroll County Public Library).

Wolfe, George "Hooper." *I drove mules on the C&O Canal.*

Chapter XII: Pow-Wow and Hex

Barry, Joseph B. *The strange story of Harpers Ferry, with legends of the surrounding country.* 1958.

Dahlgren, Madeleine V. *South Mountain magi.* 1972.

Drake, Julia Angelina and James Ridgely Ornsdorff. *From mill wheel to plough share: contributions of the Christian Ornsdorff family to the social and industrial history of the United States.* Touchstone Press, Sioux City, IA, 1936.

Draper, Virginia K. Personal communication, May 19,1995.

Conway, Grant. Archives. (Western Maryland Room).

Doddridge, Joseph. *Notes on the settlement and Indian wars of the western part of Virginia and Pennsylvania from 1763 to 1787...*3d ed.Pittsburgh. 1912.

The friend in need, or, Sympathetic knowledge, a useful book for everybody, tr. from the German by Michael Zittle, Boonsboro. 1845. (Photocopy, Western Maryland Room).

Glass, Jesse. "Pow-wowing" undated clipping. *Carroll County Times.* (Carroll County Public Library).

Harbaugh, Thomas Chalmers. *Middletown valley in song and story.* 1910.

Parke, Francis Neale. "Witchcraft in Maryland." *Maryland Historical Magazine*, v.31 no. 4. Dec.1930, p.271ff.

Senior Citizens, Wolfsville, Md. Personal communications at luncheon meeting, May 23, 1995.

Warner, Harry. "Tales of early residents with strange powers." Undated, unidentified clipping (Western Maryland Room).

Wetzel, George. *A wizard of South Mountain.* Jan.1953 (MSS) (Western Maryland Room).

"Witches."*Baltimore Sun*, Jan. 13, 1909 p.3. Typescript (Maryland Historical Society).

Chapter XIII: "Most Horrid Murder and Arson"

Cannon, Timothy L. and Nancy F. Whitmore. *Ghosts and legends of Frederick County.* 1980.

Draper, Virginia and other members of Wolfsville Senior Luncheon Group. May 23, 1995.

Nourse, Gabriel. "Narrative of the life, trial, conviction on John Markley for the murder perpetuated by him on the bodies of John Newey & wife…29th December, 1830." (1831) (Frederick County Historical Society).

Warfield, Sandra. Compiler. *A newspaper history of Washington county, 1820–1835.* Washington County Free Library. 1990.

Warfield, Sandra. Personal communication, May 1, 1991. In this she identified the papers used as *The Maryland Herald* and *Hagerstown Advertiser*; the *Hagerstown Torch Light* and *Public Advertiser*, the *Hagerstown Mail*, but did not say which paper carried which story.

Chapter XIV: Jack and the Cat's Paw

This is an expanded version of an imperfectly recalled story told me by a woman at the meeting of the Wolfsville Senior Luncheon Group on superstitions. A similar story, "Jack and the Sop Paws," was collected in Virginia in the 1920s.

Chapter XV: Was it Treason?

Archives of Maryland, v.XLV, p.467,469–70, 482,491,v.XLVII, p.297–8, 328–31, 382, 413, 415–16, 568, V XII.469.

Bowie, Lucie Leigh. "German prisoners in the American Revolution." *Maryland Historical Magazine.* v.40, 1945, p.165–200.

Brannon, Sheldon W. *Historic Hampshire.* McLain Publishing, 1976, p.91–2.

Cooper, H. Austin. *Church of the singing hills: a source book...*Mt. Airy, Locust Grove Church of the Brethren. 1988.

Drake, Julia Angelina and James Ridgley Orendorff. *From mill wheel to plough share: the story of the contributions of the Christian Orendorff family to the social and industrial history of the United* States. Cedar Rapids, IA. Torch Press. 1938.

Frederick Treason Trials. (MSS Box 526) (Maryland Historical Society).

Harling, Frederick F. and Martin Kaufman. "The ethnic contribution to the American Revolution." *Warfield Bicentennial Commission and Historical Journal of Western Massachusetts.* Warfield, Mass. 1976.

Naglack, Jacob. *The Germans.*

"Henry Shell's acceptance of pardon." *Maryland Historical Magazine*, v.6, 1911, p.30.

Hoffman, Ronald. *A spirit of dissension: economc politics...*Johns Hopkins University Press. 1973.

Jackson, Elmer Martin. *Keeping the lamp of remembrance lighted: a genealogical narrative...about the Jackson and allied families...*Hagerstown Bookbinding and Publishing Co. 1988.

Jackson, Elmer Martin. Personal communication. Dec. 20, 1990.

Jackson, Elmer Martin. Remarks to Sergeant Laurence Everhart chapter, SAR. April 13, 1986.

Kiddoo, Nancy Rice. "Of Revolutionary mercenaries: German mercenaries who immigrated to western Maryland." *Journal of Pennsylvania German Society*, v.23, p. 43–80, 1989.

Maryland Sun and *Baltimore Advertiser*. Issues no.414 of Aug.7, 1781 and no.417 of Aug. 28, 1781 (Maryland Historical Society).

Maxwell, Hu and H.L. Swisher. *History of Hampshire County, West Virginia from its earliest settlement to the present*. 1887, p.62–3.

Miles, Lion G. "Prisoners of war in Frederick County, Maryland, during the American Revolution." *Journal of the Pennsylvania German Society*, v.23, p.41–3, 1980.

Quynn, Dorothy. "The Loyalist plot in Frederick." *Maryland Historical Magazine*, v.40, p.201–10, 1945.

Steiner, Berhard. "Western Maryland in the Revolution…" Johns Hopkins University Press, 1902. (*J.H.U. Historical and Political Science*, no.1).

Chapter XVI: A Contract with the Devil

Beard, Leslie C. Unidentified, undated clipping in Beard's Church folder. (Western Maryland Room).

Schroeder, Johann Georg. "Exorcism 1789: The noteworthy story of a man who entered a pact with the devil for 18 years and was released again through Christ." *Quarterly of the Pennsylvania German Society*, v.9 no.2, p.2–17, Summer 1975.

St. Peter's Church Anniversary Program. Beard's Church file (Western Maryland Room).

Chapter XVII: Blackberry Theft

Feare, Ronald. *History of Elias Lutheran Church. 1972.*

History of Cumberland and Adams Counties, Pennsylvania.

Nakhleh, Emile A. and Mary B. Nakhleh. *Emmitsburg: history and society.* 1972.

Schildknecht, C.E. ed. *Monocacy and Catoctin, some early settlers of Frederick and Carroll County, Md., Cumberland and Adams County, Pa.* v.1. Bedial Publishing Co., Shippensburg, Pa.

Chapter XVIII: Rosaline and the Indian

This story has been told in several variations in the local histories of Washington County. The earliest account I found was in E. Russell Hicks, *Our county history*, prepared in 1974 for county school use.

In retelling the story, I assume Belinda Spring is the eighteenth century name, now unknown. The hopeful owner of a new resort named the spring after his wife in 1824.

Here I relate the story in the words of a 19th century traveler.

Chapter XIX: Murder in Monocazy

Archives of Maryland. "Proceedings of the Council of Maryland, 1698–1731." v.XXV, p.379–80, 382–3.

Marye, William, B. "Potowmack above ye inhabitants." *Maryland Historical Magazine*, v.30, p.14–25, 1935 and v.33, p. 293–8, 1937.

"Pennsylvania Minutes of the Provincial Council." Proceedings from May 31, 1687 to Jan. 23, 1735. p.145–157, 162–5.

Chapter XX: In-Comers in Four Colors

Red

Barry, Joseph. *The strange story of Harpers Ferry...*1958.

The first 150 years: a pictorial history of Carroll county, Md., 1837–1987. Historical Society of Carroll County. 1987.

Helman, James A. *History of Emmitsburg.* 1906.

Kester, John G. "Charles Polke: Indian trader on the Potomac...1703–1753." *Maryland Historical Magazine*, v.90, p.447–465, Winter 1995.

Martz, Ralph Fraley. "History of Indians in our county." *Montgomery County Sentinel*, n.d. (clipping).

Marye, William B. "Notes on the primitive history of western Maryland." *Maryland Historical Magazine*, v. 8 p.161–6. 1948.

McCary, Ben C. *Indians in seventeeenth-century Virginia*. Virginia 305th Anniversary Celebration Corporation. Williamsburg, Va. 1957.

Ridder, Dixie. "Josie Dixon of Elk Garden." *Journal of the Alleghenies*, v.8 p.3–4. 1972.

C.E. ed. *Monocacy and Catoctin: some early settlers of Frederick and Carroll counties, Md., and Cumberland and Adams Counties, Pa.* v.1. Bedial Publishing Co. 1986–1987.

Tracey, Grace L. "From distance darts." n.d. (MSS) (Carroll County Historical Society).

Tracey, Grace L. and John P. Dean. *Pioneers of old Monocacy: the early years of Frederick County, Md .1721–1747*. Genealogical Publications. 1987.

Wallace, Paul A.W. *Indians in Pennsylvania*. Pennsylvania Historical and Museum Commission. 1961.

Wallace, Paul A.W., ed. and compiler. *The travels of John Heckenwelder in frontier America.* University of Pittsburgh Press. 1958.

White

Bode, Carl. *Maryland : A bicentennial history.* 1971.

Bayard, Ferdinand Maria. *Travels of a Frenchman in Maryland and Virginia in 1781,* tr. by Ben C. McCary. Williamsburg, Va. 1950.

Helman, James A. *History of Emmitsburg.* 1906.

Minutes and proceedings of Washington County Court held in Elizabeth Town, 1776–1791. compiled by Gerald J. Sward, 1965, completed 1988. (Western Maryland Room).

Schultz, Edward T. "First settlement of Germans in Maryland." a paper read before Frederick County Historical Society, Jan.17, 1896. (Carroll County Public Library).

Smith, Elmer P. "The ethnic culture in Shenandoah Valley." *Journal of the Alleghenies*, v.5 p.17–19. 1968.

Black

Bayard, Ferdinand Maria. *Travels of a Frenchman in Maryland and Virginia in 1781...*tr. by Ben C. McCary, Williamsburg, Va. 1958.

Cohen, Anthony. *The underground railway in Montgomery County, MD, a history and driving guide.* Montgomery County Historical Society. 1995.

Conway, Grant. Archives. (Western Maryland Room).

Doleman, Marguerite. *We, the blacks of Washington County.* n.d. (Western Maryland Room).

"Early religious experiences, Carroll County." *Maryland Pendulum*, Maryland Commission on Afro-American history, v.4 no.1. Winter 1983–4. (Carroll County Public Library).

Erbst, Nora. Clippings on slavery. (Western Maryland Room).

Hoover, Sherry. *History of slavery in Washington county, 1986.* (MSS) (Washington County Board of Education, Resource Center).

Libby, Jean. *African iron-making in the New World, with an emphasis on western Maryland, 1790–1829.* 1987 (MSS) (Western Maryland Room).

Mullinix, James W. *Economic history of Washington County to 1869.*

Nesbitt, Otho. Diary. (Clear Spring Historical Society).

Shellman, Mary Westwood. "The pioneers of the early days of Westminster." (A speech before the Carroll County Historical Society) n.d.

Warner, Nancy M, Ralph B. Levery, and Margaret Taylor Weltz. *Carroll County, Maryland, a history, 1873–1971.* Carroll County Bicentennial Commission. 1976.

White, Laurie. *Account of black history in Carroll county, 1723 to 1960.* n.d. (MSS) (Carroll County Library).

Green

Beasley, F.W. *The forests of Washington County.* n.d. Maryland State Board of Forestry, Jan.1927. (pamphlet).

Maryland Bicentennial trees: a list of species of trees believed to be living in Maryland in 1776. Maryland Department of Natural Resources Forest Service. 1976.

Chapter XXI: Wilderness Maryland

"The Ashleys of Great Glades Settlement; the last buffalo." *Glades Star*, Dec. 31, 1947 v.25 no. 269.

Barrett, Todd J. "Tobacco planters, tenants, and slaves: a picture of Montgomery County in 1783." *Maryland Historical Magazine*, v.89 no.2. Summer 1994, p.184–203.

Bayard, Ferdinand Maria. *Travels of a Frenchman in Maryland and Virginia in 1791*, tr. by Ben C. McCarey. 1959.

Besley, F.W. *Forests of Washington County*. Maryland State Board of Forestry. 1922.

Browning, Meshach. *Forty-five years of the life of a hunter, being reminiscences of Meshach Browning, a Maryland hunter*, roughly written down by himself, revised and edited by G. Stabler. Lippincott. 1859.

Doddridge, Joseph. *Notes on the settlement and Indian wars of the western parts of Virginia and Pennsylvania from 1783 to 1824 inclusive*; 3rd ed. 1912.

Ducatel, Julius Timoleum. "Report on the projected survey of Maryland." n.d. (L.C. call no. GA429.D87)

A *hearthstone history of Washington County*. Hagerstown Arts and Craft Club, 1935–1936.

Kincaid, Robert L. *The wilderness road*. 1947.

Leopold, Aldo. "A passing in Cincinnati, Sept.1,1914." (U.S. Dept. of Interior, Historical Vignettes 1770–1976). Sept. 1976.

Mansueti, Romeo. "Extinct and vanishing mammals of Maryland and the District of Columbia." *Maryland Naturalist*, v.XX, nos.1&2, Winter-Spring 1950, p.3–48.

Marye, William E. "The Baltimore garrison and the old Garrison Road." *Maryland Historical Magazine*, v.16, 1921, p.105–49, 209–59.

Marye, William E. "The great Maryland Barrens." *Maryland Historical Magazine*, v.50, 1955 p.11–23, 120–42, 234–63.

Marye, William E. "Notes on primitive history of western Maryland." *Maryland Historical Magazine.* v.38, 1948. p.161–06.

Marye, William E. "The old Indian road." *Maryland Historical Magazine*, v.15, 1920 p.208–29, 270–69,345–89.

Marye, William E. "Patowmeck above ye Inhabitants." *Maryland Historical Magazine.* v.30, 1937 p.114–5., v.33, 1938 p.293–300.

Marye, William E. "Warriors' paths." *Pennsylvania Archaeologist.* v.XII, 1943, p.4–26. v.XIV 1945, p.4–22.

Maryland bicenntenial list: A list of species of trees believed to be living in Maryland in 1776. Maryland Dept. of Natural Resources, Maryland Forest Service. 1976.

Maxwell, Hu. "The use and cause of forests by the Virginia Indians." *William & Mary Quarterly Historical Magazine*, v.19, 1910, p.73–101, 1910.

Metcalf, Paul. *Waters of Patowmak.* North Point Press. 1982.

Meyer, William E. "Indian trails of the Southeast." (42d Annual Report, Bureau of American Ethnology 1924–1925) 1928.

Paradiso, John L. "Mammals of Maryland." U.S. Bureau of Sport Fisheries and Wildlife. *(North American Fauna,* no.66) 1969.

Porter J. Marshall. "The summer of the pigeons." *Journal of the Alleghenies*, v.11. 1975, p.33–35.

Pyne, Stephen J. *Fire in America: a cultural history of wildland and rural fires.* Princeton University Press. 1982.

Roe, Frank Albert. *The North American buffalo: a critical study of the species in the wild,* 2d ed. University of Toronto Press. 1970.

Rustland, Erhart. "Geographic range of the historic bison of the Southeast." *Annals,* Association of American Geographers, v.58, 1960, p.395–407.

Rustland, Erhart. "Myth of a natural prairie belt in Alabama: an interpretation of historical records." *Annals*. Association of American Geographers, v.47, 1957, p.392–411.

C.E., ed. *Monocacy and Catoctin: some early settlers of Frederick and Carroll County, Md., and Adams County, Penna, also descendants, c.1725–1985.* v.1. Bedial Publishing, Shippensburg Pa. 1985.

Schreven, Forrest. *The plant life of Maryland.* Johns Hopkins University Press. 1910.

Tracey, Grace Louise. Notes from the records of *Old Monocacy.* 1958.

Tracey, Grace Louise and John P. Dean. *Pioneers of Old Monocacy, early settlers of Frederick County, Md. 1741–1743.* Genealogical Publishing Co. 1987.

Vokes, Harold E. "Geography and geology of Maryland." Maryland Department of Geology, Mines and Water Resources, 1937. (Bulletin 19).

Wallace, Paul. *Indian trails of Pennsylvania.* Historical and Museum Commission of Pennsylvania, 1965.

Wood, Sumner, Sr. *The horseshoe of the Potomac in the days of witches, wonders and cannibals, 1648–1883.* 1973. (MSS) (Montgomery County Historical Society).

978-0-595-38004-6
0-595-38004-2